Islam and the West

Islam and the West

Critical Perspectives on Modernity

Edited by
Michael J. Thompson

ROWMAN & LITTLEFIELD PUBLISHERS, INC.
Lanham • Boulder • New York • Oxford

ROWMAN & LITTLEFIELD PUBLISHERS, INC.

Published in the United States of America
by Rowman & Littlefield Publishers, Inc.
A Member of the Rowman & Littlefield Publishing Group
4501 Forbes Boulevard, Suite 200, Lanham, Maryland 20706
www.rowmanlittlefield.com

PO Box 317
Oxford
OX2 9RU, UK

British Library Cataloguing in Publication Information Available

Library of Congress Cataloging-in-Publication Data

Islam and the West : critical perspectives on modernity / edited by
Michael J. Thompson.
    p. cm.
Includes bibliographical references and index.
    ISBN 0-7425-3106-6 (alk. paper)—ISBN 0-7425-3107-4 (pbk. : alk.
paper)
    1. Islamic modernism. 2. Islam—21st century. 3. Islamic renewal.
I. Thompson, Michael, 1973–
    BP166.14.M63I87 2003
    303.48'21767101821—dc21

                                            2003005644

Printed in the United States of America

∞™ The paper used in this publication meets the minimum requirements of American
National Standard for Information Sciences—Permanence of Paper for Printed Library
Materials, ANSI/NISO Z39.48-1992.

Contents

Introduction

$\mathcal{T}$he events of September 11, 2001, have been characterized as a turning point in the course of international affairs. For many experts and observers in the West—specifically in the United States—it was a moment that demarcates a new orientation of Islamic countries toward the West, its ideas and values, as well as its "way of life." For other more critical analysts, September 11th turned the attention of much of the West—and, again, mainly those in the United States—to what has been a persistent problem in the Middle East of political oppression and manipulation, as well as victimization by foreign economic imperatives. The result has been a plethora of attempts through books, articles, and newspaper editorials to conceptualize the apparent "divide" between western culture and society and that which is broadly defined as Islam. The primary theme around which most of this discourse has focused has been around the idea of modernity and the West's sometimes unique status as being modern.

Indeed, the very idea of modernity is associated almost exclusively with the West, its culture and its political and economic institutions. In the West, the construction of modernity was an outgrowth of the impulses of Enlightenment humanism, of technological expansiveness, and the emergence of new political, economic, and social forms of organization. The transformation of western society and culture was a convulsive one, the product of bloody revolutions, as well as of brilliant ideas. At the same time, the experience of modernity was characterized by a crisis of identity, the breakdown of traditional forms of thought and collective identity, and the emergence of the individual, both in political and philosophical terms. Modernity, in other words, comes with a price, one that is still being paid in the West and is reaching outward through the expansion of globalization.

In many ways, it is this price that, when we consider the relationship be-tween Islam, the West, and modernity, is of prime importance. The most extreme antiwestern attitudes and ideas—many of which are at the foundation of the most militant Islamic terrorist movements—come not from some impulse of aggres-sion, but, rather, from a discourse of *defense*: defense against the effects of western-ization, modernization, western rationalism, capitalism, and alienation. Therefore, the crucial question has been raised: does modernization entail westernization? Or is this question simply unimportant? Clearly, the time is ripe for leaving behind the social scientific conception of modernization, one that sees "modernity" as defined by a matrix of political, economic, and social institutions at the expense of culture and ideas, the dominant paradigm throughout the post-war period. In its place, analysis must focus on the interaction between history, economics, poli-tics, and philosophy in order to articulate a more sophisticated conception of modernization and modernity itself.

Thinkers like Alexander Gershenkron and H. H. Rostow, among others, emphasized the importance of certain institutional features of western modern-ization. This paradigm set forth the notion that development and modernization was path-dependent; that once certain institutional and ideational concerns were set in motion with the proper synchronization, modernization would be an in-evitable result. For Rostow, it was the idea set of Newtonian physics and its abil-ity to exploit nature that was essential with respect to the intellectual orientation of any modernizing culture, whereas for Gershenkron, it was a specific matrix of economic and political institutions that would foster economic development and social modernization.

But whatever the discourse the development literature may contain, the cen-tral problem of the relation between the West, modernity, and Islam is still para-mount. Since the terrorist attacks of September 11th the topic of Islam's political, cultural, religious, and spiritual tendencies and beliefs has been thrust into the spotlight. Even more, the so-called clash of civilizations that ostensibly appears to be emerging is of even more interest. The encounter between the militant strains of Islamic fundamentalism and western culture, politics, and values touches on is-sues that extend deep into the historical consciousness of the West itself. Indeed, it should be seen that the struggle between Enlightenment notions of reason, sec-ularism, universalism, civil society, and the like have always been in conflict with the *volkish* tendencies of cultural particularism, nativism, provincialism, and spiri-tualism both within the West and elsewhere. The fault lines that divide Islamic extremism and western modernity are by no means new to the western mind. At the same time, historical and political context needs to be kept firmly in mind. There is no way to talk about the relation between the West and Islam without dealing with Europe's imperial past in the region, as well as the contemporary po-litical and economic manipulation of Islamic societies.

In this sense, conceptualizing the current encounter between western modernity and the fundamentalist notions of Islamic culture is not simply one of ideas. Indeed, although it has become quite fashionable today to argue that there exists a war of ideologies—the West's defined as heralding freedom, democracy, and markets and Islam's upholding notions of tradition, custom, and community—what must also be seen is that there are concrete political concerns that need to be highlighted. It is not simply the case that western modernity—inspired by the Enlightenment and pushed forward by the development of certain social and political values and institutions—is a distinct product of western culture as thinkers such as Samuel Huntington have tried to argue. It is rather the case that there are rational and irrational segments within every culture and that the very stuff of history is a struggle between these elements once rationalism has developed to such an extent, and tradition and custom become questioned and are interrogated. In this sense, it must be kept in mind that the West is still undergoing its own struggle whereas, perhaps, this struggle is simply beginning in Islamic culture.

The complexity of the current problem is therefore not so much in the historical evidence, something that is in fact quite clear, in that regard, but rather in the perspective we take. It is simply wrong to reduce the apparent failure of modernity in Middle Eastern Islamic states to a set of religious or cultural variables, as has been so common in the popular media, and simply ignore the historical impact of colonialism and the contemporary interests of international capital and its political consequences. At the same time, it is equally wrong to pursue what has become, on the left, an economic determinist approach emphasizing the interests of western capital at the expense of certain historical tendencies of Islamic societies away from the western Enlightenment ideas and values.

To elaborate on this point means that taking a critical perspective on this subject therefore means analyzing it from a multilayered point of view. It has been fashionable for analyses of Arab-Islamic/western relations to take on one of two primary perspectives. First, there is what we may term the *materialist approach* that gives explanatory primacy to the economic interests of international actors and their linkages with domestic elites. This interpretive framework therefore sees relations between the West and Islamic Middle Eastern states as being determined by a Realpolitik that seeks to make the most optimal political arrangements for capital. Oil is the prime sector that is seen to drive these interests, and the extent that oil reserves are controlled by domestic governments translates into a kind of "friction" for the interests of capital. The political elites within Islamic states are, in this reading, tied to the interests of the West (especially the policies of the United States), and modern forms of democracy are prevented from developing since national self-determination would be an obstacle to the circuit of economic interests between foreign developed states and domestic elites.

Second, there is the *culturalist approach* that emphasizes the inherent differences of cultural values and the outlook of various actors. Whereas the materialist approach is largely informed by neo-Marxian notions of imperialism and the dynamics of capital, or by the core-periphery relations of power that result from international power (economic) inequities, the culturalist approach is not as easy to pin down in terms of its categories of analysis. Thinkers as diverse as Max Weber and Samuel Huntington can be grouped under this interpretive framework, which gives primacy to the historical substance of *ideas* and *values* over that of the deterministic character of economic and political institutions. However, in the current context, this approach has been vulgarized and there is a more simplistic analysis where complexity is needed. A common charge against the culturalist approach is that of orientalism, a charge that also, at times, tends toward simplicity of analysis.

But what is clearly required is the fusion of these perspectives. Indeed, it is through an overlapping of social, historical, economic, and cultural/philosophical layers that the complexity of Islam's relation to the West and the idea of modernity is best characterized. It is simply no longer sufficient to argue that Islam has yet to embrace a reformation of its religious institutions as had been done in the West. Nor is the charge that the legacy of western imperialism and the continuation of economic and political interference in the affairs of Islamic states is any more capable of capturing, on its own, the sophistication of the problem. Moving beyond methodological rigidity is therefore a first step toward breaking away from the narrow mode of analysis that has currently infected the analysis of this topic.

The chapters collected in this volume each attempt to deal with the problem of Islam's relation to modernity through this complex prism of analysis. Indeed, the perspectives presented here are not at all in agreement with respect to their ultimate findings and positions. However, there is no question that each of them move beyond the methodological narrowness of the two perspectives outlined above and attempt to broaden the discussion of the relationship between Islam, the West, and modernity through political, historical, philosophical, and social scientific lenses—complex historical and social phenomena require "thicker" methods of analysis. Indeed, it was the great nineteenth-century Swiss historian Jacob Burckhardt who claimed that what was needed in historical analysis was not great simplifiers, of which there was always an excess, but rather great *complexifiers*, those who were able to generate new insights through a more concentrated analysis of multiple layers of historical reality. This claim has not lost currency over a century and a half later, and it is precisely what the present volume attempts to achieve and, through it, a more nuanced, and hopefully more lucid understanding of one of the great historical, political, and cultural tensions of modern times.

1

Muslims and the West: A Paradigm for Polarization

Haroun Er-Rashid

$\mathcal{P}$olarization between the West and Muslims greatly accelerated after September 11, 2001, and now this bipolarity threatens to become a universal paradigm. The predictions of Daniel Pipes, Bernard Lewis, and Samuel Huntington seem to be unfolding before our very eyes.[1] Suddenly, all Muslims have become suspect in the West and Islam itself has been openly labeled "evil" by mainstream and fundamentalist evangelists and politicians. As events unfold in many different countries it is clear that America, if not all in the West, is waging a struggle to control, and whenever possible, destroy an enemy that appears in various forms as an ideology, a number of disparate cultures, a religion, and even a whole civilization. This has bewildered Muslims the world over, not least those who have identified themselves with the democratic aspirations of the West.

1. Say: "O you who deny the truth!
2. I do not worship that which you worship,
3. and neither do you worship that which I worship.
4. And I will not worship that which you have [ever] worshipped
5. And neither will you [ever] worship that which I worship.
6. Unto you, your moral law, and unto me, mine!"

Surah Al-Kafirun
Al Quran

Muslims take this *surah* to be the ultimate exhortation for toleration. It says very clearly that in matters of religion, Muslims will tolerate other religions provided they are given the same toleration in return. It says, again very clearly, that non-Muslims are not expected to convert or to curb their religious practices. Surah Al-Kafirun and others of similar vein form the kernel of injunctions, which guide the great majority of Muslims in their relationships with non-Muslims. Fortunately, the great majority of non-Muslims also believe in toleration. Otherwise, over the past fourteen centuries there would have been endless wars, forced conversions, massacres, expulsions, and immense misery. That in the main this has not been so is ample proof of a fair degree of toleration on both sides.

Nothing in human affairs is angelic or perfect. There has been discrimination, periodic persecutions, unjust legal measures, and occasional wars and expulsions by both sides. The majority of the different Muslim and non-Muslim peoples have absorbed cultural shocks, adjusted to new situations, and reached an accommodation with new regimes and new neighbors. Throughout history this has been the "live and let live" principle, which has safely guided societies out of intolerable situations. It is the misfortune of existing Muslim societies to be faced with a time of trials and tribulations. Over the past half century, there have been many small conflicts in Muslim countries, precisely because the Muslims in those areas lived or continue to live in intolerable situations. According to Samuel Huntington, the "borders are bloody" but that is because Muslims have tried to redress situations imposed upon them.[2]

One often reads and hears through the media that the events of 9/11 have profoundly changed the world. This is not correct. What it did was enable the radical elements in the West to push through their agenda for world hegemony. In retrospect it seems as if they were waiting for some event to happen and strengthen their hand. Almost like the seizure of Kuwait by Saddam Hussein, a decade earlier. Allusions to "profound change" are a red herring that serves to misguide the western public who know so little of the non-West. Today's events that anger and bewilder the westerner have their roots in colonialism and in some instances go back 500 years. The seeds of this whirlwind are to be found in the fifteenth-century European voyages of discovery and colonialism. The first wave was of massive plunder and merciless exploitation of Mexico and Peru, with a smaller, but ultimately more significant, series of raids and expropriations in Asia.[3] Asian trade increased, often under duress, and as Asian empires and kingdoms declined, the appetite for overseas possessions increased. From the very beginning, the expansion of European power was primarily for economic exploitation and only secondarily for the expansion of legitimate trade, the settlement of colonists, and the spread of Christianity. This expansion was possible mainly as a result of superior technology and management skills. After two centuries of gradually building up their prowess in these two areas, Europeans began the second phase of their power-play by conquering Bengal and Java.[4] These eighteenth-century colonial gains laid the foundation for an almost complete conquest of the world in the next century. What is being witnessed today are the reverberations of that reckless enterprise.

During the century or two of physical colonialism in different parts of Asia and Africa, Europeans engaged in the vicious intellectual enterprise of demeaning and denigrating the cultures of subject peoples. Using their superior management of academic disciplines Europeans fabricated the falsely academic edifice of Oriental Studies, whereby all subject people, and Muslims in particular, were reviled, and shown fit for subjugation.[5]

Colonialism dehumanizes the colonial more than the colonized. A civilization built on economic exploitation and cultural falsehoods will sooner or later turn on itself. This is what happened in the two World Wars, with their fifty million dead. Western civilization, it may be said cynically, was too successful for its own good. Not only did it make magnificent advances in the sciences but it also constructed philosophies that made man the "ultimate reality." Seen from a nonwestern point of view, and with the advantage of hindsight, it seems that a few superficial successes made the western imagination dream of immortality and deification. The results were existentialism, fascism, and communism, all three of which troubled, and continues to trouble, not only the West but the rest of the world as well.

The legacy of a West that is apparently in decline[6] consists of a bipolar economic order, a unipolar military order, and heightened tensions among all cultural groups. The United States has over the past few years become virtually synonymous with the West. It is larger, richer, and more vocal than the European Union (EU). Its culture, or rather subculture, has penetrated into every culture of the world and threatens to alter each of them. Its economic power seems virtually overwhelming, even after massive accounting errors.[7] With globalization the economic power of the United States may reach such proportions that in many countries nothing may be left of local economies. This prospect arouses not just fear but great alarm. Even more alarming is the enormous destructive power of the U.S. armed forces. Alarming not because it is in the hands of Americans but because humans are fallible. No one should have such power. Absolute power can corrupt absolutely. It is this possibility of the misuse of power that deeply worries the rest of the world, including Europeans. The United States is fully aware of this and does not mind reminding others of their overwhelming might.

For heightened tensions between different cultures one needs only to consider the sorry state of the African continent, where over half the population is Muslim. The nation-state, a very artificial social construct in Africa, divides, discriminates, and destroys local cultures. Ties with the West bring rewards to the elite, who are themselves in large measure alienated from the masses by education, wealth, power, and sometimes even by the preferred western language. Exploitation did not stop after the end of colonialism, rather it deepened through transnational corporations and trade barriers. The mineral resources of the African continent has brought the Africans much misery in this century. One needs to only look at the forces that kept Angola and Congo (Zaire) in civil strife for decades, and the new scramble for oil.[8] With the decline of its near absolute power, the West has resorted to the old colonial politics of setting off one community or nation against another. The West in this case is not the ordinary people of the West but the economic interests within the West that exploit in order to provide acceptable dividends to their shareholders. This is the face of the West in nonwestern countries and that is why there is so much misunderstanding. The West that most of the world sees is that of the unfeeling, cold-blooded economic exploiter.

Is it any surprise then that nonwesterners feel that the West speaks with a forked-tongue when it preaches democracy, liberalism, and free trade but practices racial profiling, shows scant regard for environmental laws, resorts to strong-arm tactics, and earns far more from the developing countries than it invests there? The brunt of the West's double standards is borne by Muslims, and therefore they stand up and challenge the West.

Who are the Muslims? They are the people who accept Islam and are therefore guided by the Quran and the Sunnah.[9] For many of them this acceptance is nominal, but for the majority it is a real commitment. They are not one people in the sense that they do not have the same culture. People of many different cultures have become Muslims over the centuries. Accepting the Islamic faith did not necessarily mean rejection of the former culture. In many cases the former religion would be formally and ceremonially rejected but even in these instances the language, dress, and house patterns would remain the same. Sleeping patterns changed insofar as the feet would not be pointed toward the direction to Makkah (*Kibla*). There would be dietary changes since meat would have to be *halal*. Obviously former religious songs would be totally avoided and new ones would be introduced. Musical instruments would remain and judging by historical legacy it seems that tunes and modes remained as they were.[10] Changes in cultural patterns are inherent in the dynamics of the particular society. In some cultures changes were rapid and in others slow. The adoption of Islam did not necessarily lead to great changes. The passage of time and societal urge to reinvent themselves could over time lead to a greater adoption of Islamic symbols and trappings. This seems to be true for Bangladeshi and Bengali-speaking Indian Muslims, who together number no fewer than 140 million people. This large group of Muslims in the eastern part of South Asia share the language and much of the music, food, and dress patterns with Bengali-speaking Hindus. Is this very unusual in the Muslim world? Probably not. Palestinian and Egyptian Muslims and Christians share many cultural attributes such as the language, dress, many food items, and much of the music. The same can be said of the Yorubas, the Swaheli, the Thai, and Gujeratis, for example.[11]

There are also many places where Muslims and non-Muslims prefer to be different, for example in Cambodia and Malaysia. The explanation is simple. In Cambodia the Muslims are from a different ethnic (*Cham*) group than the dominant Khmer. In Malaysia virtually all Malays are Muslim, and virtually none of the Chinese or Tamil are. By and large Muslim cultural groups do not look or behave very differently from their neighbors. The Muslims and their neighboring non-Muslims have *overlapping cultures*.[12] They coexist in varying degrees of amiability. Political, economic, or environmental stresses may, however, lead to a drifting apart. In the majority of such cases the cause is political: the ambition of one or more persons to capitalize on communal feelings. It takes a great deal of statesmanship on the part of the other community to steer clear of the collision course. Not only is statesmanship in short supply in every community but a challenge is usually met by a counterchallenge. The old territorial defense mechanism always comes up front. The more nervous of the two communities shows more belligerency, again in keeping with biological principles. The result could be a conflict that neither community wanted.

The Muslims are not a monolithic community except when the non-Muslim threat is perceived to be life threatening for the community as a whole.[13] Otherwise there are tensions and occasionally even conflicts among Muslim communities of the same culture and between cultures. When it is felt that the religion, and that part of culture based on religion, are not in danger of annihilation then other forces take over. Conflict over space, natural resources, trading privileges, and other, pettier problems can and do result in tensions from the family to the national level. This is not unusual in other cultures or "civilizations." However these tensions are more numerous in societies that are economically poor because of the greater scramble for resources. This alone could explain many of the numerous "fault line" conflicts cited by Huntington. He, however, deliberately minimizes the many historical instances of conflicts between Muslims.[14] The longest running of these was the Ottoman-Safavid series of wars and invasions. Then again there was the series of wars and invasions between the Durranis and the Mughals. Armed conflict between different Muslim kingdoms in North Africa matched the continuous conflicts between Christian countries and communities in southern Europe for a thousand years. It was only when the two different religious groups fought each other that these conflicts were seen as epochal. This magnification was due to the fear of being culturally strangled. The colonial conquests in the eighteen and nineteenth centuries were different in that they were overtly and loudly for economic exploitation and thus in most cases let religion go on as before. Efforts to convert were a pale shadow of the economic effort. Wherever the missionaries were given a free hand there were immediate conflicts, some of which continues into the present.[15]

Huntington provides us with a very handy set of indicators of modernization. He says that "modernization involves industrialization, urbanization, increasing levels of literacy, education, wealth, and social mobilization, and more complex and diversified occupational structures."[16] One wonders if that is all. If it is then every city in the non-West is modernizing and their vast, teeming countryside are not. Every one of the changes cited above are happening in nearly every Muslim country, but when can they declare they are modern? When they have urbanized more than half their population and industries to feed the consumer society that has ruined the environment? Surely modernization involves a change in mindset. Huntington reserves that for the West. It is unique to the West because it requires the classical legacy, western Christianity, European languages, separation of spiritual and temporal authority, rule of law, social pluralism, representative bodies and, above all, individualism.[17] Essentially this is an exclusionist view, because by definition no non-westerner can westernize without that unique legacy. No matter, he implies, since they can modernize and in the process copy western mannerisms. The real world shows that the non-West has modernized for over a century and the process could have been faster if it were not for economic exploitation by the West. As for the mindset, it is hard to see why individualism, which implicitly rejects family values, is essential for modernization. On the other hand, democratic norms would seem to be essential.

Western intellectuals present *individualism* as the core concept in westernization, which is of course equated with modernization.[18] Muslims, moderate and radical, reject individualism of the type extolled by the West because their emphasis is on the *family*. They point out that individualism has resulted in the self-centered western (or westernized) person, heedless of the needs of others, indulging in consumerism, willing to destroy nature and man to keep up the lifestyle that accompanies the market economy. Those who subscribe to such a lifestyle are the lifeblood of the culture of consumerism, which destroys the world's ecosystems through ever-increasing demand and sustains the transnational corporations that so completely dominate the world economic order. In this worldview, the concerns of environmentalists (both western and non-western) and of the poor people of the world (of all religions) overlap with the concerns of most Muslims. If westernization/modernization means consumerism, individualism, and unsustainable "development" then the great mass of the world's people will sooner or later reject it.[19]

Democracy as it has evolved in the twentieth century means that the majority of the people of a particular political area wish to be ruled by laws that do not discriminate against minorities. It also assumes that the will of the people is ascertained by periodic elections, that governments operate within a constitution, that the law of the land is supreme, and that this law protects fundamental rights and liberties. Everything in this formulation is in consonance with Islamic tenets. The concept of democracy can be argued over but the very fact that democratic norms do not suppress Islam, or oppress Muslims, shows that they can be compatible. Despotic regimes may be cloaked in democratic forms of governance (elections, parliament, etc.) but they are exposed when it comes to freedom of the media. This is the freedom that distinguishes democracies from authoritarian forms of government. Freedom of the media is not allowed in any authoritarian country because then the arbitrariness, nepotism, wastefulness, lack of accountability, and extralegal measures are exposed to the public, which then creates resistance to officialdom and the ruling clique. No doubt there are countries with democratic procedures but authoritarian structure. As long as these borderline cases have a free press, they have the chance to become fully democratic. Not that democratic societies cannot be, at least in the short term, oppressive to other societies. Democracy without human compassion is not what Muslims are looking for.

Much has been said about the "failure of democracy" in Muslim societies.[20] The extent of this "failure" has been overdrawn. If only countries that have a Muslim majority are counted then out of the forty-five countries, eighteen have democratic institutions (elections, majority rule, critical media, market economy, etc.) and twenty-seven are authoritarian. By sheer number of countries, big and small, it cannot be said that democracy cannot establish itself in Muslim countries. It is correct that the majority of the countries in the Middle East and North Africa are authoritarian, but recent history makes it transparent that behind these nondemocratic regimes lie French, British, or American financial, political, and military assistance. It is not correct to say that Arabs cannot be democratic. The truth is that they are not allowed to be democratic. Since the notorious Sykes-Picot Pact the West has deliberately fostered enmities and undermined all efforts to create powerful and democratic regimes. The West is not to be blamed solely. Assad's suppression of the uprising in Homs or Saddam's suppression of the uprising in Basra were not dictated by the West. There are no doubt deeply entrenched groups who oppose any democracy but they are clearly tribal, clan, or ethnic entities.[21] They are neither popular nor Islamic. It is therefore very misleading to dismiss Muslim societies as being inherently incapable of democracy. In fact if people rather than countries are counted then over half of the total Muslim population of the world live in Muslim countries with a fair degree of democracy. This is not the picture usually presented, even by many Muslim scholars, because the Muslim- (read Arab-) biased paradigm is so prevalent in western media and even some of its academia.[22]

Looking back at their history, and immediate past events, every community separates into those who would like to negotiate and resolve differences with the West and those who think that there can be no negotiations. Across the dividing line the radicals, extremists if you will, see other radicals and are reassured of their confrontational stance.[23] The moderates are by definition not aggressive and stand aside when radicals take over. The radical Muslims have a long-standing grouse against the West.[24] They contend that the West, in one guise or another, has exploited Muslims for several centuries, and worse, that they have tried and are still trying to wean Muslims away from their religion. First they tried to convert them to Christianity and then, when that failed rather miserably, to tempt them away through existentialist, hedonistic secularism. This has succeeded somewhat more and raised the hackles of the radicals. Their anger at moderate Muslims is arguably even more than against the West. In their thinking all Muslims must stand together or they will fall together. They do not allow for any cultural variations or nationalistic feelings.

Against the West, their constant enemy, the Muslim radicals bring three main changes to bear. First, that the West tries to destroy family-centered Muslim life through the promotion of lax sexual mores and deviant behavior. Second, that there is economic exploitation, depriving Muslim countries of their just dues and thus keeping them in poverty. The encouragement to move earnings by Muslims rulers, officials, and businessmen to the West is seen as part of the effort to keep the Muslim masses powerless. Third, that the West brutally imposed their political domination on most Muslim countries and created the divisions, including the fracturing of Palestine, that weakens the Muslim countries. The West, they argue, continues to meddle directly in the politics of Muslim countries only to undermine their stability and thereby keep them politically and economically powerless. The moderate Muslims, who comprise the great majority, do not necessarily disagree on these issues, but they do disagree on ways of dealing with them. The radicals contend that the West grew on the basis of warfare, conquest, and exploitation and is therefore an inherently aggressive civilization. The moderates see changes over the past fifty years that indicate that there can be negotiations with the West.

Family values are the very essence of Muslim community life. They have been eroded by modernization or westernization, but Muslims consider the family to be the bedrock of the Islamic communal structure. Anything that challenges the traditional roles is viewed with a jaundiced eye. Sexual mores, to put it bluntly, is one of the sorest issues between the West and the Muslims. Muslims disapprove of the free mixing of sexes, outside the family circle. Increasingly they insist on the *hijab*. They abhor the rise of gay groups and see in this phenomena one of the surest signs that the West has become irremediably decadent. They also cite that in many western counties half or more of the children are born outside wedlock. Citing passages in the Quran (and the Old Testament) they find in these phenomena proof that the West is rotting at the heart. Western societies reject these charges as a coverup for the oppression of women in Muslim societies. Their countercharges range from female mutilation to habitual domestic violence to inequality before the law. Whereas moderate Muslims see some truth in both points of view, the radicals insist that decline of traditional family values is a sure sign of decadence. It is in the nature of radicalization that they become blind to their own shortcomings. However, some good may yet come of this largely verbal conflict. Having been accused and challenged by the West, many Muslim scholars, both moderate and radical, are reexamining the role of women in Islam. Judging by the debate it seems that they have found that the treatment of women has varied greatly between different Muslim cultures. Whereas Bangladesh elected a woman to be the prime minister in 1990 (and the next two have also been women) and Pakistan in 1992, it is as yet unthinkable in some other Muslim countries that women should even hold public posts. Modernization will invariably challenge traditions, but it does not change the basics of Muslim cultures. However postmodern, westernization—with its setting aside of family values and emphasis on individualism and consumerism—is unlikely to ever become acceptable.

The West has enormous economic strength, indeed more than is healthy for the rest of the world. The combined gross national product (GNP) of the G-7 countries was $13,382 billion (U.S.) in 1999, whereas that of the rest of the world was $9,850 billion (U.S.). The Muslim-majority countries are mostly very poor and their combined GNP in 1999 was probably not more than $1,250 billion (U.S.).[25] If that is compared to the U.S. economy of $8,351 billion (U.S.), it becomes quite apparent that with continuing globalization the economies of the Muslim countries can be virtually taken over. The Asian financial crisis of 1997–1998 has heightened these fears. Malaysia was the only country that arrested the slide by imposing restrictions on transfers, which of course drew indignant protests from the West. These experiences only increase distrust of the West's financial power and maneuvering. While the moderates call for a restructuring of the world's financial system, the radicals call for its dismantling. Huntington, probably unwittingly, identified the real source of power in the world when he wrote about the *Davos Culture*.[26] The powerful military-industrial establishment and their political and academic hangers-on are not just figments of liberal or leftist thinking. They exist and they try to act in concert, with the profit motive guiding them through thick and thin. Their unconcern with the common person angers not only nonwesterners but many in the West as well.[27] The excessive speeding up of the global flow of funds increases the exploitation of people and resources and at the same time threatens to upset the entire trade and investment system. The Muslim world views this with great suspicion because, poor as they are, they cannot afford the slightest regress.

The most direct effect of the enormous economic disparity is on military strength. Once again Huntington's thesis is biased when he writes that Muslim countries are more militarized than non-Muslims countries.[28] Lacking seriously heavy firepower most poor countries rely on rifle-toting infantry. Even if his figures are correct (and they are suspect) they do not translate directly into military power. Huntington surely knows that if firepower is compared it may be a ratio of a hundred to one between the West and the Muslim countries. Nearly all of the Muslim countries purchase their armaments from the West and therefore are totally dependent on them for maintenance and replacement. The few countries that do have armament industries (Iran, Iraq, Pakistan, Turkey) manufacture a small range of products. There cannot therefore be protracted conventional warfare between the two sides. This knowledge is probably an important factor in compelling several governments to go for a nuclear arsenal and the radicals to opt for suicidal tactics.

Huntington is quite wrong when he says the conflict is between Islam and the West.[29] The anger of the Muslim world is certainly not anger against Christians or Christianity. The religious challenge was successfully met in the nineteenth century. The anger and angst is now against the triple threat of ultra-liberal culture, economic exploitation, and political domination. These threats vary in time and space. There are differences between Morocco and Mindanao and from one year to another. However, all three are present and they reinforce each other. Islam is not the issue, except for a radical fringe in the West. All responsible leaders in the West have repeatedly said that Islam is not the target and judging by the freedom of assembly and speech in western countries that cannot be denied. The West's political conflict is with Muslim countries and communities for a variety of reasons. The most long-standing, most rancorous, most divisive issue between the two sides is Palestine.[30] Many Muslims see in the recent history of Palestine the worst aspects of the West: their duplicity when it comes to Muslim interests, their long-term strategy of keeping Muslim nations under tutelage, and their denial of basic human rights to Muslims when their hegemonic interests are at stake. The denial of Palestinian rights is the core cause of the recent worldwide conflict.[31] There are Muslims who point out that Israel was created by denying Palestinians their right to ancestral property. The radical Muslims contend that this denial is based on a myth as monstrous as that of the Nazis. Moderates may not go so far, but they too see the situation as intolerable and unacceptable. Time after time Israel has denied the Palestinians their basic rights and flouted dozens of UN resolutions calling on them to respect international law. How is it that Israel can go on violating international conventions and UN resolutions? Because the United States is blindly on their side. Muslims of all shades consider this to be the single biggest fault of the United States, and by extension of the West, too. Unless the Palestinians are given an adequate homeland, with some form of control over the Al-Aqsa complex, the confrontation and struggle will continue. This is likely to be very costly for Muslims but not necessarily for Evangelical Christians and their Zionist allies. This extremist segment of the West welcomes the conflict because they are able to direct the military might of the United States, at least for the next few years. Extremists in the West seek confrontation and conflict with all Muslim nations, which threaten, or may threaten, the unchallenged supremacy of Israel. Seen in this light it becomes obvious why a Republican government would use all possible excuses to go to war with Iraq first and then with Iran.

Muslims perceive the labeling of Iraq and Iran as being in the "axis of evil," frequent references to Libya, Sudan, and Syria as "rogue states," and the pro-Israeli policy of the United States as being antagonistic to both moderates and radicals for the sake of protecting and enlarging America's economic interests.[32] This will lead many Muslim countries to seek accommodation with Russia and China. Some may look toward the EU, even though it has a long colonial history. Over the past two decades the growth of Muslim communities in the EU has caused some problems but overall they have been well received.[33] Only recently, in Belgium and Denmark, there were some anti-Muslim political campaigns, and after 9/11 there was an understandable surge in anxieties. That seems to be ebbing and the EU emerged with honors, in Muslim eyes, when Germany and France refused to tow the U.S. line on Iraq. If this trend continues it will of course be applauded by moderate Muslims because they are wary of too close ties by their countries with the basically totalitarian bureaucracies of Russia and China.

The media has created most of our recent history, and one of their favorite creations is that Marxism is dead and the 1989 breakup of the Soviet Union was an epochal turning point. This is a short-sighted myth with absolutely no political value. Not only is Marxism a strong social paradigm in China but, over much of the world, Marxism is alive and making something of a comeback. As for Russia it is not a toothless bear. It still has enough nuclear weapons to blow up the world and this should not be forgotten. Russia has lined up with the West for short-term gains. After a breathing pause Russia is most likely to rise up once again as a major power. That time may just have begun, with Russia unwilling to sanction U.S. military action against Iraq. The implications are clear: Russia will side with the West, or the Muslim countries, or even with China, as and when that suits her. The tendency to underestimate the Russian potential has been so pervasive in the western press that great disservice has been done to geopolitical realism. As long as the Soviet Union was willing to stand up as a credible threat the Muslim countries could, and did, counter western pressures by opening a dialogue with the "East." With the collapse of the Soviet empire this alternative was gone and within two years the

West unleashed the Gulf War and the only superpower has gone from strength to strength. However, geopolitics is as dynamic as energetics, and the lone superpower is bound to be challenged increasingly.

With Russia keeping a low profile for the time being, Israel is taking advantage of the situation by using the United States to re-create the total regional supremacy it had prior to 1973. At the same time their policy will enable the United States to assert its total control of the petroleum resources of the Middle East and also cow down Muslim thoughts of parity in world affairs. Triple benefits from a deliberate conflict. As long as this remains the policy of the West they will do nothing to give the Palestinians their legitimate dues. Keeping the Palestinian wound open creates a war psychosis in Israel that works in favor of the extreme Zionists, greatly infuriates the radical Arabs, and sustains the Intifada. It also greatly irritates moderate Muslims throughout the world, who then maintain their anti-U.S. stance, which in turn fuels the anxieties of evangelical rightists and makes them drum up a war psychosis in the United States. For the arms manufacturers this is music.

Modernity, as a set of objective conditions has never been a problem with Muslims. Conflating modernity with westernization certainly has, on the other hand, created serious problems, and the fusion has been rejected by almost all Muslim cultures.[34] The problem, as the Muslims see it, lies in the overwhelming economic and military power of the West, specifically the United States, which is used to economically exploit and culturally subvert the Muslim cultures, and also the other nonwestern cultures. The West's hegemonic interests only lead to distrust and continuing clash. In Huntington's thesis the West is in decline,[35] and if this is so then the present is but a prelude to the future. The efforts of the West to arrest this decline could be the cause of the present confrontation. It is then up to the West to reexamine its ultimately untenable position and to reconcile itself to a situation of greater parity with the non-West. This ideal is unlikely to happen as long as western intellectuals like Bernard Lewis and Samuel Huntington keep blaming "Islam" and minimize the overwhelming impact of the West on the rest. A different, nonconfrontational approach is called for.[36] This is being tried in various Muslim-Christian dialogues but unfortunately this promising trend is virtually confined to academics in the West. The healing dialogue has to be extended to the media, the politicians, and to the various institutions of civil society in Muslim countries and in the West.

NOTES

1. Huntington's article and book on the "clash of civilizations" contains many wrong assumptions and many wrong ideas, but he is not always wrong. When he says

that "within both Muslim and Christian societies, tolerance for the other declined sharply in the 1980s and 1990s" he is certainly correct. Samuel Huntington, *The Clash of Civilizations and the Remaking of World Order* (New York: Simon & Schuster, 1996), 211. See also Daniel Pipes, *In the Path of God: Islam and Political Power* (New York: Basic Books, 1983); Bernard Lewis, *Islam and the West* (New York: Oxford University Press, 1993); S. Rashid, ed., *The Clash of Civilizations? Asian Responses* (New York: Oxford University Press, 1997); Colin Chapman, *Islam and the West: Conflict, Coexistence or Conversion?* (Carlisle: Paternoster, 1998); and Ralph Braibanti, *Islam and the West: Common Cause or Clash?* (Washington, D.C.: The Center for Muslim-Christian Understanding, Georgetown University, 1999).

2. Huntington's remark that "Islam's borders are bloody, and so are its innards," (Huntington, *The Clash of Civilizations and the Remaking of World Order,* 258) is outrageous because he deliberately avoids mentioning that most of the conflicts resulted from Muslim efforts to be liberated from oppression. Misunderstandings abound and it is difficult to see how the conflict will be resolved. See S. Rashid, "Can this War End?" *Journal of the Historical Society* 2, no. 3 (fall 2002).

3. K. M. Panikkar's study is now a classic. The cruelty and the avarice of the conquistadors has been all too apparent in the centuries of colonialism in the East. For far too long the West had read with self-satisfaction one-sided accounts of the Age of Colonialism (disguised as the Age of Enlightenment). In the past forty or so years an increasing number of intellectuals, many from the West, have challenged the "*conventional*" view. Also see William Hardy McNeill, *The Pursuit of Power: Technology, Armed Force, and Society Since A.D. 1000* (Chicago: University of Chicago Press, 1982); Deepak Lal, "Asia and Western Dominance: Retrospect and Prospect," UCLA Department of Economics Working Paper, no. 813, delivered as Annual Lecture for the International Institute for Asian Studies, Leiden, the Netherlands, October 2000.

4. Edward Said's brilliant study was essentially about the Middle East, but the West conquered that part of the "*East*" *after* conquering many places further east. At the time of its downfall in 1757 Bengal had more wealth and population than the entire Arab Middle East. Colin McEvedy, *The Penguin Atlas of Modern History (to 1815)* (Harmondsworth, U.K.: Penguin, 1972) and Colin McEvedy and Richard Jones, *Atlas of World Population History* (London: A. Lane, 1978).

5. Edward Said's *Orientalism* is surely a classic. Its detailed scholarly exposition of the intellectual arrogance and shallowness of self-proclaimed western experts explains to a great extent the troubles of our times. Edward W. Said, *Orientalism* (New York: Vintage Books, 1979). See also particularly Martin W. Lewis and Kären E. Wigen, particularly chapter 3, *The Myth of Continents: A Critique of Metageography* (Berkeley: Univeristy of California Press, 1997).

6. Huntington's entire thesis is based on his certainty that the West has and will continue to decline in relative strength to other civilizations (chapter 4, "The Fading of the West"). He assumes that "civilizations" act like nation-states when it suits his arguments, but when citing many actual events he illustrates that nation-states act in their self-interest.

7. The bankruptcies declared by Enron and WorldCom together are bigger than the combined GNPs of Indonesia and Bangladesh. If globalization means opening up the

economy to free transfer of funds then transnational (so-called multinationals) will own not just assets but whole economies.

8. The exploitation of the Niger delta for oil and the dreadful environmental mess it created is one of the sorriest instances of "development" in Africa. It led to the judicial murder of Ken Saro-Wiwa and others and continues to be a human rights disaster. Right now the exploitation of oil resources in Gabon and Angola threatens to create more environmental and social disasters.

9. The use of the word Islam to describe various subjects, objects, attitudes, arts, and concepts has been criticized in many works (by Edward Said and others) but the tendency continues. It seems to be an effort to debase the religion and make it look restricted in time and space. There needs to be a clear distinction between the terms Islam and Muslim. Muslims are people who have accepted Islam as their religion, and they are, as people are wont to be, very diverse in their social patterns. As the author wrote earlier, "There are no Islamic countries and no Islamic societies, only countries and societies that are Muslim, and their failings cannot be attributed to the religion of Islam," Haroun Er-Rashid, "Huntington's Prediction Refuted," *Journal of the Historical Society* 2, no. 2 (spring 2002).

10. Some Muslim communities think music and singing is allowed only if it is for "sacred" purpose (praise of Allah and his Prophet). Most Muslim communities, however, think this is too restrictive and allow a great deal of "profane" music and singing.

11. A word of caution: no matter how similar Muslim and non-Muslim communities look to the westerner there are fundamental differences that are not readily apparent. Their language could be nine-tenths similar (with regional variations) but the tenth that is dissimilar immediately separates the two, because it relates to religious symbols, festivals, anniversaries, commemorations, family relationships, etc. In short, the differences relate to the cores of the cultures while the rest belong to shared geographical proximity. See Lewis and Wigenk, *The Myth of Continents,* for fresh perspectives on cultures.

12. In another place the author refers to "cellular" societies, borrowing from E. A. G. Dobby, see Haroun Er-Rashid, *Conflict of Cultures: Lessons From Bosnia* (Dhaka: University Press Limited, 1998). This term is applicable to situations when two communities do not share the same language, as in Malaysia. In situations where two (or more) communities share the same mother tongue they are not strictly cellular. Their cultures obviously overlap. The overlap is even greater when the different cultural communities share many occupations and also a long history.

13. The entire lot of Muslims in the world comprise the Muslim *Ummah*. According to Ahmed S. Dallal "it has often been used to express the essential unity of Muslims in *diverse* cultural settings," Ahmed Dallal, "Ummah," in the *Oxford Encyclopedia of the Modern Islamic World* (New York: Oxford University Press,1995).

14. Huntington is correct that there have been many conflicts between Muslims and non-Muslims (Huntington, *The Clash of Civilizations and the Remaking of World Order,* 254–65) in the past half century but he self-servingly glosses over Russian, French, and British conquests in the nineteenth century that are the immediate causes of most of the recent conflicts. He makes a great deal out of conflicts that have simpler explanations. In terms of conflict duration and scale, the border (fault line?) between Sunni

and Shia in Iraq, and Iran could be shown to be as volatile as any between Muslims and Christians. That would not, however, fit Huntington's thesis.

15. G. H. Jensen, in his *Militant Islam* (London: Pan Books, 1979), cites instances in Algeria, Sudan, and Java when overzealous Christian missionary activity aroused immediate reactions and long-term effects. Though on the whole, Christian missionary activity in Bengal was subdued there are many instances, particularly from the nineteenth century, when there were agitations and petitions against them.

16. Huntington, *The Clash of Civilizations and the Remaking of World Order*, 68.

17. Huntington, *The Clash of Civilizations and the Remaking of World Order*, 68, 69–72.

18. Huntington, *The Clash of Civilizations and the Remaking of World Order*, 72, emphasizes that "again and again both westerners and non-westerners point to individualism as the central distinguishing mark of the West."

19. For a powerful exposition of the case against westernization see Mehmet, 1999. For more views on modernization see Fazlur Rahman, *Islam and Modernity: Transformation of an Intellectual Tradition* (Chicago: University of Chicago Press, 1984); Tariq Ramadan, *To Be a European Muslim* (Markfield, U.K.: The Islamic Foundation, 2000); and Gema Martin Muñoz, ed., *Islam, Modernism and the West* (London: I. B. Tauris, 1999).

20. For a westernized view see Ömer Çaha, "The Deficiency of Democracy in the Islamic World," chapter 3 in this volume. For more on Muslims and Democracy see Ahmed Moussalli, *The Islamic Quest for Democracy, Pluralism, and Human Rights* (Gainesville: University of Florida Press, 2001), and John Esposito and John Voll, *Islam and Democracy* (New York: Oxford University Press, 1996).

21. Clan and tribal allegiances have always weakened the solidarity of the Muslim *Ummah*. A leading Pashtun politician once said that his allegiances were firstly with his family, and then his clan, next his tribe, and then only with other Muslims. Allegiance to his nation-state came last of all.

22. For those who think American antagonism to Islam is a post 9/11 phenomena consider the following analysis by an academic, D. D. Newsom, in the mid-1980s: "If there is a broadly negative view of Islam in the United States, it springs primarily from two perceptions. One is that Islam, particularly fundamentalist Islam, represents a threat to the interests of the United States. The other is that Islam is basically an inhumane religion," in John L. Esposito, ed., *Islam in Asia: Religion, Politics, and Society* (New York: Oxford University Press, 1987). For an interesting counterview see Paul Findley, *Silent No More—Confronting America's False Images of Islam* (Beltsville, Md.: Amana, 2001).

23. Muslim radicals consider themselves as idealists and therefore espouse goals (such as a return to the simple lifestyles of the early Khalifas) that are not achievable or may not even be desirable given the flow of history. Moderates, on the other hand, are more rational, realizing that a return to the past is not a practical goal for the future.

24. Whereas Muslim radicals tend to see only evil in the West, moderates see both good and evil. The refusal of the radicals to see any good in western cultures is what marks them out in Muslim societies. Fundamentalism may not be the right word for such an attitude. Readers may also consult John Esposito, *Unholy War: Terror in the Name of Islam* (New York: Oxford University Press, 2002) for more on this.

25. Accounting by the PPP method (World Bank 2001) should be more favorable to the poorer countries, but even by this method the GNP of all Muslim-majority

countries comes to a mere 7.9 percent of total world income. Huntington's statement that "Islamic civilization" accounted for 11 percent of the world's gross economic product in 1992 is surely a gross overestimation. Huntington, *The Clash of Civilizations and the Remaking of World Order*, 87.

26. Huntington, *The Clash of Civilizations and the Remaking of World Order*, 57.

27. For arguments against consumerism (essentially the *Davos Culture*) see William Ophuls, *Ecology and the Politics of Scarcity: Prologue to a Political Theory of the Steady State* (San Francisco: W. H. Freeman, 1977) and *Requiem for Modern Polities—The Tragedy of the Enlightenment and the Challenge of the New Millenium* (Boulder, Colo.: Westview Press, 1997), as well as Bruce Rich, *Mortgaging the Earth* (Boston: Beacon Press, 1994).

28. Huntington, *The Clash of Civilizations and the Remaking of World Order*, 88–91.

29. Huntington, *The Clash of Civilizations and the Remaking of World Order*, 88–91, 209–16.

30. At present, major geographical areas of Muslim concern are Palestine, Chechnya, Kashmir, and Mindanao. A few years ago there were also Bosnia and Kosovo. The Muslims of these two countries were ultimately rescued from their sufferings by the West, a fact that is seen very positively by moderate Muslims. However, in the case of Bosnia the motive of the West is somewhat suspect (see Rashid, *Conflict of Cultures*).

31. Over half a century of human rights violations against them have taught the Palestinians that extremism is the only way out of this misery. The path of brutal repression by Sharon is creating its own equal and opposite reaction, which in double-talk is terrorism.

32. Ahmed Rashid, *Taliban: Islam, Oil and the New Great Game in Central Asia* (London: I. B. Tauris, 1999), and John Cooley, *Unholy Wars: Afghanistan, America and International Terrorism* (London: Pluto Press, 1999) make interesting reading.

33. Tariq Ramadan, *Muslims in France: The Way Towards Coexistence* (Markfield, U.K.: The Islamic Foundation, 1999) and *To Be A European Muslim*. See also Aristide Zolberg and Long Litt Woon, "Why Islam is Like Spanish: Cultural Incorporation in Europe and the United States," *Politics and Society* 27, no. 1 (March 1999), for an optimistic view before 9/11.

34. Tariq Ramadan, *Islam, The West and the Challenges of Modernity*.

35. Huntington, *The Clash of Civilizations and the Remaking of World Order*, chapter 4.

36. From the Muslim perspective one of the best expositions of what they want is by Abdessalam Yassine, *Winning the Modern World for Islam* (Iowa City: Justice and Spirituality, 2000).

2

Islam, Modernity,
and the Dialectic of Dogmatism

Michael J. Thompson

A scene from Youssef Chahine's film *Destiny* shows the twelfth-century Islamic philosopher and jurist Averroes (Ibn Rushd) in dispute with one of his students who, being a follower of a literalist conservative religious sect in Moorish Spain, argues that faith is superior to the use of knowledge when it comes to the comprehension of religious texts. For Averroes, the answer is clear, "revelation can be interpreted only by study," and the messages of religion are to be seen through the gaze of reason. For the traditionalists, the answer is equally clear: religious texts allow for no interpretation.

Far from being a mere slice of historical trivia or even of intellectualized cultural atavism, Chahine's film frames an interesting and crucial problem when considering the state of contemporary Islamic societies and their relation to modernity. It captures a dynamic moment in the history of Islamic thought, encapsulating, in its own way, what Chahine represents as the loss—in his depiction, a tragic one—of rationalism to irrationalism, of the impulse of critical thought to dogma, and of rational enlightenment to the blindness of custom and tradition. The tension between reason and its implications for the idea of interpretation, universal understanding, and rational inquiry on the one hand, and the dogmatic acceptance of religious doctrine on the other, is a problem that extends deep into the intellectual history of Islamic thought. To grasp this tension is the key to seeing the development of certain intellectual traditions, which can be viewed as structuring the specific ways that ideas have impacted the historical development of society and politics.

But the implications of this twist of fate in classical Islamic thought are issues that Chahine, as a contemporary filmmaker, merely hints toward. Through Chahine's lens, Averroes's struggle with the fundamentalist interpreters of the Quran, and Islamic faith more broadly, is a metaphor of the contemporary rational critic of Islam from within. As a film concerned with historical events and, implicitly, with contemporary problems, it operates on two distinct levels: first, as a historical documentary of that point in Islamic thought when the project of reasoned interpretation loses its struggle with Islam's more conservative, dogmatic forces, those grounded in a more mystical and literalist set of traditions themselves not at all separate from certain political imperatives; and second, as a metaphorical, even allegorical, representation of reasoned, critical thought in the face of more irrational forces of religion, custom, and tradition. For Chahine, this would be a grandiose representation of the critical Islamic thinker within the Islamic context; but what should be initially explored is the first, more complex reading. One that has deep implications and should be investigated when discussing Islam's relation to modernity, as well as its relation to the West.

But even more, it is in the character of culture that many attributes of modernity are rooted. In many ways, this is an Aristotelian insight: that the character of any culture or community, its *ethos*, is a primary determining factor in the character of its polity.[1] However, it has become common to view modernization and the process of political, economic, and social development solely as a process of institutional evolution: the development of legal-rational institutions, free markets, and a liberal civil society. But the role of ideas, of the ways that people cognitively shape their social, political, and cultural environment needs to be emphasized. There needs to be a space opened up for the role that ideas play in the process of social change while still accounting for the structural realities of economy, polity, and society. When I say "ideas," I mean political-philosophical ideas, as well as moral values and ethical conceptions that affect the way we conceive of the world and human beings. Ideas that shape the specific way that a culture views its political, ethical, moral, and cultural self; the way it shapes its political and legal institutions, which serve as receptors, in a certain way, for foreign ideas. In this sense, the development of modernity—itself a concept that is defined by both structural and cultural variables—needs to be recast as an interaction between ideas and institutions, as the promulgation of a particular political *tradition.*[2] Be this as it may, any attention paid to ideas means an attention paid to the history of those ideas. In this sense, it is in the history of Islam itself and the different ideas that it has produced over time that can give us a glimpse into its relation to modernity and the West.

REASON AND FAITH

In his polemical book of 1866, *Averroès et l'averroisme: Essai historique*, Ernest Renan used the figure of Averroes in his intellectual struggle against religious authority in France in the nineteenth century.[3] For Renan, Averroes was a figure who spoke rational truth to traditional, dogmatic power. Against the precepts of religion and its stifling effect on free thought, Renan's Averroes was the last of a rationalist tradition in Islamic culture:

> Averroes's life occupies almost the whole twelfth century and is linked to all events of this decisive era for the history of Muslim civilization. The twelfth century saw the definitive failure of the attempt made by the Abbasids of the Orient and the Umayyads of Spain to create in Islam a rationalist and scientific development. When Ibn Rushd [Averroes] died in 1198 Arab philosophy lost in him its last representative, and the triumph over free thought was assured for at least six hundred years.[4]

In Renan's highly interpretive reading, after Averroes there would not be free thought in Islamic society until his own day, when a renaissance (*nahda*) within Islamic culture was being born. Irrespective of Renan's eurocentric approach to Islamic studies, his championing of Averroes as a figure of rational enlightenment battling dogmatic faith should still be taken seriously, although perhaps not in the literal terms that he may have expressed it.

The idea of enlightenment, both in the West and elsewhere, has always been problematic, not so much for what it achieved but for what it represents and what its various implications have always been. The Enlightenment was a major force in the modernization of western social and political institutions. It gave primacy to reason as a force for social change and privileged reason and science against the precepts of tradition and religion. It paved the way to modernity by establishing the institutions as well as the mindset for an entire culture—institutions and a mindset that continue to exert their force on and within the world to this very day. Of course, this has always meant that established "truths" and ideas were the object of Enlightenment critique. It was Immanuel Kant who made the crucial distinction between that of dogmatism (*Dogmatismus*) and criticism (*Kritizismus*)—the perennial distinction between reasoned analysis and blind acceptance that Enlightenment thinkers had always placed at the core of their worldview.

Today, the cultural content of Islam is seen by many to denote a religious doctrine unreflexive in nature, its society characterized by extreme economic inequality and political oppression. The most commonplace views of contemporary Islamic society and its politics therefore reflect a convenient "other" to the developed world of the West where economic affluence, cultural complexity, and political freedoms are the norm; where religion is private, the state is democratic, and we can claim for ourselves the most enviable mantle of being "modern." In contradistinction to the "enlightened" West, Islamic states are seen to reflect unenlightened, despotic rule and this has led to culturalist assumptions as to the very roots of enlightenment and rationality itself, that it is the unique product of the historical-cultural trajectory of western society.[5]

Nevertheless, the question that is most pressing is this: what are the factors that historically inhibited the growth of at least some aspects of modernity in contemporary Islamic states? Of course, colonialism, war, the predominant existence of tyrannical political rule, all play an essential role in grappling with this question. But the role of ideas must also be examined. Enlightenment is not, contrary to most of the critical literature on the subject, a purely western product. The idea of enlightenment—as the privileging of reason over unreason, of demonstrative logic over that of blind faith, and of inquiry and proof over passive acceptance and tradition—is not something unique to the West. As Amartya Sen has shown, the fundamental ideas of political tolerance and the privileging of reason over that of custom and tradition can also be found on other classical cultures such as in his discussion of India's King Akbar:

> Akbar's emphasis on reason and scrutiny serves as a reminder that "cultural boundaries" are not as limiting as is sometimes alleged (as, for example, in the view, discussed earlier, that "justice," "right," "reason," and "love of humanity" are "predominantly, perhaps even uniquely, Western values"). Indeed, many features of the European Enlightenment can be linked with questions that were raised earlier—not just in Europe but widely across the world.[6]

The relevance of this for the philosophical ideas of classical Islam—more specifically, the philosophical ideas of those thinkers that embraced Greek philosophical thought and merged it with the humanistic interpretation of Islamic religious teachings, a group of thinkers known more specifically as *falasifa*[7]—must be emphasized. These Islamic thinkers engaged in a humanistic ethos that emphasized the role of human reason and also gave primacy to the act of rationalistic *interpretation* (*ta'wil*) over that of faith.[8] This emphasis on human reason put humanism and rationality at the core of their thought, and it can be seen that the effects of the loss of this tradition in Islamic thought is severe. For the *falasifa*, reason was wedded to the ends of human happiness and fulfillment, reason was given emphasis, and the ability of human beings to reason was at the core of their thinking, and it is this humanistic notion and the kind of ethical, normative, and ultimately political stances that it supports, which I will call "rational humanism."

This rational humanistic ethos was prevented from developing into a full-fledged intellectual and cultural tradition—one that could have had profound impact on political and social development—in Islamic culture not because of what Renan called the "Quranic yoke," but because of the loss of the rational strain of Islamic philosophy within the context of the more traditionalist strains of Quranic teaching. To put it in a more simplistic, even crude light, with the decline of the rationalist tradition of the *falasifa*, Islam loses its struggle with the enlightenment tendencies that were growing within it. Indeed, it is simply not the case that thinkers like Averroes and Avicenna represent an atheistic impulse hidden within the dark abyss of religious ignorance and intolerance. It is also true that small shreds of this humanistic and rational tradition in philosophy remained among some elite scholars in Islam who were followers of Alfarabi, Avicenna, and Averroes—themselves not particularly popular in mainstream religious circles and certainly antithetical to the more traditional forces within the religion—such as Ibn Khaldun, Al Iji, and, as late as the nineteenth century, Al Bajuri. Renan's analysis has therefore been discredited in that respect; but it would be wrong to simply dismiss the insight as an orientalist, even racist view of Islam. Renan's basic view is also echoed by the German philosopher Ernst Bloch who argued that the work of the *falasifa* constituted an "anti-feudalist" philosophy opposed to orthodox Islam. In Bloch's interpretation, "[p]hilosophy became in the Orient as dangerous as natural sciences in Italy after the Galilei case."[9]

However we may wish to conceptualize the role of rationalist philosophy in Islamic thought, it is more important to show how this discussion is related to the ideas of the western Enlightenment. The Islamic encounter with Enlightenment ideas during the eighteenth and nineteenth centuries was therefore met by an Islamic culture that could find no real intellectual or cultural affinity with those ideas. In addition, as Shlomo Avineri has argued, there was also the problem of the method by which these ideas were delivered to the Islamic world.

> When Europeans think of Napoleon's abortive campaign in Egypt, they associate it with Champollion and the Rosetta Stone. For Arabs, it was the first of many European military incursions—incursions that spelled defeat for Muslim (and Arab) forces but that also brought the ideas of the Enlightenment to the Middle East. European ideas became associated both with military conquest and Christian missionary activity. Consequently, the emancipatory messages of the Enlightenment and the French Revolution were tainted.[10]

Of course, Avineri is right—but his conclusion cannot rest solely on the realities of western imperialism. The ideas of the Enlightenment were also just that: ideas. What needs to be seen is that there was a tradition in Islamic philosophy that was essentially defined by the interpenetration of different cultural ideas. The emergence of the religion itself was an outgrowth of Hebraic and Christian religious ideas and symbols, and its philosophical tradition was fundamentally shaped by its discovery of Greek philosophical thought. This was done not merely through cultural and intellectual osmosis; it was also a self-conscious activity on the part of the *falasifa*, especially those associated with the ideas of Averroes. Indeed, there is no way to minimize the effects of imperialism on Islamic countries and the way this shaped their political and social development, but it should also be seen that the less any culture privileges reason and the general precepts of enlightenment, the less likely there can ever be a way out of the cycles of history that confine people to domination and unfreedom. It is simply not the case that western ideas—as Sen has shown[11]—were rejected in those places throughout the world where imperialism occurred. What is important to see in the case of Islamic history is that there was the lack of any philosophical substrate to which Enlightenment ideas could attach themselves and, as a result, root themselves within the broader fabric of thought, culture, and values of Islam. In many ways, the lack of a thriving rational humanistic ethic within the tradition of Islamic thought made any affinity with western Enlightenment ideas nearly impossible.

In terms of Islam itself, the history of philosophy in its "golden age" shows us that coming to terms with reason and faith was a central problem that was deemed solvable by the philosophical thinkers associated with the tradition of *falsafa*. *Falsafa* was that branch of Islamic thought that was concerned with incorporating Greek rational philosophy into the religious apparatus of Islam. This, in and of itself, was not an act of dissent like that of the *philosophes* and *Aufklären* of eighteenth-century Europe. It was an attempt at harmonizing what were seen to be two separate but consistent truisms about the world, humanity, and nature. First, there was Islamic law, *sharia*, which was the revealed law given to Muhammad, which served as the central core of Islamic civilization codifying its belief structure and values. Next, there was the realm of science, of demonstrative logic that was passed down from the Greeks and the rational laws, the *nomoi*, that it purported to discover. Demonstrative logic was also seen as possessing truth content since it too revealed laws about the nature of the world.

Both were inherently concerned with the notion of law. *Sharia* was divine, religious law, whereas the Greek conception of law, *nomos*, although not divine in any way, still expressed truisms about the working of nature and politics. What the Islamic philosophers of the ninth, tenth, and eleventh centuries were attempting was not a theological worldview immune to the insights of philosophical science; they sought to sustain and to integrate the insights of Greek philosophy with the cultural values of Islamic civilization and the deeper meaning that they felt the religious texts offered. When I speak of a dialectic of dogmatism, I am therefore referring to that crucial turn in Islamic philosophical thought that broke with this tendency. I am referring to the critical turn away from reason, from the tradition of reason as a logical, in the sense of demonstrative logic, rational worldview that was reflexive and dynamic in its dealings with nature and religion. This is a logic that dealt with objective reality in objective terms, terms that, the *falasifa* believed, were *universal* in nature and not *particular*. Universalism was something inherent in both *sharia* and *nomos*: God, on the one hand, had revealed absolute, universal truths through *sharia* just as *nomos* was demonstratively true for all times and places—the former being mystically communicated, the latter reasoned and discovered by human beings. They need not be accepted on faith, but determined by reason and demonstrated *through* reason and accepted by a community composed of reasoned persons. There was, then, a failure on the part of the *falasifa* to extend and develop their ideas of rational humanism and, as a result, modernity would be seen as an "other" incapable of synthesis with Islamic culture and faith, their ideas drowned out by the more dogmatic, conservative notions of Islamic faith grounded in the communitarian structure of society.[12]

The core idea here is not that these trends in Islamic philosophy, in the thought of the various *falasifa*, would have led to an intellectual period comparable to the western Enlightenment—this would have required a multitude of other variables to produce—but that the component of rational thought (as demonstrative logic) and its position as an essential component of faith and religion would have kept open a space within which a rational "dialogue of civilizations" could have emerged. Western Enlightenment ideas could have had some affinity with an Islamic tradition of rational humanism as laid out by the *falasifa*. In this way, the political, moral, and ethical traditions of Islam and the West could have had a wider circuit of communication and the orientation of Islam to modernity would have been, today, more positive. Openness to what we have come to identify as western values and ideas does not necessarily require westernization. Indeed, it is possible that the notions and political values of liberty, justice, democracy, equality, etc., can take on new forms and be shaped by the cultural context within which it is introduced. But such a situation would require that these ideas, values and, inevitably, institutions are acquired through the means of civilizational dialogue, not through their violent importation and forced implementation.[13]

But did the seeds for such a rational humanism really exist in Islamic thought? The question is centered around the particular way that the *falasifa* conceptualized the relationship between man and God. As Lenn Goodman has argued, there are three core theses that need to be considered when thinking about the classical age of Islamic thought:

1. The seemingly ineffable content of religious experience can be articulated through symbols and so made a social reality, as imagery, ritual, myth, and law.

2. To know God we must study the world. Since man is made in the image of God, one can learn about God by studying humanity.
3. God executes justice in history by visiting upon us the consequences of our actions, communally and individually.[14]

The first two theses are most relevant when considering the shift in Islamic thought away from articulating a rational humanistic ethos within its religious scope and, throughout this development, a progressive force culturally, politically, and intellectually and toward a situation where the doctrines of religion have the effect of arresting this development and, in the end, constructing a boundary to the reception of certain ideas that will allow modernity to take root.

As we have seen, the *falasifa* of classical Islam sought a continuity between the notion of law derived from Greek philosophy (*nomos*) and the doctrines of sacred, divine law derived from Islamic thought (*sharia*). This project was linked to the three theses mentioned above. In the first sense, the idea of religious practice was a pragmatic concern. The ethical ideas illuminated by religious thought were to be communicated to the masses of people, not via direct rational argumentation or persuasion but through the communication of symbols and rituals, through religious practice. These symbols would therefore make these abstract principles and teachings concrete through social practice. Similarly, the second thesis indicates an emphasis on the study of the link between God and man; the primary entrance into a kind of humanism that would have been responsive to the impulses of the modernizing West or, at least, instrumental in the formation of a kind of humanism that would have led to an Islamic modernity.

Islamic philosophy of this "Golden Age" held to the notion, echoed by its greatest Jewish student, Maimonides, that one cannot believe unless one thinks. The primary impulse behind the rational inquiry into human affairs was to show how the efforts of Greek rational thought were one with the divinely revealed truths of Islam contained in *sharia*. Greek rational philosophy presented an interpretation of the world that was rational and understandable; it was potentially accessible to everyone and it was an explanatory medium that—in the eyes of thinkers like Alfarabi, specifically—did not diminish Islam but instead fortified it through the provision of a rational account to that which was divinely prescribed.[15] This was the initial justification for the confluence of Greek thought and Islamic religious belief from the beginning, and it is the loss of this tradition, of this perception of the interlock between reason and faith, science and religion that has had such an important impact on the capacity of contemporary Islamic culture to receive and absorb the tenants of western modernity.

In this vein, Avicenna argued that revelation was not simply a matter of divine, religious insight, but was primarily the product of a kind of access to the realm of ultimate truth, something that, in and of itself, was the divine. Thus, Plato, Aristotle, Pythagoras, and other ancient thinkers were prophets in this sense. Although they did not express truths in the manner of the Quran and Islamic teachings, it was through their teachings and their philosophies that they were able to articulate a form of truth in the world through rational means. What this expresses is the close connection these thinkers felt between a philosophical tradition that was secular and anthropocentric, and revealed religion—a connection that was diametrically opposed to any form of dogmatic interpretation of religious faith. This is not dissimilar from Alfarabi's claim that there existed a harmony "between their divine law and the practical intention of classical political philosophy."[16] The ideas of the practical Greeks was therefore fulfilled in the revelation of divine law, of *sharia*.

Of course, this view was not the dominant one in Islamic thought. Those thinkers that embraced Greek philosophy and tried to apply it to Islamic teachings and their interpretation were opposed, in many ways, by those thinkers who saw in Greek philosophy not a form of rationality that could be used to enhance the doctrines of Islamic civilization, but a form of naturalism that was foreign and dangerous to the teachings of Islamic faith and, ultimately, to the very core of Islamic civilization itself. This view was a product of *kalam*, or dialectical theology, a form of religious interpretation where meaning was "anchored in speculative premises extracted from an adversary or (even more suppositiously), from scripture."[17] More importantly, it was opposed to *falsafa* through its opposition of what many of the *falasifa* put at the center of their method: Aristotelian syllogism.[18] Thus, within Islamic thought, there was a burgeoning rift between those thinkers that privileged reason in conjunction with religion, and those that directly opposed this privileging.

But it is precisely this turn away from rational inquiry within the tradition of Islamic thought that Chahine, in his cinematic portrayal of Averroes, seeks to depict. What in film can be seen as an allegorical confrontation between reason and dogma is something that still permeates the intellectual framework of Islamic thought. To embrace the impulses of reason imparted by Greek thought was therefore, for a figure like Averroes, not a matter of rebellion against religion per se—as Renan and Bloch argue that it was, an act of atheism—in the face of enlightened reason. The answer is more subtle than this, and more complex. Rather than philosophizing with a hammer, Averroes develops rational philosophy within the context of Islamic thinking and emphasizes rational interpretations of religious doctrine rather than dogmatic, literalist ones. *Sharia* and *nomos* are not in opposition, as the antirationalist theologians would have it; rather, religion had a rationalist base and *sharia* was not mystical and therefore unapproachable by reason:

> It is very clear . . . what Averroes wants to say about prophecy and *sharia* . . . , that it provides exactly the same information as philosophy, albeit in a different form. *Sharia* does have a decisive superiority, he makes it clear elsewhere in that it is available to a far wider cross-section of the community than philosophy, yet there is nothing in *sharia* that contradicts "ancient wisdom," by which he means Greek thought.[19]

With this in mind, it is not a picture of Averroes as the subversive that we should privilege. On the contrary, we should see that he was weaving a rational humanism that would put human interpretation at the core of human activity and an ethics informed by religious principles, which in and of themselves were rationally interpreted. In this sense, rational humanism becomes the ultimate enemy of dogmatism: it questions the authority of belief and the hierarchy of religious elites that espouse them, and it also places universal emphasis on human beings as the ends of ethical acts. In this way, traditional authority can be combated, irrational norms critiqued, and the inception of enlightenment can be glimpsed. The West therefore may have articulated the basic ideas of enlightenment and in their most politically viable form, but, as the ideas of Averroes and the *falasifa* indicate, it cannot claim an absolute monopoly on its principles.

If we extend this argument it cannot be said that modernity needs to be a specifically western enterprise or that the institutions of modernity require the transposition of one culture into another. The cross-pollination that occurred between Greek learning and Islamic faith shows that the mixture of a rational outlook was compatible with the cultural content of Islam. As a metaphorical figure, Chahine's Averroes is not merely a historical figure, he is a symbol of this mixture of rationalism, moderation and criticism against dogmatism, irrationalism, political inflexibility, and social intolerance. Even more, he is a figure who represents the cultural values of Islamic civilization and who, at the same time, embraces the principles of reason and the drive to gradually attain truth through the activity of demonstrative logic. The highest form of science in Islamic civilization was jurisprudence (*fiqh*), or the study of divine law. This involved the interpretation, study, and application of divine law. Revelation was taken by some to be absolute and the expressions of religious law were interpreted either literally or were seen—through the eyes of the *falasifa*—through the eyes of human reason. Religious practices and symbols were not, in this latter interpretative framework, expressions of absolute truth. They were symbols and practices that were meant for the consumption and education of the masses. Intellectual study of truth required training in philosophy and this, as it was for Plato, was rare indeed:

For it is only with great strain that [the common people] can comprehend the true states of such matters; it is only the very few among them that can understand the truth of divine "unicity" and divine "remoteness." The rest would inevitably come to deny the truth of such existence, fall into dissensions, and indulge in disputations and analogical arguments that stand in the way of their political duties. This might even lead them to adopt views contrary to the city's welfare, opposed to the imperatives of truth. Their complaints and doubts will multiply making it difficult for a man to control them. For divine wisdom is not easily acquired by everyone.[20]

Religious custom and belief were therefore not to be seen as literal acts that were performed due to the dictates of custom. Rather, they were meant to inspire goodness on the part of the individual and to bring them closer to that essence within themselves that was "good"; the role of reason was to control the animalistic instincts of man and to encourage ethical and political goodness. This last point is important since, for the *falasifa*, ethics and politics were at the core of their philosophies. Politics was meant, as Alfarabi argued, to sustain happiness. The good regime was one that did not allow the excesses of want, domination, possession, sensual pleasures, and honor. Rather, the role of the ideal political regime, the "virtuous city," was to concern itself with the right opinions of its citizens, with their moral attainment of goodness and happiness.[21]

Once again, it is not the point here that these ideas in some form presaged modernity, enlightenment, or democratic forms of government. What it is meant to show is that there was a vibrant form of rational humanism that evolved and had currency among those thinkers that tried to explore the linkage between faith and reason, between *sharia* and *nomos*, Islamic religion and Greek philosophical thought. The broader relevance of this point is that there existed an intellectual struggle of *Weltanschauungen* between this rational humanism, on the one hand, and a tradition-bound, interpretation of scripture on the other—between reason and dogma. The core essence of this struggle was between the place of human reason in the context of revelation, the same intellectual struggle that characterized the rise of rational logic within Christianity and its humanistic implications by thinkers such as Abelard in the twelfth-century Renaissance and beyond, as Majid Fakhry has argued:

> contrary to the widespread view that Arabic philosophy was engrossed with the methodological question of the reconciliation of philosophy and religion with its obvious metaphysical implications and undertones, the philosophers of Islam were equally concerned with the kind of "humanist" enquiry that has been the hallmark of modern philosophy since the time of Rene Descartes.[22]

But this brings us back to the three theses laid out by Goodman. The ethics of Islamic humanism were current in the philosophical language and concerns of the *falasifa*. The decline of this tradition was not, in itself, the cause for the current dissonance between western modernity and Islamic ideas and values. Quite to the contrary, what it is essential to see is that ideas are important when discussing social and political development; that the ideas that any particular culture may possess will not inherently lead toward fostering the processes of modernization. There is always a struggle within any culture, any tradition that is intellectual in any form, between the forces of enlightenment—or those forces that privilege rational aspects of that civilization and its ideas and its values—and those of custom and tradition. My contention here is simply that what Chahine portrays in his film is something that resonates deeply within the history of philosophical and political ideas within Islam and that this resonance is still felt today. The more concrete form of this argument centers on the ideas of development and modernization that the West employs and the way this discourse is formed. Ideas are therefore important, but it must now be shown how they are central in the process of social and political development.

MODERNITY, ENLIGHTENMENT, AND DEVELOPMENT

The connection between faith and reason in Medieval Islamic thought should not be seen as irrelevant when considering the process of modernization. The core issue here, as raised most recently by Bernard Lewis, is whether or not modernization implies, or if not, even requires westernization.[23] Modernization is a process of developing certain kinds of institutions in the spheres of government, economics, and the application and advancement of technology in the manipulation of nature. Westernization is the evolution of certain values such as individualism, liberty, the separation of secular and sacred realms within government, the evolution of a public sphere, and the values of political and social equality.

On the whole, the discourse around the concept of modernization is predominantly defined as a matter of material development, as a development of economic and social institutions, which in the end, aid in the solution of social problems of various types. The materialist conception of development is not as much wrong as it is misguided in its emphasis on the category of economic institutions and their development. Ideas matter, and it is this side of development that has been neglected in the analysis of questions such as those posed here. It was the central contention of Max Weber that both the material (i.e., institutional) and ideational domains spark social change and development through the notion, borrowed from Goethe, of the "elective affinity." For Weber, the modernity of Western Europe was an outgrowth of an elective affinity between emerging mercantile interests and institutions of trade and small scale production on the one hand, and the worldly asceticism determined by a Protestant ethic—specifically by Calvinism—combined to produce a new social context where capitalism could emerge and develop. A Protestant ethic was merged with these newer economic institutions to produce a spirit of capitalism. The lesson taken from Weber here is not the typical one, that of content—i.e., that lacking a Protestant past and certain types of mercantile interests, Islamic societies could not develop capitalist institutions and, hence, modernity—but one of form: that ideas and the material conditions of existence (whether they be economic or political, in the form of political organization) interrelate in a constant, fluid manner. There can be no resting in a purely economic explanation before slipping back into the sphere of values and ideas to see how actors viewed and inevitably shaped their social world and then back again to see how these values and ideas were constrained or shaped by institutions. Institutions, although correctly defined separately from ideas, cannot be properly conceived outside of the "thick" historical description that incorporates values and ideas.

With this in mind, the discussion of Islam's development into modernity is severely affected by considering the question of the interaction between ideas and institutions. If the great Islamic philosophical tradition did lose, as I have been arguing here, the struggle between Enlightenment reason defined by its emphasis on demonstrative logic, the independence of reason and a rational humanism derived from the confluence of religious values and human rationality on the one hand, and dogmatic faith where the emphasis was on a literal interpretation of Quranic teachings and institutions, then the question of the development of ideas takes on a more central concern since the devolution of a tradition of rational critique was subordinated to the simplistic doctrines of faith. The current clash between Islamic and western *values* should therefore not be interpreted as a clash between *civilizations*, as it has been so fashionable to argue as of late. Nor should it be seen as a mere function of political oppression and global economic imperatives, of the broad hand of imperialism. Without question, as an explanatory path, the latter is elucidating, but also, in the end, incomplete. The absence of a firm, consistent intellectual tradition that privileged reason over dogma is, I would assert, a central aspect in the continued struggle of Islamic states with the notion of modernity. And, even more, it is important to see that the lack of what I have been calling here rational humanism to develop and grow into a political tradition is of historical importance when it comes to understanding the relationship between Islam and the West. Indeed, the problem is therefore too broad to be confined within the bounds of mere political science, sociology, or economics alone, spilling over into that of philosophical and intellectual history as well.

But, not unlike Weber, and even Marx, the dialectic between ideas and institutions throughout history is key. It would be absurd to assert that it is simply through the content of philosophical history that modern institutions are born and evolve—ideas develop in a dialectic between the material forms of life that are always already present, and vice versa. What this means in the current context is that, insofar as the Islamic world is concerned, the ideas of the Enlightenment need to be injected into the dialogue of civilizations that is current among Islamic and western intellectuals.[24] Modernization does not, however, require westernization. Enlightenment ideas need not imply, nor do they compel, cultural imperialism. Indeed, what the globalization and development literature has been lax to point out is that different cultures can, and must, emphasize the rational elements already inherent within themselves thereby effecting a turn to rational institutions and social, political, and economic modernization from the inside. Islam's relation to the West and to modernity is therefore not simply an issue of how certain religious precepts and customs interfere with the capitalist ethic, or how it has affected political thought and the emergence of civil society. Lacking a tradition of rational humanism— something that was simply undeveloped, not nonexistent as we have seen—is essential for the emergence of modernity in the Islamic world. As Majid Fakhry has further argued:

> it seems to me that it is the essence of modernity (or active participation in the life of the modern age) that humanism in some form or other, should be placed at the center of our intellectual, economic, social or political concerns. On this view, humanism becomes the most important element in any program of reform or social change, for which the Arab world has been searching, and continues to search today. Here the philosopher can do a great deal to clarify issues, define objectives of an ideological or ethical nature, and finally contribute to the development of practical reform programs.[25]

This perspective would seem to fly in the face of most of the social scientific literature on social and political development. It is not the case that ideas and the traditions within which they are articulated have no role in social and political modernization. In place of ideas—usually given a tertiary role as "ideology" in the literature on development and modernization—economic structure, property relations, and class formation are seen as being the prerequisites for democracy and political and social modernity throughout history.[26] But what I have been trying to show is that this development literature fails to put emphasis on the role of political *tradition*: that there is an active element that ideas possess in history and in politics, and the developmental path of societies.[27] In this sense, the loss of a tradition of rational humanism in Islamic thought is a contributor to the reception of Enlightenment ideas from the West that would have provided a barrier to the kind of religious dogmatism that became so prevalent in Islamic society and would also have contributed to the historical articulation of the ideas we associate with western modernity, or at least to their prerequisites. At the same time, this rational humanism can still serve as the core of a new political tradition in Islamic culture and thought and, in turn, help with the vision of new political and economic institutions paving a path to modernity.

The question is, today, why democratic movements have failed to take root, capture the imagination of broad segments of most of Arab Islamic societies, and begin to transform them. This is in the process of happening in Iran, where the ideas of political modernity—women's suffrage, electoral institutions, and a constitution promising certain basic rights—were put in place after the Islamic Revolution in 1979, and the legacy of these rights are only now beginning to shake Iranian society to its foundations. Also, there are figures, such as Saad Eddin Ibrahim, in Egypt that actively advocate for political and social reform. Ibrahim's base of operations is the Ibn Khaldun Center, named for the fourteenth-century Islamic philosopher who treated history as a science and introduced methods of sociology and political economy into his analysis of history. These forces of modernity are, no doubt, inspired by the West, but their source is from within the Islamic tradition itself.

Modernity, in this sense, and enlightenment go hand in hand. In terms of politics this was the key insight by Kant when he argued that "this enlightenment, and with it a certain sympathetic interest which the enlightened man inevitably feels for anything good which he comprehends fully, must gradually spread upwards towards the thrones and even influence their principles of government."[28] It is not only enlightened government that encourages political progress into political modernity; rather, it must rise from a *culture* of enlightenment. This was an insight generated by Aristotle where politics was seen as an outgrowth of the views and moral fabric of its community and not the other way around. In this sense, for Kant, it is through combating the irrational elements of culture, of custom and belief, and replacing this with the free public use of reason that is necessary for the development of a modern sensibility.

What this means is that what looks, at least on the surface, as a clash of civilizations is nothing of the kind. There is no inherent tendency within Islamic civilization toward despotism or theocracy. On the other hand, to explain the persistent state of Islamic political and social life—with respect to its more despotic characteristics—as a result of the particular regimes and institutions that make up and define the political landscape of contemporary Islamic states, is also misleading. The more complex explanation may, in the end, be the most accurate one: that Islam's struggle within its own philosophical heritage between what I have called its roots of rational humanism and the dogmatic tendencies of religion and tradition hindered its own growth toward modernity.

In light of this discussion, what we may see as the tragic tale of Averroes is actually something much more than a mere historical turn to religious dogmatism. It is, rather, a key element in the understanding of the concept of modernity itself and modernization as opposed to westernization. Chahine's film gives us a glimpse into a fundamental problematic that resonates through the ages of Arab-Islamic thought and culture—into the historical and political implication of ideas. Today it is brought once again into the spotlight as a result of the West's contentious relationship with Islamic states, and vice versa. But, it would be absurd to argue that this contentious relationship is grounded in some kind of civilizational divide. For, not unlike the emanations of a penumbra, rational enlightenment can always be glimpsed on the edges of Islamic religious dogmatism, the sources of both being one and the same, hidden deep within the complex fabric of history.

NOTES

1. See the *Politics* for a further discussion. For an interpretive discussion, see James Bernard Murphy, "Nature, Custom, and Reason as the Explanatory and Practical Principles of Aristotelian Political Science," *The Review of Politics* 64, no. 3 (summer 2002).

2. This concept of tradition is laid out by Stephen Eric Bronner as follows:

> Traditions are forged from a given complex of ideas and goals, material interests and institutional strategies, as well as divergent styles and constituencies. Each has its normative features and practical interests. Each also retains an existential dimension and thereby provides a mode of self-definition in relation to others. Tradition is, in short, different from the way metaphysicians, positivists, and phenomenologists conceive it. It can evidence various conflicting tendencies or subtraditions. But it is inherently informed by a *project*, an expressly political commitment, to transform its ideas into reality. Future forms of political theory, if they seek to remain relevant, must more self-consciously focus upon the role of traditions and their projects: the ideas they have utilized, the institutional constraints they have navigated, and the material interests they have embraced.

Bronner, *Ideas in Action: Political Tradition in the Twentieth Century* (Lanham, Md.: Rowman & Littlefield, 1999), 9.

3. See *Oeuvres Complétés,* vol. 3 (Paris: Calmann-Levy, 1949).

4. *Oeuvres Complétés,* 1f.

5. For this view, see Samuel Huntington, "The West: Unique, Not Universal," *Foreign Affairs* (November–December 1996): 29–35.

6. "East and West: The Reach of Reason," *The New York Review of Books*, July 20, 2000. For more on Akbar and his enlightened policies and ideas, see Irfan Habib, ed., *Akbar and His India* (Delhi: Oxford University Press, 1997).

7. The word itself is a variant of the word *falsafa*, a direct Arabic transliteration of the Greek term, φιλοσοφία.

8. For Averroes, *ta'wil* was defined by taking the overt, apparent meaning of some Quranic verse and penetrating to its essential meaning one hidden by its overt expression. This was an idea put forth by Avicenna and also has reverberations in the Hegelian distinction between *essence* and *appearance*.

9. *Avicenna und die Aristotelische Linke* (Berlin: Rütten & Loening, 1952), 62. For Bloch, the aim of this work was to discover a "subversive" tradition within the philosophies of Avicenna and Averroes. For Bloch, this tradition was defined by *atheism* and *materialism* and was inherently subversive to the religious beliefs of orthodox Islam. For an interpretation, see Stefan Wild, "Between Ernest Renan and Ernst Bloch: Averroes Remembered, Discovered, and Invented—The European Reception Since the Nineteenth Century," in *Averroes and the Enlightenment*, Mourad Wahba and Mona Abousenna, eds. (New York: Prometheus Books, 1994).

10. "Failed Democratization in the Arab World," *Dissent* (fall 2002): 22.

11. Also see Amartya Sen's discussion of this topic in his *Development As Freedom* (New York: Knopf, 2001), chapter 10.

12. It should be pointed out that some scholars have argued that the period of "free-thinking" in Islam ended much earlier than with Averroes. Sarah Stroumsa argues that: "[i]t appears that after the tenth century, blunt prose expression of freethinking was no longer possible." *Freethinkers of Medieval Islam* (Leiden: Brill, 1999), 241. For a classic statement of this view, see H. Steiner, *Die Mu'taziliten oder die Freidenker im Islam* (Leipzig, 1865).

13. This is essentially the argument of Alexis de Tocqueville in his "Second Letter On Algeria: 1837," included in this volume.

14. Lenn Goodman, *Jewish and Islamic Philosophy: Cross-pollinations in the Classic Age* (New Brunswick, N.J.: Rutgers University Press, 1999), 3.

15. See Mushin Mahdi, "Alfarabi," in Leo Strauss and Joseph Cropsey, eds., *History of Political Philosophy* (Chicago: University of Chicago Press, 1972), 182–202.

16. Mahdi, "Alfarabi," 184.

17. Lenn Goodman, "Humanism and Islamic Ethics," *Logos: A Journal of Modern Society & Culture* 1, no. 2 (spring 2002): 2, at: www.logosjournal.com.

18. See Goodman, "Humanism and Islamic Ethics."

19. Oliver Leamann, *Averroes and His Philosophy* (Oxford: Oxford University Press, 1988), 124. For more on the relation in Averroes's thought between reason and *Theos*, see Mushin Mahdi, "Remarks of Averroes's *Decisive Treatise*," in *Islamic Theology and Philosophy: Studies in Honor of George F. Hourani* (Albany, N.Y.: SUNY Press, 1984).

20. Avicenna, "Healing Metaphysics," in Ralph Lerner and Mushin Mahdi, eds., *Medieval Political Philosophy* (Ithaca, N.Y.: Cornell University Press, 1989), 100.

21. See "The Political Regime," in Lerner and Mahdi, eds., *Medieval Political Philosophy*.

22. Majid Fakhry, "Arabs and the Encounter with Philosophy," in M. Fakhry, *Philosophy, Dogma and the Impact of Greek Thought in Islam* (Manchester, U.K.: Varorium, 1994), 10.

23. Bernard Lewis, *What Went Wrong?: Western Impact and Middle Eastern Response* (New York: Oxford University Press, 2002).

24. This point is also made by Shlomo Avineri, op. cit., p. 24.

25. "Humanism and Modernity in the Arab World Today," in M. Fakhry, *Philosophy, Dogma and the Impact of Greek Thought in Islam,* 177.

26. For examples of these perspectives, see Adam Przeworski, *Democracy and Development: Political Institutions and Material Well-Being in the World, 1950–1990* (Cambridge: Cambridge University Press, 2000); Adam Przeworski, "Political Regimes and Economic Growth," *Journal of Economic Literature* (May 1993); Rueschemeyer, Stephens, and Stephens, *Capitalist Development and Democracy* (Chicago: Chicago University Press, 1992); Huber, Rueschemeyer, and Stephens, "The Impact of Economic Development on Democracy," *Journal of Economic Literature* (May 1993). For an analysis of the primary role of ideology as an organizational tool in the history of political transitions, see Theda Skocpol, *States and Social Revolutions* (Cambridge: Cambridge University Press, 1979).

27. It is important to distinguish *political tradition* from *political culture*. Political culture are the norms and values inherent within a political society whereas a political tradition, although it evolves out of culture, is not limited by any one specific cultural context. It can be exported, selectively appropriated, and used by foreign cultures to elucidate new paths out of the institutional constraints that are present. See Bronner, op. cit., for more on this concept of tradition. For the most coherent statement of political culture, see Gabriel Almond and Sydney Verba, *The Civic Culture: Political Attitudes and Democracy in Five Nations, An Analytic Study* (Boston: Little Brown, 1965).

28. "The Idea for a Universal History With a Cosmopolitan Purpose," in Hans Reiss, ed., *Kant: Political Writings,* H. B. Nisbet, trans. (Cambridge: Cambridge University Press, 1991), 51.

• 3 •

The Deficiency of Democracy in the Islamic World

Ömer Çaha

$\mathcal{T}$he attack on the World Trade Center on September 11, 2001, has once again drawn attention to the reconciliation of Islam with democracy. It is generally accepted that today, among the five religious and cultural blocs that predominate in the world—namely Christianity, Confucianism, Buddhism, Judaism, and Islam—it is the Muslim societies that have been furthest from democracy. Most countries in the Islamic world are governed by authoritarian or totalitarian regimes. Some of these regimes have constructed authoritarian structures under the absolute rule of a cult or party leader, an ideology, a king, or an emir. One can appreciate how vital it is for Muslim intellectuals to focus a great deal of their energy on the reasons behind the deficiency of democracy in the Islamic world. Once we consider that democracy not only brings about political freedom and human rights, but that it is also a driving force behind economic growth and development, we can better appreciate the significance and urgency of this issue for Muslim societies.

ISLAM AT THE CROSSROADS OF DEMOCRACY AND DESPOTISM

Before discussing the relationship between Islam and democracy, we should clarify the actual meaning of democracy. Democracy is a mode of governance that came to the fore and evolved as an alternative to despotic regimes prevailing in both traditional and modern societies. The most fundamental values of democracy are human rights and individual liberties. It has been evident that democracy, among its various alternatives, is a unique form of government that strives to guarantee the rights of all minorities and individuals on the basis of the rule of law. A democratic system requires the existence of certain procedural (formal) conditions in order to guarantee its fundamental principles, i.e., human rights and liberties. Periodical elections, constitutional government, majority rule, the accessibility of the media, and the free market economy, multiparty system, separation of powers are all ultimately intended to protect fundamental rights and liberties. In a democratic society the relationship between the state and society is founded on "contract." By means of social contract democracy limits the absolute and unlimited autonomy enjoyed by the state on the basis of societal will and the principle of the rule of law.

Political systems opposed to democracy may manifest themselves in different forms. Such modes of government may display authoritarian characteristics, while others are totalitarian in nature. Needless to say, in terms of state-society relationships and from the perspective of human rights, there is hardly any difference between the two regimes. Indeed, both types of regimes are disposed toward force and compulsion. In both, the state exercises arbitrary control over society. The political initiative remains entirely in the hands of the ruling elite. In short, both authoritarian and totalitarian regimes hinge on a coercive and despotic state. Here, the state is everything and the individual nothing.

In trying to understand the position of Islam between these two systems of government and to single out the one that comes closest to the Islamic approach to political governance, we observe that neither the Quran nor the Sunnah (the deeds and the words of the Prophet of Islam) contains a comprehensive list of injunctions about the theory of political governance. The Quran only mentions about a number of moral principles (consent and fairness) relevant to the political values, and not about the organizational structure of political governance. Likewise, the Sunnah does not touch upon the organizational structure of political governance, but contains advice geared to rulers on principles of justice, compassion, mercy, and obedience to God.

Given that the Quran and Sunnah do not admonish clearly defined and binding principles about political governance, Muslims have been left free to establish their own organizational structure in matters of politics, in accordance with the social conditions of their times. This was indeed the case for the Four Caliphs period (which emerged immediately after the death of the Prophet Muhammad) and thereafter. The caliphate system, established during the Four Caliphs period, emanated from the de facto will and choice of Muslims rather than stemming from Islamic theology. Therefore, it hardly seems difficult to see a certain type of government as an ideal model in Islamic theology and its practice in history. The flexibility in the structure of political systems in Islam gives an opportunity for Muslims to adapt any political system that serves their aims over time.

Islam primarily addresses the human individual—basic rights are accorded to the individual, and not to collective entities. Islam guarantees the human rights to life and property, protection of honor, freedom of conscience and enterprise. Moreover, Islam has abolished the legal hierarchy between human beings and put them under equal status. There is no distinction between the ruler and the ruled in terms of their standing before God. Both have the dignified privilege of being human. One can only speak of the superiority of a person to the extent of his or her fear and obedience of God *(takva)*, i.e., his goodness.

In addition to its theology, the practice of Islam by Muslims in their long history also indicates that Islam is far from being an organic unity of religion and state. In other words, neither Islamic theology nor Islamic practice over the course of centuries, under different empires (Umayyads, Abbasids, Seljukians, Ottomans, etc.), have obtained a political basis for the construction of a theocratic state. What we see however, is that, throughout Islamic history, a distinction was always made between *common law* (secular law) and *religious law (Shariah)*, and the rulers could enact laws that met the needs of their age. The Quran itself opens a space for common law by holding, "don't disregard common usage *(orf)* in your commands." This Quranic verse in fact permits the contribution of a particular culture to the construction of government and thus gives opportunity for the relativity of the governmental structure.

In short, in analyzing the question as to whether Islam is closer to democratic or despotic regimes, we ought to conclude, in the light of the criteria examined above, that democratic regimes, rather than despotic regimes, ought actually to be more compatible with Islam. We must not hereby disregard the fact that democracy is a political system that has been an outcome of historical conditions (ancient Greek ideas and institutions, feudalism, industrialization, etc., in the West), whereas Islam is a religion containing moral principles that admonish the exaltation of human spirit. Needless to say, democracy serves the aim of Islam with respect to the basic human rights it gives to Muslims, as well as in respect to the construction of the government it envisages, i.e., the construction of government by the consent of the subjects.

THE FAILURE OF DEMOCRACY IN THE ISLAMIC WORLD

It has been stated that the teachings of Islam are not opposed to democracy. Despite this, most Islamic countries are today governed by authoritarian rather than democratic systems. Most Islamic countries are beset by rigid and centralized political structures shaped around a tribal chief, party leader, member of the army, king, or emir. Why is it then that democracy cannot take root in this part of the world? The relative absence of liberal democracy in the Islamic world in general, and the Arab world in particular, has been taken up by many scholars dealing with the subject. Scholars measuring the level of modernization would link the development of democracy with the existence of various indicators of modernity such as the level of per capita GNP, literacy rates, urban life and other industry indexes, the level of media consumption, the degree of the development of social classes, and population levels. This mode of analysis suggested that, in order to achieve transition to democracy, non-western societies had to complete their processes of economic modernization in a manner similar to western societies.

This was the most common explanation for the lack of democracy in the Arab world in the 1970s. However, although GNP per capita in countries like Saudi Arabia and Kuwait has reached a level comparable to western countries, this has not resulted in the arrival of democracy there. Authoritarian regimes still survive in petroleum exporting Arab countries in spite of the fact that the economic infrastructure of some conforms with western standards. This suggests that the lack of democracy in the Islamic world depends on factors other than the indicators of modernization. There are historical and contemporary factors that make the concentration of political authority in the hands of a clique or a small group of elite possible in Islamic world.

When looked at from the angle of history, it is to be seen that the social classes that played a leading role in the course of sweeping social and political changes during western feudalism and capitalism, and therefore, acted as an intermediary between society and state, never took hold in Muslim societies. While economics and the social classes emanating from the economic sphere were the driving forces behind civil society in the West, this function has been performed by a central authority in Islamic societies. Although the incontrovertible truths of Islam consider property in a positive vein, in Islamic states of the past, societies were mostly estranged from economic life and therefore inevitably came to depend on the states as the property holders. We cannot speak of the existence of market-based economic exchange nor of social classes that would guarantee the survival of the market in traditional Muslim societies based on agriculture. No doubt in the past there existed some intermediary institutions that played the role of civil societal ingredients. However, since they were established on *cultural* rather than *economic* foundations, they could not transform themselves into strong organizations. Instead they came to operate not unlike a branch of the state. The segments of society, such as the caste of religious scholars, foundations, and guilds, acted like functionaries of the state in the provinces. This traditional relationship between state and society hindered the emergence of politically and economically powerful social groups over time.

In addition to this historical background, the colonization of the Islamic world at the beginning of the twentieth century seems to be another fundamental factor lying behind the deficiency of democratic systems in the Islamic world. In most Muslim societies, people piled up around the central government and the ruling elite with full force in order to throw off the colonial yoke and to gain independence throughout the first half of the twentieth century. The countries carved out of vast empires in Europe easily furnished themselves with democratic systems by building up national states. By contrast, the Islamic countries, which broke off from vast empires, failed to build up national states and fell prey to colonial empires such as Britain, France, and Italy. While countries like Bulgaria and Greece, which had been split from the Ottoman Empire, managed to acquaint themselves with democracy in the early twentieth century, Muslim countries such as Egypt, Lebanon, Algeria, Iraq, and Syria came under colonial domination during the same period. Saudi Arabia and Egypt aside, which gained independence in 1922, the Arab world was under the colonial rule of Britain, France, or Italy in the early twentieth century. Therefore, the priority in these countries did not lie in the dissolution of power between the centralized political authority and people, but in concentrating around a political authority for the purpose of liberating their countries.

The experience of colonialism in the Islamic world reinforced the centralized political culture that had solid foundations in traditional Muslim societies. The charismatic power of the rulers who had presented themselves as the representatives of God on earth during the Umayyad and Abbasid eras, was sadly reinforced in the postcolonial era of the twentieth century. Some leaders, by virtue of their essential role in independence struggles, came to be idolized in their country, and most of them used this charisma to disregard their people. Many groups or leaders who played a pivotal role in the struggles for independence, began, perhaps inevitably, to perceive people as their own property, thus resisting demands for sharing power with them. Many Islamic countries that gained independence after the Second World War naturally developed an aversion toward democratic institutions that had evolved in western countries like France and Britain, since they were the same countries against which they had been fighting for independence. For this reason, most of the Islamic countries were lured into the Russian way of socialism in the aftermath of World War II.

The case of Ottoman/Republican Turkey, which was not colonized by western countries, is a very clear indication of the impact of colonization over the mode of political systems in the Islamic world under colonization. The Ottoman Empire acquainted itself with democratic mechanisms such as parliament, multiparty politics, and elections beginning from 1876 up to 1918.

However, such democratic mechanisms were disbanded following the outbreak of the War of Independence beginning in 1918 against Greece and such other western countries as France, Italy, and Britain. The question of how to liberate the country then came to take the central care of political elite and even of the subjects rather than the discussions about democratic mechanisms. The society felt a strong need to unite around leaders promising independence against the West. Indeed, the need for independence and the construction of a national state as the representative of national independence created an authoritarian single-party regime in Turkey until 1950.

REACTIONARY MOVEMENTS AND DEMOCRACY

One of the main obstacles that undermine the arrival of democracy in Muslim societies is the existence of reactionary movements. Radical and revolutionary Islam, which emerged as reactions to colonialism, were inspired more by socialist values than by liberal democratic values, and they formulated their principles in line with this outlook. It was common in the Islamic world until the 1980s to consider Islam as a source of ideology as well as a revolutionary ideology. It was particularly the Iranian revolution, which became an inspirational reference for Islamic movements at that time. In this period, Islam was taken by Muslim thinkers of Iranian origin as well as by those of North African origin, almost as a kind of state religion, a revolutionary ideology, and a theocratic political structure.

Such interpretations of Islam can be traced back, in the case of some North African countries, to the period between the second half of the nineteenth century and up to the first half of the twentieth century. At that point in time, Muslim countries began to suffer a long and painful setback in the face of the incredible economic growth and the development western countries were experiencing. Moreover, the colonial ambitions of western countries directly over Islamic territories evoked strong reactions from Muslim thinkers of North Africa who began to think in terms of Leninism. This explains a great deal about the distance, which Muslims began to feel toward liberalism, democracy, capitalism, and other similar systems and ideas.

The two key concepts that these thinkers borrowed from Leninism were the "state" and "revolution." It was, in their view, the state that symbolized social justice, social unity, and the struggle against the West. Such a state could only be established through revolution, this being under the leadership of a pioneering group. The works of Sayyid Qutb, an Egyptian Islamic intellectual who was hanged by the Nasser regime in 1966, for instance, emphasize the role of a revolutionary group. Largely on account of his Leninist background, Qutb envisaged the establishment of an Islamic state by means of a revolution led by a specially trained group versed in Islamic values. The project toward the creation of such a group, indeed, can be seen as an attempt to replace Lenin's proletarian vanguards with their Muslim counterparts. For Qutb, the salvation of Muslims, as well as the entirety of humanity depended on an Islamic state that would represent a third way, i.e., an alternative to socialism and capitalism. Although critical of socialism, many Islamic intellectuals, as in the case of Sayyid Qutb, operated on values that might be combined with a Leninist style of state socialism in some form through its emphasis on collectivity, brotherhood, revolution, equality, salvation, a centralized state, anticapitalism, and antidemocracy among others.

Hence, both authoritarian regimes and Muslim intellectuals with a firsthand experience of colonial domination completely refused the West, and sought to set up alternative institutions, which were authoritarian in character. When realizing that traditional interpretation of Islam fell short of enabling the deployment of adequate means by which to resolve existing problems, they began to borrow concepts and perspectives from Russian socialism, which was anticapitalist and antiliberalist in character, to develop an Islamic myth as an alternative. The concepts of "nation" and "centralized state," the latter of which emerged out of the former, raised the greatest difficulty for such intellectuals. Although initially these intellectuals emphasized the universality of the Islamic message, following the ascendancy of nationalism and of the idea of national state, they chose to transpose Islam into a national context, thus they organized nationalist movements as responses to the western challenge.

As for the intellectuals who came from noncolonized countries, they sought to understand the West rather than reject it entirely and made use of western ideas and institutions that they considered to be useful. While, by the end of the nineteenth century, the foundations of a reactive movement of an antiwestern character were being laid in countries under colonial domination, the Ottoman intellectuals, who had no such experience, had a vision of society that was open to interaction with the West. The vanguards of the movement toward Ottoman Enlightenment, such as Namık Kemal, Ziya Paşa, and Ali Suavi, advocated institutions and values such as freedom, democracy, and constitutional and parliamentary government in a western sense. The appearance of democracy in Turkey despite occasional setbacks, as opposed to the lack of democracy in other Islamic countries, should be linked to the above. Whereas the intellectuals in Ottoman society pursued a strategy of modernization, which, inter alia, embraced western institutions, the colonization of other Islamic countries by the West was the prime cause of the rejectionist attitude developed by Muslim intellectuals against western values.

Present-day revolutionary radical Islamic movements emphasize the sovereignty of God, rather than human beings in the world. These movements strive to consolidate their version of sovereignty, which relies on various Islamic interpretations, instead of embarking on projects designed to improve the living conditions of Muslims and those who live with Muslims. However, it is obvious that God never acts as sovereign, this being true for all times and places; therefore, those who rule in the name of God in fact represent a particular interpretation of religion. It is correct to assert for all religions, including Islam, that there are always more than one equally valid interpretations of a given religion. Those who claim to be acting on behalf of God, in truth, rule on the basis of one of such interpretations. Granting that the human person is the most exalted among all of God's creations, the services designed to respond to the needs of human beings should of necessity constitute part of God's sovereignty. In God's reckoning, political rule should be based on assembly and consultation. In modern societies, this can only materialize by means of principles such as an oath of allegiance, elections, contract, consultation, consensus of the learned, constitutional government, and the separation of powers. The entitlement to the right to govern through elections is the synonym of the principle of consultation admonished by Islam; surely this authority is not intended to act as the sacred shadow of God on earth, but as the representative of Muslims for a defined period.

The verse of the Quran, which is all too often cited by revolutionary and radical Islamic circles, that "sovereignty belongs to no one save God," does not in any way imply legal, legislative, or political authority. The verses that speak of "God's sovereignty" are expressions of God's creative role in the entire universe. Those who first distorted the meaning of these verses to give them a political bent, were the *Haricis*. The *Haricis*, in their time, used such verses to shake the legitimacy of rulers whom they opposed. The Quran enjoins believers to conduct their affairs by consultation, which means that it is a moral principle related to governance. As in the verse, "their affairs are a matter of counsel," there are numerous verses that hold that believers, in conducting their affairs, consult one another. This suggests that people should resolve political-administrative problems on the basis of consultation among themselves, or else, they will entrust an able person with the task of resolving the problem. There is no model better than democracy to sort things out in this way. In conclusion, we can assert that sovereignty lies in the people (the source from which the authority emanates), and those who exercise sovereignty should act in accordance with the commands of God so as to enjoy legitimacy. Good and useful works done by human beings are mentioned in the Quran among the deeds that earn the approval of God.

Since radical Islamic approaches are primarily reactionary movements, they have a propensity for wholesale rejection of everything that comes from the West. This attitude in fact contradicts with sociological reality. We cannot perceive a particular way of life simply as black or white, as good or bad. There are always elements to learn and borrow from different cultures, ideas, and life experiences; to be more accurate, societies, of necessity, exchange cultural elements and products. What is more, we need to *understand* western civilization. Today, we observe that political institutions and values, which are most in tune with the essence of Islam, are in fact to be found in the democratic political structures of the West, and not in the despotic political structures prevailing in Islamic countries. When regard is made to the political institutions current in western societies, we come across with institutions and the system of fundamental rights and liberties whose level of perfection have rarely been seen in the course of Muslim history.

Those who advocate political Islam are no lovers of freedom. Instead of defending their freedom alongside that of others, they are after a hegemonic system under their political control. After all, sustenance of political domination at the exclusion of others is a fundamental problem that Muslim countries have had to face in the past as well as today. Replacing a dictatorship, which relies on the army, a tribe or a clan, the state bureaucracy, or the leader's charisma, with another dictatorship grounded in a particular interpretation of Islam, is apparently futile. The perspective of political Islam is full of malice, hatred, and fury. This mode of thinking is in fact far from being able to comprehend the autonomous human person; instead it considers him or her as an object of political domination.

This mode of thinking also operates at the level of identities. Its adherents approach social actors from the perspective of "us" and "them." A greater part of such movements could easily accuse others—if Muslim—of blasphemy rather like *Haricis*, and consider violence an acceptable method of struggle. Such movements focus their energy on distinctive characteristics that separate them from others and are therefore likely to accuse others of blasphemy and to exclude and look down upon them instead of underlining the points of convergence that make space for peaceful coexistence. Since this mode of thinking falls into the trap of dogmatism by failing to approach issues from a critical perspective and idealizes elements or values that belong to them, it fails to identify the contemporary problems for which Islam has already provided answers and those that it has not.

The state is that sphere in which human ambitions, interests, and the "will to power" are set in motion and where they act themselves out. The transposition of religion into the realm of the state distorts the primary purpose of religion; it results in its defamation and exploitation, and allows freedom for only one religious approach or interpretation (and, by this logic, a single religious group). While the state is an entity that constantly transforms in response to changing sociological needs and conditions, religion, by contrast, possesses immutable universal principles. Because of this, when the state and religion merge, the sphere of everyday life is inevitably held outside the process of change. The demand for political authority and the peculiar consecration of sovereignty enjoyed by this authority has aborted the emergence of a tradition of critical thinking among radical groups in the Islamic world; and this has paved the way for the stifling of ideas and intellectual fertility.

· 4 ·

The Roots of Terror

Lauren Langman and Douglas Morris

INTRODUCTION

𝒯he profound tragedy of 9/11 may seem beyond explanation. But we will proffer an understanding of the event as a product of a history of contention and more
recent geopolitical realities. Islamic fundamentalism in general, and terrorism in
particular, must be located within a larger social-historical context. Marx re-
minded us that men may make history, but not under circumstances of their own
choosing—the legacy of earlier eras weighs down upon the present. Such an understanding must not ignore individual agents. More specifically, as C. Wright
Mills argued, the "sociological imagination" should locate individuals in their
historical context. This is not to suggest that the past "determines" the present,
there are a number of mediations and variable contexts for human agency, but this
agency can only be expressed within the limits of a historically based social context. The tragic consequences brought on by a few individuals must be understood in terms of the ascent and decline of hegemonic powers, more specifically:
(1) the waning of Islamic hegemony after the fourteenth century; (2) the ascent
of Christian Europe as a hegemon; and (3) the postwar expansion and extension
of the United States as a hegemonic power with "interests" in the Middle East,
imposing policies, abetting certain leaders, and thwarting progressive moments.
All three stand in the background of recent events.

From the moment the Prophet heard Gabriel speak the words of Allah,
(words that included some Judeo-Christian teachings), to the Crusades, to the
Islamic influence on the Renaissance, to the contentious relationships of
today, the fate of Christendom and Islam have been intertwined.[1] At the end
of the fourteenth century, Islamic societies stood at an economic, political,
and cultural apex. They were affluent as well as philosophically, scientifically,

technologically, and administratively advanced. Mighty armies of "heroic warriors" and vast trade networks had spread Islamic culture from the Atlantic coast through the southern Mediterranean and North Africa to the Middle East, Southeast Asia, and parts of China. Yet the *same* factors that enabled Islam's rise to power, would *later limit* growth. Economic weakness and political turmoil, wars over succession, led to religious conservatism and an intellectual ossification, which spread throughout Islam. Meanwhile Europe had just begun its Renaissance, based in large part on Islamic intellectual influences.

Christian Europe in the fourteenth century was a collection of poor, ignorant, and politically fragmented kingdoms, duchies, fiefdoms, and bishophorics. Save the Italian city-states, Europe was far less culturally advanced than Islamic societies. Yet, following the *Reconquista*, and Spain ascendant, its sailors reached the New World, stole its gold, and initiated the rise of Europe as a major world civilization spread through imperialism.[2] When the Spanish Armada was defeated in 1588, commerce moved from the Mediterranean to the Atlantic. The Dutch (United Provinces), then the British and French became imperialist powers. In the nineteenth-century capitalist, industrial Europe eventually joined with American capital to produce unprecedented wealth and power; by then the Islamic world had become a number of peripheral and semiperipheral areas that would never regain its hegemonic status. By the nineteenth century much of the Islamic world had been colonized or controlled by European powers. Following World War I, the decline and defeat of the Ottoman Empire marked the end of Islamic power. By the end of the twentieth century former colonies became independent nations; while the United States had become the dominant hegemonic power. But by then, with greater information available to better-educated populations, the Islamic world became much more aware of its underdevelopment and lack of democracy, often due to American oil-based geopolitics. Given both internal barriers and external factors, Islamic countries remained poor while other countries would prosper. In the face of these conditions, following the failure of secular agendas, often thwarted by the West, there has been a growing embrace of fundamentalist versions of Islam in which spiritual renewal might act as compensation to material deprivation.[3] But in some few instances, with Islamisms (fundamentalist Islams) flourishing, the legacy of the knightly warrior, a "heroic masculinity" has been resurrected within a framework of a modern holy war, *jihad*. In some cases, the warrior took the form of the *shaheed*, martyr.[4]

THE RISE OF HEGEMONS

Max Weber asked how and why only western Christendom gave rise to rational capitalism, democratic nation-states, and the massive applications of science to technology.[5] Questions of the ascent and decline of history's major hegemonic powers such as states, empires, caliphates, or nations, require considerations of several levels of analysis, material conditions, social institutions, orientations to the world, and the subjective meanings and dispositions of actors. With Marx we would interrogate class relations and legitimating ideologies.[6] With Weber, the ascendance of modern capital depended on (1) the rise of a bourgeois class engaged in rational commerce; together with (2) more bureaucratic administration; (3) a demystified worldview; and (4) a "Protestant ethic" of ascetic work as a "calling" that demanded a methodological orientation to everyday life. But with Nietzsche and Freud, we must remember the individual and her desires, frustrations, *ressentiments*, and defenses.

THE RISE OF ISLAM

In the seventh century, the conflicts between Persia and Byzantium fostered a southerly movement of trade routes through the deserts of Arabia that were largely populated by warring nomadic tribes ever involved in vendetta and countervendetta. Further, particularistic tribal religions stood as barriers to the expansion of the urban, merchant classes and threatened the security of their caravans. These conditions would dispose the merchant classes to embrace a unifying religion that would extend across many lands, uniting (controlling) the populations, and securing the general conditions for aggressive commerce and trade. Muhammad, a merchant, articulated a divine message, the word of Allah, the Quran, which became the foundation of a new faith. Islam provided a monotheistic salvation religion rooted in Jewish and Christian traditions of prophesy, incorporating some of their ethics, Christian eschatology, and many of their customs. Islam was more than a religion; it was an entire way of life. Muhammad, as a prophet and skilled arbiter, found a ready audience among the growing classes of merchants, whose status disposed an "elective affinity" for a salvation religion that would establish an "imagined community" of people united by faith that provided members with valorized, sacralized identities, and a God-ordained ethical regulation of everyday conduct conducive to the expansion of commerce. As Weber noted in the case of Protestantism, ethical standards between members of the religious "brotherhood" of a "world" religion, even if strangers, were important for the conduct of business in large markets. In its formative period, Islam was often spread by conquest or *jihad*, holy war.

> At the time of its origin in Mecca, the eschatological religion of Muhammad developed in pietistic urban conventicles that were likely to withdraw

from the world: subsequently in Medina and in the evolution of early Islamic communities, the religion was transformed into a widespread Arabic, status oriented, warrior religion.[7]

For Islam, political control was more important than the conversion of the conquered. However, there was an active destruction of polytheistic folk religions and ways such as idol worship. Violence was used to eliminate tribal parochialism and create and enforce religious universalism. Indeed, compared to other religions, once Islam subjugated a population, it was highly tolerant of Judaism and Christianity, the Prophet saw as Abraham, Moses and Jesus preceding his work. In Islamic societies, monotheistic religions were sometimes celebrated in the same shrines. The tolerance of the major monotheisms enabled the flow of ideas as well as facilitated cultural exchange and political stability. Another factor enabling the expansion of Islamic political control was that early converts to Islam came from powerful merchant families. Given economic interests in social stability and thus profitable trade, and their own high social status, they were economically, culturally, and socially disposed to assent to the rule of other elites. Thus, unlike the Christianity of poor, marginal, artisans under Roman domination, Islam began as a religion of ruling stratum, a *Herrenreligion*.[8] There was no *ressentiment* of the rich and powerful.

Early Islam, as a religion of knightly warriors, had little room for sin, humility, or vocational asceticism. But so too was Islam a religion of merchants who prospered across the pacified lands that however diverse the peoples, were united by a common religion with strict regulations of everyday life conducive to economic growth. Along its secured trade routes there emerged a vast network of cities not only advantageous to trade, but cities like Cordoba, Cairo, and Baghdad became advanced cultural centers for the codification of laws and the encouragement of scholarship, science, and philosophy. In its Golden Age, there were great advances in science, astronomy, mathematics, medicine, literature, philosophy, architecture, music, and art.

Prebendial Feudalism

Following Barrington Moore's classical understanding of landlord/tenant class relations impacting the directions of later politics, the differences between Islamic and Christian feudalism would dispose different historical trajectories that lead either to the embrace of modernity or to active resistance.[9] The tribal nature of early Islamic societies, coupled with state-based landownership, would lead to dissimilar forms of land tenure, land use and, in turn, different historical trajectories. The Latinized, Christian Germanic chieftains who overthrew Rome claimed "conquered" territory, giving a distinctively military hue to landownership. Eventually, European feudalism was based on the fiefdom and vassalage; a self-contained manor depended on serf/slave labor. Christian feudalism could be seen "as a military system . . . of fiefs, military service, and gradations of vassalage and sovereignty," as well "as a mode of production based on serfdom and the manorial economy."[10] Ownership of land, the fief, including its subject serfs, was parceled out to knightly vassals, specialized military elites, in exchange for loyalty and service, especially military service. It was a complex system of obligations bound by personal ties and codes of honor. "A complex parcellization of sovereignty was maintained, tolerating some alloidal holdings by peasants and some time certain autonomous towns for the burghers, two vital sources of creativity under late feudalism." This decentralized form of enfeoffed vassalage was also conducive to "constitutionalism" in which nobles and notables could organize and join together to limit royal authority. The legacies of these clearly established constraints would eventually make democratic nation-states possible.[11] (These moments were unique to Europe.)

The ruling classes were landowners as well as military elites ever ready to battle and often were engaged in combat against invaders (Arabs, Maygars, or Norsemen). More often than not, they fought each other. Moreover, Christianity provided a common faith and legitimated secular rule as "God ordained," priests dispensed "magical forms of protection" for their flocks and patrons in exchange for protection and upkeep of monasteries, lands, and estates. Notwithstanding a common Christianity, feudalism was a highly decentralized system of local authority dependent on particularistic ties often subject to rapid changes of allegiance, riven with treachery and deceit. The system was violent, chaotic, and often dangerous. Its ruling classes were in constant battle; it produced little surplus, little creativity, and little impetus to change. Nevertheless it proved remarkably stable, enduring till the ascent of the bourgeoisie and rational capitalism. Further, it did manage to halt Muslim expansion and create the conditions for constitutionalism and the military revolution.[12]

Islamic feudalism was radically different. Landownership held by the State was placed under the control of caliphs, monarchs, and sheiks, while villages retained a great deal of autonomy. Land may have been provided as a fiscal benefit, an *iqta'* where military service could be rewarded by rights of tax farming designated properties, but without political/juridical power over subjects or hereditary transmission of ownership. The *iqta'* was not a feudal fiefdom leading to a seigneurial system. Peasants retained the rights of usufruct and could sell land.[13] Thus the European system of parcelized fiefdoms and vassalage did not emerge. There was no symbiosis of ownership, military service, and landownership.[14] In the "Maghreb [for example] the presence of warrior herdsmen and montagnards made such a development impossible, given the strength of tribal and state structures. The vassal system could not emerge because of the strength of tribal structures and the permanent nature of the State Structures imposed on them."[15]

Meanwhile the Islamic world became organized into large states ruled by caliphates and kingdoms. Eventually, under the Ottomans, an Islamic empire was administered (and often defended) by large bureaucracies, Janissaries, children of Christians recruited and trained to serve the Sultan.

Caliphates and Sultanates

Islamic societies emerged in the shadows of the great agrarian empires of Egypt, Babylonia, and Persia. Like them, a Church-State elite ruled through control of the military and the scribal bureaucracies. Literati classes of religious virtuosos gave the system and its elites religiously based legitimacy. Muhammad was a religious prophet as well as a secular political leader; accordingly, the ideal typical form of governance became the Islamic community, the *umma*, living according to Quranic law, led by a caliph, a descendent of the Prophet. Despite its formal egalitarianism of believers, it disposed the acceptance of Caliphism, Sultanism, and/or other forms of strong, centralized, dynastic, hierarchical, authoritarian dynastic rule, more often than not legitimated suppression of democratization or pluralism—legacies yet found in some societies. Islamic societies did not develop the feudal system with alternative bases of landed power, like the nobility of Europe, the English Gentry, the Boyars of Russia, or Daimyo of Japan that might challenge centralized power. Moreover, given peasant usufruct, peasant agriculture sparked few revolts. (In the nineteenth and twentieth centuries, there would be such conflicts.) Islam was spared the endless conflicts from within. As a result, the basic forms of Islamic governance remained fairly stable. In Turkey, a non-Arabic society, quite tolerant of its subject populations, the system endured for over 700 years. Islamic societies of the Middle East thus did not have either internal contradictions or class pressures to modernize. The seamless web of religion everyday was unchallenged by currents from without, especially European ideas such as the Reformation or the Enlightenment. The Reformation was a political struggle between the rising merchant classes and the dynastic rule based on land played out on the terrain of religion. The religious wars ended with the Treaty of Westphalia, that while sustaining religious-based rule, was itself a secular agreement. Islam had been established by merchants. An upstart, alternative merchant class was unlikely. Finally, insofar as leaders were descendents of the Prophet, and legitimacy was unquestioned, there were few challenges to dynastic rule.[16] Meanwhile, the decentralized nature of Islam, without a hierarchical clergy, did not lend itself to a Reformation. Sects from Sufi to Wahabbism served similar functions in containing diversity and eliding fundamental challenges to Islam. Then Enlightenment, with its division of sacred and secular, flew in the face of the seamless world of Islam. Thus without a class bearing ideas of either religious challenge or the embrace of reason, there was little material or ideological basis for change. When the better-armed European armies claimed the Islamic lands, the colonial forces encouraged docility and compliance.[17] Change, when it came, was largely through petit bourgeois military revolts, e.g., Turkey, Lebanon, or Egypt, or anticolonial struggles in which European educated leaders/intellectuals, learning of the Enlightenment, democracy, etc., returned and inspired peasant revolts, e.g., Algeria, Pakistan.[18]

The Law, Hanafi Codes, and Roman Law. For Islam, the law was the word of Allah as revealed in the Quran. There was no distinction of sacred and secular law and all law was sacred.[19] This is not to ignore the law of the book and the laws of actual practice. Islam, as a set of laws and ethical regulations that applied to all pacified and unified diverse peoples enabled vast networks of trade and commerce. The fairly universal, but flexible, Islamic law, *sharia*, enabled the expansion of trade throughout the region. Sacred law eliminated the space for rational, predictable legal procedures such as in Indian law or even Roman law that *did not claim* theological justifications. As Weber noted, in the western system, legislative bodies passed laws based on formal rationality and rules of evidence. Judges dispensed justice. But Islamic law, *kadi* justice, was jurist in nature. The great jurists who established the legal traditions of Islam were more "legal prophets" establishing substantive-theological "stereotyped jurists law . . . that opposed secularization"; formal-juridical (rational) legal codes were wanting.[20] Its system of trained *mufti*, legal scholars, and *kadi*, judges, appointed by the central authority, were yet frequently antagonistic to the central authority. This often gave the judge administrative authority that nevertheless made him loyal to the central authority and prevented local powers or landed classes from emerging.[21] Lawyers and administrators regulated traditional Islamic society, not a clergy, the jurists, the *muftis* and *kadis*, were religiously trained, but they were not *immans*, *mullahs*, or religious virtuosos. While they may have been appointed by the State, absent legislative bodies, jurism in Islam was not centrally litigated or legislated; it was based on interpretation and local conditions. It was highly important that for Islamic societies, social rationality was closely tied to the foundations of specific religious categories, beliefs, and exercises in relation to everyday life, commerce, and governance. This is not to imply that such justice was random, haphazard, or without formal training.

The economic practices that were subject to Quranic law, namely *kadi* justice and *Hanafi* codes, regularized the resolutions of agricultural disputes or caravan-based, merchant trade and thus established conditions conducive for economic growth. The "unity" of sacred and secular law was routinized but not rationalized, localized not generalized. At later times this law became an *impediment* to the expansion of the economy both from within and without. More specifically, the legal codes of the *Hanafi* School, based in large part on what had been local traditions, would facilitate the rapid growth of Islamic commerce, but would eventually acquire a fixity that would act to prevent later generations from making revisions as material conditions changed.[22]

Firstly, Islamic merchant trading associations, whether or not familial, could not assume the legal form of a corporation with juridical rights independent of the owners. Quranic laws limited the growth of a secular, commercial, sphere; Muslim merchants were unable to practice the kinds of economic rationality, e.g., double entry bookkeeping, joint stock corporations, or risk insurance: as did the Italian merchants whose commerce flourished.[23] Secondly, Islamic succession and inheritance laws meant that when one of the associates died, a partnership was terminated and inheritance was divided in egalitarian ways as opposed to European laws that allowed limited inheritance, e.g., a single person could inherit a share of an enterprise that nevertheless survived the loss of a partner. Thus, a business could continue to grow and amass fortunes long after the death of a founder(s). Indeed many of the successful merchants of Italy were families such as the Medici's. Islamic codes kept business small, limited, and ephemeral, no great merchant families emerged.[24] As a result, Muslim merchants were unlikely to become bearers of a "worldly ethic of practical action" as were their Christian counterparts whose diversity of occupations declined while military and bureaucratic occupations grew, Islamic economies then began to stagnate.[25] The commercial-legal *Hanafi* codes that had once promoted expansion and regional trade, thwarted economic growth, precluded large-scale economic enterprises, and deterred foreign investment.[26] To allow economic growth, Quranic law would need to be jettisoned, as has been done in Turkey, Morocco, Malaysia, Indonesia, or Egypt that now embrace modern, western commercial law.

Medieval European law was derived from Canon law as well as Roman law. But with the expansion of trade, the rational nature of Roman law, its dependence on philosophical principles, precedence, procedures, and evidence, facilitated the expansion of commerce and trade as well as greater centralization.[27] Perhaps the most important aspect of European commercial codes was their rational origins in Roman law, that were revised along secular, rational lines, as for example the codes of Amalfi in 1329. Decisions were based on precedent, cases were judged on the basis of evidence, and justice was dispensed without the personal "feelings of the judge." While at the time very few people were very much affected by fourteenth-century commercial codes, *legal principles were established that would allow investment banking, joint holdings (the early form of corporations), and risk insurance.* While we often focus on economic agents, their agency depends on the social conditions; the rationalization of commercial law would become one of the pillars of modern capital. As Weber noted, while elements of rationality were present in other systems, only in Europe would such codes be fully rationalized, only in Europe would capitalism flourish.

Banking. Islam, a trading culture, was the pioneer of transnational commerce. A banking network (with a checking system/exchange) formed that greatly facilitated the growth of trade and commerce. One could write a check in Cordoba that would be honored in Tashkent. As progressive as that system might have been for its age, it depended on personal relationships and particularistic ties and thus never achieved either the rationality of the later western banking nor the economies of scale that would take place in the West where large banks (and stock markets) would finance factories, railroads, etc. Thus, while one could invest in a particular venture that would produce profits, there was not much incentive to large-scale investment banking or lending at a interest-deemed usury. The proscriptions on either long-term investments or short-term usury meant that financing of economic enterprises was limited. Hence, borrowing was not rationalized and banking institutions and systems remained small. Like medieval Christianity, proscriptions against usury limited the growth of banks and in turn commercial growth. (In Europe, the landless, untitled Jews filled this need and were evermore needed and for this reason, often resented.)

War, Warfare, and Warriors. Often little considered, war, warriors, and technologies of war are salient moments of social change. Discipline originated in the Spartan warriors.[28] Such discipline, later undergirded by Protestantism, enabled the triumph of Cromwell's Ironmen over the more individualistic Cavaliers. Further, military discipline, from the Hoplites to the guild armies was a precondition of democracy. For our purposes, it is important to note that the rise and spread of early Islam depended in large part on military conquest. This would establish the basis for a legacy of "heroic masculinity" that would be continually retold and refashioned long after the demise of Islamic hegemony:

> Muhammad was both an ethical prophet and a charismatic politico-military leader. He overcame tribal particularism by surpassing its polytheism and ritualism with monotheism and a legal ethic, and by transforming feuding tribes into a national-Arabic movement of conquest. . . . Muhammad was . . . not a marginalized prophet of doom, and certainly not a wandering charismatic preacher; instead, he was a religio-political leader who knew how to realize his intentions step by step, especially through the skillful use of time honored tribal practices of the creation and resolution of conflict. . . . With the successful reception in Medina, the transformation of Islam from an eschatological

religiosity into a political religion into a religion of national-Arabic warriors was inaugurated.[29]

After conquering Medina, Muhammad went on to capture Mecca; he eventually united and pacified the nomadic tribes and sedentary peoples. Islamic societies continued the tradition of religious justifications, if not mandates for political/territorial expansion, as in the case of the conquest of Andalusia or, later, the imperialist armies of the Ottoman Turks.[30]

Nomadic tribesmen, by virtue of their habitat, horsemanship/camelmanship, courage, and warlike spirits were excellent warriors, often defeating more advanced sedentary populations and/or defended merchant caravans. The extensive use of horse and camel cavalry enabled the spread of Islam and eventually created a vast hegemon stretching from the Andalusian peninsula to parts of China and Asia.

Such an empire naturally invited attack from without. The ferocious bravery of the Muslim warriors, their superior weapons (Damascus steel), and the distance of Christian supply lines, combined with homeland defense and the surety of heaven for fallen warriors, contributed the expulsion of the Crusaders by Saladin. But at the same time, nomadic warriors were difficult to tax and control, ultimately leading to the growing power of the agricultural societies of conquered lands in which state monopolies of land supported the cities and centers of learning where Islamic scholarship and science flourished. This would become the Golden Age of Islam; caliphs, descendants of the Prophet, ruled a vast network. (Like most systems of dynastic rule, there was a lot of controversy over lineage and claims of succession.) Notwithstanding, its limits and constraints, its hegemony endured until the sixteenth century. The Ottoman Turks held power until 1923 when overthrown by the Kemalists, petit bourgeois military officers.

Most civilizations typically exalt their warriors, the brave military heroes who exemplify "heroic masculinity." Such heroes are celebrated in myth, history, song, and poetry. In the feudal eras, both Christian and Muslim knights were highly esteemed and respected. But Christian knights were typically landed elites whereas Muslim warriors typically came from backgrounds where everyone had combat training. But changes in weapons and tactics would eventually transform the European military. The small, decentralized, local armies, with little communication or coordination faced serious threats from the larger Muslim armies. With variable levels of military ability, without coordinated training, little discipline, often shifting loyalties, and uncertain terms of service weakened feudal armies.[31] Between changing technologies of combat, favoring infantry over mounted knights, growing use of gunpowder, internal and external factors, feudal military organizations began to decline in the fourteenth century. Meanwhile, in the sixteenth and seventeenth centuries, facing large, powerful Muslim (Turkish) armies after the fall of Byzantium and defeats of the Hungarians and Austrians, Europe underwent a military revolution in the face of the growing threat. Infantry (archers) and gunpowder (artillery) began to play a larger role.[32] Armies became larger, they employed more advanced weapons and techniques while administered by expanded central organizations.[33] Soldiers became more specialized, better trained, disciplined, and supplied. And slowly but surely, as noted above, by now Islam had become economically stagnant, militarily surpassed, politically riven by internal conflict, and intellectually ossified. Meanwhile, European armies and navies, with ever-more sophisticated military technologies and organizational capacities, would become larger and stronger than those of Islam. But more recently, with the rise of fundamentalism, the warrior legacy of *jihad* for the sake of Allah became rekindled.[34] But as is also evident, given the asymmetrical nature of western and Muslim militaries, the warrior would be refashioned as martyr, *shaheed*.

THE WANING OF ISLAMIC HEGEMONY: WHY IT WENT WRONG—ISLAMIC BARRIERS TO MODERNITY

Toynbee noted that ascendant societies were open to new ideas, change, and diversity, while declining societies became closed and rigid. Islamic civilization fits his observation, it attained a level of cultural, scientific, and intellectual development previously comparable only to India or China. While a very advanced, affluent civilization, a number of factors led to an erosion of its dynamism and in turn stagnation, dogmatism, and a turning inward and waning of its hegemony. Today much of the Middle East remains mired in preindustrialism. Most people still work in agriculture or in handicraft production.[35] Given the prosperity of its Golden Age and the richness and level of its civilization—in radical contrast to its current poverty, lack of democracy, intolerance, fervent fundamentalisms, and spawning grounds of terror, Lewis (1993) and others have asked, "What went wrong?" Why did Islam not have a Reformation? Why did it wane? Why has the march to modernity faced such barriers compared to other cultures?[36] Such questions require considerations of historical legacies long past. But at the same time, we should remember that *only* in postfeudal, Christian Europe did all the elements first come together that led to modernity, industrialization, and representative democracy.

From all that has been said, while a number of factors must be considered, we noted material factors in this case: trade, commerce, commercial law, land-ownership, and tenure. Islam was shaped by the needs of merchants who wanted secure caravan routes and thus supported warriors to make sure they lived in a tranquil empire of trade. The land was owned by the state, while most people may have been sedentary farmers or nomadic pastoralists, there did not develop a landed class of nobles and hence there were few peasant revolutions or uprisings against landowners that might herald major social change as in China or Russia.[37] It would follow that like the great civilizations of antiquity, a church-state elite would emerge whose literati, typically religious virtuosos, found theological justifications and blessings for the social arrangements that secured their power.[38] This was evident in the legal system in which sacred law, *sharia*, together with the *Hadith* and religiously based codes of *Hanafi*, became the basis of legal scholarship articulated by the *ulema*, *muftis*, and administered by the *kadi*. And indeed Islamic civilization reached great heights, but later turned to orthodoxy and stability would eventually lead to its demise as an ascendant Christendom was emerging from its feudal past.

In its maturity, Islamic government, facing challenges from without, weakened by "internal" strife, failed to garner needed revenues. After the collapse of the Almohad Empire, Islamic societies turned to orthodoxy and became resistant to change.[39] Indeed, in sharp contrast to its early eras, after the fourteenth century, Islamic societies actively maintained various barriers to external cultural influences. While this preserved Islamic cultures, bred stagnation, and reproduced social arrangements, it also precluded later incorporation of western innovations from commercial practices to industrial factories to nationalism, etc.[40] The highly advanced Islamic pursuits of science, medicine, and philosophy ceased to develop. "Independent inquiry virtually came to an end, and science was for the most part reduced to a veneration of a corpus of approved knowledge."[41]

As we have noted, there were a number of reasons, both internal and external, why Islam did not, indeed, could not, embrace democratic, industrial modernity starting with material factors. For Islam, the symbiosis between the merchants and rulers precluded the rise of an upstart bourgeois class qua agents for social change through private appropriation of the means of production, organizing, and coordinating investment and innovation.[42] Nor would merchants challenge dynastic rule or *sharia* law.

Islam, which had encouraged great advances in science and medicine, erected a number of barriers to a transition to technologically based industrialization.[43] There was no single factor to explain this, but in Europe, the merchants and artisans of postmedieval towns were more disposed to utilitarian innovations than for example were the Ottoman Sultans or *ulema*, religious scholars. Meanwhile, in the land masses of Islam, wide-scale agricultural and/or cotton production and separation of science from technologies of production were not conducive to early industrialization. Nor did its leaders initiate "revolutions from above."[44] (In the twentieth century we would see army coups such as in Turkey, Iraq, and Egypt.)

We might also note the profound impact of printing. The Arabs had learned the art of papermaking from the Chinese. But they preferred elaborate calligraphy to simple type and as result, while many books were to be found in their libraries, in Europe, printing would foster mass literacy. Literacy itself has independent consequences, not the least of which is the empowerment of the reader. With increased availability of information, people could find alternative sources of information and understanding that might interrogate the "received wisdom of clerics and kings." But crucial for fostering modernity, widespread literacy was the prerequisite for the wide emergence and distribution of the scientific tracts of the sixteenth and seventeenth centuries that would encourage the Enlightenment and the emergence of the bourgeois "public sphere." New ideas about science, politics, and culture would be debated and discussed. These ideas included critiques of despotism, inalienable rights, and popular sovereignty. Such emancipatory ideas gave legitimacy to power struggles. While we thus argue that no single factor was crucial, the legacies of feudal Europe would give rise to democratic industrial capitalist societies while the legacies of feudal Islam would act as barriers to a secular, capitalist, democratic western modernity. But this is not to blame the victims; indeed, imperialist powers actively sustained the lack of development.

Imperialism, Conquest, and Subalterity

The capitalist mode of production transformed the world. And while the bourgeoisie would extol limited democracy and freedom at home, more typically at levels of ideology than practice, they would become imperialist conquerors around the globe. The Islamic societies of the Maghreb and Levant of the eighteenth and nineteenth centuries were relatively weak, powerless societies or colonies. Ottoman Turkey was clearly in decline. European interests held considerable sway over much of the Islamic world from the Maghreb to Southeast Asia. By the nineteenth century, European imperialism was in its heyday; its armies, especially the English and French claimed vast areas of Islamic lands, e.g., Egypt, Algeria, trans-Jordan, etc. Oriental cultures were deemed inferior, the people lazy, criminal, and oversexed. Whether by direct colonial rule or through governors, viceroys, intermediaries, or simply asymmetrical market situations, Europeans maintained dependency relationships over markets and politics. They actively suppressed anticolonial independence movements. There were tendencies in some areas for the emergence of large-scale commercial agriculture owned by a landlord class producing foods for (European) export markets or, as in Egypt and the Sudan, or cotton for the English textile industries. But such decisions meant that there was almost no European investment in local industrial production. This sustained dependency and peripheral status. Following World War II, the United States became more involved in the region, supporting the House of Saud, the establishment of

Israel, support for Shah Palevi, and otherwise aligning itself with "friendly" conservative, antidemocratic forces that however dictatorial, were allies against communism.[45] Progressive "western" movements or ideas such as socialism or nationalism were suppressed by the West, resulting in political stagnation.

It is now evident that a number of factors colluded that led to the decline of Islamic civilization. A once great hegemon was reduced to agrarian or handicraft economies with limited possibilities for industrialization and/or modernization. Notwithstanding the indigenous structural, legal, and ideological barriers that were noted, legacies of colonialism, imperialism, and now globalization sustain dependency and subalterity. Even today, except for oil-producing Gulf States, most Muslim societies remain agrarian or in some cases, extractive. At the end of World War II, the Islamic countries stood at basically the same economic levels of Asian countries like Taiwan, Korea, or Thailand. But the Asian "tigers" have prospered, as has Israel—while Islamic countries have remained poor, backward, and stagnant. While Turkey has become an industrializing country, and some high-tech assembly factories can be found in Malaysia, and garment/toy production in Pakistan or Qatar, the industrial output of all the Islamic countries is about $5 billion, the same as Nokia of Finland.

The dominant economic and cultural force in the world today is globalization. Except for some tourism, minerals, or garment/toy assembly, the economies of the Middle East have not become integrated into world markets. Between dictatorial governments, archaic legal systems, rampant corruption, and antiwestern feelings, most global corporations sell their goods and services, but are reluctant to make major financial investments in production—especially when capital can find more stable places with cheaper workers elsewhere. Nevertheless, globalization has had a great deal of impact on the Islamic from unequal distributions of oil wealth, impositions of structural adjustment programs, and infrastructure investments that benefit few people, etc. There is little economic growth, little economic opportunity for most people, few factories, and even fewer state-of-the-art science research centers.[46] A number of postcolonial crises have had dire consequences, especially for the more urban-educated populations.[47] We find a wide swath of poverty, unemployment, destitution, and hopelessness that runs throughout a once glorious hegemon. Moreover, while well-paying jobs may be few, there have been rapid social dislocations as rural villagers move to cities, as women gain education, and youth become more independent of families. Finally, while globalization has had little economic benefit, there has been growth in mass media and exposure to secular western values and its hedonistic indulgence that offend conservative traditions. But this same mass media, often propaganda outlets controlled by governments, have blamed the West (Israel) for all social problems. One-party governments that tolerate little dissent foster displacement of resentments to theological terrains.

Poverty, ignorance, and despotism are the breeding grounds of Islamic fundamentalisms and terrorism, understood as reactions to multiple crises of legitimacy due to stagnant economies, unrepresentative governments, and failure to embrace western ideologies (rationality, nationalism, socialism), yet exposed to its secular materialism and hedonism. Fundamentalism, with its clear-cut moral values, its affirmation of hierarchies, designations of blameworthy "enemies" responsible for "evil," has provided many people, especially those close to rural roots, with a variety of social and psychological comforts. But furthermore, insofar as political/economic crises migrate to cultural terrains of identity and desire, we can understand how Islamic fundamentalist movements articulate *ressentiment* over subalterity. Such doctrines provide explanations of stagnation as coming from external enemies in the West and/or Zionist plots. Moreover, Islamisms grant valorized identities based on faith and ritual. In its extreme forms, its hatred, its intolerance, and love of death turn fundamentalism into "clerical fascism." Such fundamentalisms take two forms, classical ethnoreligious movements in which a "people united" by faith engage in either anticolonial struggles, and/or struggles against secular governments. Algeria has seen both, first seeking independence from the French and then to conflicts between modernists and fundamentalists. The Iranian revolution of 1979 was a struggle against a secular government, today, that fundamentalism is under assault.[48] Finally, insofar as western globalization (read America) can be framed as the "enemy" of Islam, we have seen the recent fusion of twelfth-century ideologies and twentieth-century technologies in the rise of transnational terrorist organizations like Al Qaeda that would contest the West and attempt to restore the caliphate. While this is clearly irrational and impossible to attain, and only very small, dedicated minorities embrace this view, "true believers," with atavistic goals and technological skills from computers to flying airplanes, embracing legacies of warrior martyrs, can bring mass death, destruction, and mayhem.

The Joys of Clerical Fascism

Modernity, with its values of progress, rationality, secularism, freedom, equality, and of late, hedonistic indulgence, has fostered various stresses and strains. From within, there have long been critiques ranging from Burke and de Toqueville's lament of waning aristocracy to Nietzsche's bewailing the sterility and repression of modern culture—echoed by Freud and Weber. In more recent years, especially with the globalization of capital, modernity has led to massive social transformations and dislocations. In many traditional societies, rural agricultural ways of life have waned as people flock to cities, often facing severe unemployment and in turn poverty, overcrowding, and crime. Between the loss of economic resources, and often better-educated children, and sometimes more educated women, patriarchal power faces challenges. Religious meaning systems that valorize moral piety, qua hierarchical orders and impulse control confront egalitarian, secular humanisms that celebrate the impulse life.

In response to these changes, fundamentalism, itself a *modern* movement, has emerged that would provide solace through a community of meaning linked to collective memories—or at least constructions of a "better time" from the past that will be restored. It provides a stable worldview in an unstable time, it valorizes fixed identities based on hierarchies of gender and faith in a postmodern world of multiple and transitory identities. It provides clear meanings for a world now facing contradictory meaning systems, secular ideologies, and exposure to the values and practices of infidels (especially sexuality). The social dislocations of the sixteenth century, much like those of the early twentieth century, attenuated social ties and rendered people lonely and powerless.[49] Protestantism, and later Nazism, and as we will suggest, religious fundamentalisms, created "pseudo-*Gemeinschaft*" communities of meaning that for the price of *submission* to superior authority, a rigid rule bound, pietistic orientation to everyday life, provided solidarity networks and promised desires realized, self-fulfilled, and glorious future imminent. Moreover, fundamentalisms differentiate themselves from the Other, designated as "enemies," sinners, and infidels—especially fornicators and homosexuals who must be punished and/or eliminated. Fundamentalism appeals to the weak, the powerless, and those denied recognition. It is above all, an expression of *ressentiment*.

> In this scenario, "ascetic priests" took revenge on the strong and "domesticated" the body, creating a slave morality which channels *ressentiment* inward against the body and outward against enemies of the herd. In Nietzsche's account, weaker individuals resented the prerogatives of the stronger and carried out a transvaluation of values, overturning previous master morality in favor of slave moralities which promise salvation in a future heaven in exchange for submission and obedience to social forces and institutions. Transforming powerlessness and *ressentiment* into discipline and social control, ascetic priests forge individuals into compliant "herds" who conform to the dominant morality.[50]

At this point, fundamentalisms diverge, each has its own history and vision of the future. As we noted, the waning of Islamic hegemony, as Christendom ascended, had already disposed *ressentiment* that would take the form of erecting barriers to western ideas and practices. Yet these technologies and values did come when Islamic societies became little more than client states or colonies.[51] Moreover, European imperialism and contemporary globalization, which made underdevelopment evident, constantly remind people of their "backwardness" and poverty building further *ressentiment*.

Foregrounded by barriers to modernization, subsequent colonization by the West and in turn dependency, today, except for the oil kingdoms that are yet quite dependent on imported goods, economic growth has bypassed the Middle East. Indeed even oil-based economies like Iran and Saudi Arabia show economic decline. Meanwhile changes are taking place that can be threatening, especially for those in dire economic straits. In the dense slums of Cairo, Kabul, or Jakarta, the small-world anchors of family, lineage, and local *imam* no longer serve as effective compasses for residents.[52] But there are compensatory alternatives, "mechanisms of escape"; fundamentalist mosques are eager to offer solace and compensations through virulent Islamism. So, too, in the many cities of Europe where Muslims have emigrated to find jobs they instead find not only marginalization, but also poverty and menial labor. The impersonality of the city, discrimination, and prejudice, and, to add insult to injury, they face the hedonistic lifestyles of Europeans that many find a moral affront. And, what's more, many of their young take up the same hedonistic European popular culture that is an insult to traditional morality. Fundamentalism provides a dignity-granting community of meaning based on imagined traditions and values derived from traditional forms of community, identity, and values. Frustrated needs for attachments, recognition, agency, and meaning, find gratification through the ideology, the community, and often the material benefits of Islamicist organizations. Mosque-based movements provide anchors for the rootless, services for the impoverished, and perhaps most important, they create "public spheres" where the hitherto silent find voice and articulate alternative visions.[53] Fundamentalism has thus become a powerful social movement and political force.[54] While it may indeed provide a compensatory balm, as Marx described religion, fundamentalism, rejecting modernity, is ill equipped to provide economic growth and in turn political legitimacy. It thus perpetuates the very factors that maintain the poverty and stagnation. Transnational capital avoids countries in which bribery is routine, where rational legal institutions do not exist, and where there is no corporate transparency.

TERROR, HEROIC MASCULINITY, AND THE DIGNITY OF AGENIC MEN

When facing colonization and domination, the cultures and identities of the colonized were denigrated, denied, and deemed inferior compared to the more affluent and powerful colonizer.[55] This of course leads to *ressentiment* and rage, but the subaltern's rage is often turned inward, upon the self. The violence done to the culture of the colonized, to the "wretched of the earth" fostered self-hatred and self-destructive behavior such as crime, addiction, or interpersonal violence. But violence to the colonizer was cathartic. Fanon wrote in the context of colonialism, especially the French control of Algeria and

Martinique, his homeland. Today, it is no longer colonial powers, but globalization, borderless markets, and regulatory agencies, decoupled from nation-states, that as a form of neocolonialization, controls investments, local government policies, and raw material prices, etc. But what is crucial to note is that globalization, as a deterritorialized system, does not present clear targets to oppose. Rather, resistance to globalization takes quite different forms than liberation struggles against a colonial power.

If fundamentalism is a faith of the weak, terrorism is its weapon. While fundamentalism may well be palliative, it often shades into a politics of hate, preaches death to infidels, and can impel violence. For some people, and we would note *very few*, fundamentalism often moves from prayer, piety, and purification to terrorism. As fundamentalisms would restore a mythical "Golden Age," they recover the legacies of the "heroic masculinity" of the warrior. For Islam, there linger memories of Saladin who threw the Christian Crusaders out, the Saracen victories in the Steppes, and Sultan Mehmed II who defeated the Byzantines.

For those at the margins of social change, for the victims of political changes, the "wretched of the now globalized earth," those without recognition face powerlessness, shame, humiliation. Lacking either means of effective communication to articulate grievances, and/or without state institutions that have the capacity or will to respond to the plight of such people without dignity or hope, anger, violence, and even death become the default mode articulated through irrational worldviews with legacies of heroes. Terrorism serves as a means of redemption, a violent response to the violent conditions that deny recognition, honor, and dignity. It empowers the powerless; it celebrates death to overcome a dominated, thwarted, empty life.[56] In some cases, violence may take a nationalistic form seeking autonomous nationhood in an age when the nation-state is waning. In other cases, the goal is not so much a modern State, but restoration of a premodern theocracy. It seems as if the levels of kinds of education of the leadership stratum—and their followers—determines the direction. But indeed, we often find both factions facing each other, using violence to advance their agendas, as for example, Lebanon in the 1980s, Algeria, or the Palestinians.

Thus the legacies of "heroic masculinity" embodied in "warriors" past transform degradation and despair into dignity and honor. Terrorism serves to direct rage to the oppressor and thus empowers the individual, restoring dignity and honor—qualities highly valued in Islamic societies. Violence to the oppressor is not only cathartic, but becomes viewed as the means to overcome political, economic, or cultural domination.[57] Projecting *ressentiment* outwards, a small number of radical fundamentalists, typically young, unattached, underemployed males, turn militant and turn to terrorism. And of these, an even smaller number become suicide bombers, fully accepting the belief that fallen warriors, martyred in battle, *shaheeden*, get a special place in heaven and a welcome by seventy-two virgins.[58]

While most such *shaheeden* tend to be boys from the poor and destitute classes, increasingly, better-educated young people, and even women opt for martyrdom. Universities, once the breeding grounds for socialist revolution are often spaces where Islamism is becoming widely embraced. But we should note that in many Islamic countries, there are many times more college graduates than there are jobs for them—especially for those trained in Arabic studies or Quranic studies. Moreover, there are a number of Muslim students who go to European universities and even move to Europe. But Europe, facing high unemployment, regard such Muslims with anger and contempt. They are denied jobs, relegated to inferior housing, and treated with contempt. Without dignity, without honor, they turn to fundamentalist mosques for solace and repair. And some embrace causes and action that provide "heroic masculinities." On September 11, 2001, nineteen such men changed the course of history.

TERRORISM AS FAILURE

Terrorism, as a desperate effort of the weak to wage asymmetrical warfare is most typically a sign of the failure to find other means of redress; it is indeed rare that it ever succeeds in changing a political or economic agenda.[59] In the context of Islamic terrorism, secular or sacred, as a manifestation of the underlying social psychological conditions that have been noted, not only does terrorism preclude interrogation of the internal conditions that evoke terrorism, but further, terrorism precludes amelioration of the conditions that engender the hopelessness that engenders it. Moreover, terrorism often evokes very strong forms of counterterrorism such as Mubarak's crackdown on Islamic *jihad* or Sharon's repression of the Al Aqsa Brigades, Hamas, Hezbollah, etc.[60] We are not "blaming the victim." Subalterity is not simply being colonized and/or impoverished, it is the condition of those whose selfhood is denigrated and suppressed, who are denied recognition and dignity, who see no hope.

It is of course true that terrorists articulate widely shared grievances and there are legitimate injustices starting with colonialism, fostering dependency relationships, sustaining "friendly" despots, and suppressing democratic, progressive movements. From the oil-based alliances with the house of Saud, the overthrow of Mossadeq, unqualified support to Israel, the abandonment of Afghanistan after the Russian retreat, the attacks on the Taliban, etc., there is a great deal of resentment of the West in general and the United States in particular, who are seen as being responsible for economic hardship, dictatorial governments, and the people's subalterity. Such perceptions and understandings, while having a great deal of truth, are not the whole story. Israel's occupation of Palestine does not explain why Pakistan put money into nuclear weapons and not schools, creating openings for the Saudi-funded *madrassas*. In other words, to focus on external constraints and grievances avoids dealing with the internal factors that have led to economic problems. Why is there a systematic refusal to address and confront the internal factors that sustain underdevelopment and instead attribute all misfortune to the West, especially America?

Several factors are involved, beginning with the cultural stagnation that began over five centuries ago and as a result that, unlike the West, there was never a space for rational critique. Rather, social shortcomings were seen as the will of Allah, failures of piety as, for example, Wahabbism. Further, the *ressentiment* that we described makes the Other, the blameworthy, despicable West responsible for all misfortunes, the internal conditions are thereby blameless for all adversity. This *ressentiment* is then fueled by mass mediated images of a materially abundant, sexually permissive West that further supports unpopular policies or regimes. The generally unfree press and mass media, directly controlled by political elites, castigates external enemies.[61] Few people have access to alternative sources of information that might be critical of their governments. If we then recall the tendencies of authoritarianism such as anti-intraception, projection, and an extrapunitive orientation, the conjunction of these moments disposes blame and precludes self-criticism and change. Moreover, given the frailty of civil society and the typically undemocratic nature of governance, political elites have no interest in fostering those changes—e.g., public referendums that would put themselves out of jobs. We have noted the resistance of the Iranian theocrats to the elected representatives of the Majlis.[62] (But there has been growing opposition to mullah rule as seen in the widespread support for Afghajari, a historian condemned to death for advocating a separation of church and state.)

Last but not least, and as a result, there are major barriers to progressive agendas. For the majority of Muslims—typically lower-middle-class, small landowners, shopkeepers, clerical workers, or state employees—progressive agendas, especially socialist visions are anathema. Not only do such classes feel anxious about what little status they have, and fear the "masses," but insofar as they embrace Islam, there is little space for secular doctrines, especially if critical of religion.[63] The fall of socialism in 1989 destroyed whatever allure it might have held. But even among many of the better-educated elite classes we see many of the same attitudes. The majority of Muslims in the Middle East do not believe Muslim terrorists were behind 9/11; rather, majorities believe it was a CIA-Mossad plot to justify a war against Islam. Moreover, these classes are often more aware of the "inferiority" of their systems vis-à-vis the West and foregrounded by the long-standing *ressentiment* noted, the unacknowledged shame disposes anger and rage more than insight and responsibility. This is not to say that all such elites share this perception, and indeed, there are many, often with western education who would spearhead efforts to usher in modernity.

CONCLUSION

From what we have said, following the decline of Islamic hegemony, most Muslim societies, whether in terms of their elites or commoners, shunned western secular modernity, democratic governance, and hence remained poor and undemocratic (though imperial powers that sustained authoritarian intermediaries and underdevelopment should also be noted). The legacy of Islam has disposed fundamentalism as a resistance to modernization. For example Wahabbism, a particularly stern, austere version of Islam emerged as the Ottoman waned. Its basic principles claimed that Muslims have strayed from righteousness, they must strongly reaffirm their faith to be saved, they must shun modernity and see that Jews and Christians are enemies to be slain. Various forms of Islamisms have been widely embraced as comforts to, if not expressions of *ressentiment* in the face of poverty, stagnation, and despair. Insofar as various secular western ideologies such as socialism, nationalism, and even Nasser's pan-Arabism have had little material success, many people now shun modernity; they see the core hegemons as responsible for all indignities and commit themselves to fundamentalisms. In a few cases, some opt for *jihad*. Yet fundamentalisms, especially when they embrace terrorism, foster the kinds of economic stagnation that create the conditions they would ameliorate. Following the recent bombing in Bali, Indonesian tourism has plummeted and foreign investment declined, and many companies sought other producers. Thus many Indonesians, Muslim as well as Hindu, will suffer.

Radical Islamic fundamentalisms, are *modern reactions to the pains of modernity*. They provide "memories" of a former greatness to be restored by a new caliphate; such ideological compensations promise alternatives to secular globalization would ameliorate economic, political, and cultural stresses. But fundamentalism cannot ameliorate the problems to which it promises solutions. While it might give voice and expressions to shame and anger, and its theologically sanctioned violence may be cathartic, the logic of eighth-century caravan trade does not offer a realistic alternative to modern industrial production. Yet fundamentalism, by encouraging piety and religious study at best, to homicidal terrorism at worst, cannot lead to material improvements that would make life easier for its adherents. Nor can it reverse massive social changes in which large numbers have been educated, urban masses cannot return to the countryside.

But there are other trends that are taking place as well. There are grow-ing classes of university educated Muslims, many of whom have been edu-cated in the West who would seek to modernize their lands and improve the quality of life. In the face of current events, from the conflict between Israel and the Palestinians, India and Pakistan, and a seeming resurgent Al Qaeda, one might have much reason for despair and gloom. We disagree and suggest that fundamentalism has been a failure, it has crested, is waning, and is in de-cline. Fundamentalist terrorism is a last ditch effort to attain what politics has failed to accomplish.[64] Fundamentalism appeals to those close to village life who now live in teeming cities.[65] As more people grow up in cities and be-come more cosmopolitan, fundamentalist fervor wanes. Thus we see it slow-ing and receding. The fundamentalist government of the Sudan was over-thrown. The unpopular Taliban were quickly dispatched in Afghanistan, Indonesia has again rejected *sharia* law. The theocrats of Iran are rapidly los-ing any legitimacy.

There is a growing number of intellectuals and clerics who would reject Islamisms and celebrations of the warrior hero, and resurrect another form of hero, the scholar, the open-minded, tolerant, rationalist intellectuals of the Golden Age such as Ibn Sinna (Avicenna), Ibn Rushd (Averroes), Al-Zarqali (Arzachel), and we would include Ibn Kaldun, the first sociologist. Through-out the Islamic world, there are now a growing number of moderate and mod-erating voices, often drowned out by the shouting of the angry, that would re-claim Islamic legacies of openness, learning, and toleration that would hasten the entry of Islamic countries into the modern world. This began in Turkey, is proceeding in Indonesia, Morocco, and even some of the Gulf States such as Bahrain, Qatar, and UAE. Iran is a case in point where the growing numbers of the younger and better educated are increasingly demanding more personal freedom, more occupational opportunities, and more democratic government. Bernard Lewis suggested that there are growing pressures for modernization and democratization throughout the Muslim world. He suspects that when one country becomes democratic, there will be a domino effect as throngs of people in other lands demand the same. Whatever direction, Islam takes, and each Islamic nation may very well take a different direction, each destiny will have been shaped by the demise of an earlier hegemony, each future by new syntheses of the past and present.

NOTES

1. Bernard Lewis, *Islam and the West* (New York: Oxford University Press, 1993).
2. Immanuel Wallerstein, *Historical Capitalism* (London: Verso, 1983).

3. Bassam Tibi (1998) has argued that Islamic fundamentalism grew following the failures of modernist movements such a nationalism or socialism to improve living conditions—to which we note, some of these "failures" were due to western interference.

4. *Jihad* can mean either struggle for spirituality within, or religiously based warfare.

5. Of course this was a typical question of early sociology, beginning with Marx's question of how/why European feudalism gave rise to capitalism. Weber followed Marx's leads in noting the central role of the bourgeoisie as an urban class practicing rational trade. Weber however emphasized mediating factors such as religious values and "inner determination" of actors.

6. We cannot here consider Marx's theories of the Oriental mode of production or Oriental despotism.

7. Wolfgang Schluchter, "Hindrances to Modernity, Max Weber and Islam." Toby E. Huff and Wolfgang Schluchter, eds., *Max Weber and Islam* (New Brunswick, N.J.: Transaction, 1999), 79.

8. Schluchter, "Hindrances to Modernity, Max Weber and Islam," 79.

9. Barrington Moore Jr., *Social Origins of Dictatorship and Democracy: Lord and Peasant in the Making of the Modern World* (Boston: Beacon Press, 1966).

10. Richard James Blackburn, *The Vampire of Reason: An Essay in the Philosophy of History* (London: Verso, 1990), 126.

11. Brian M. Downing, *The Military Revolution and Political Change: Origins of Democracy and Autocracy in Early Modern Europe* (Princeton, N.J.: Princeton University Press, 1991).

12. Downing, *The Military Revolution and Political Change.*

13. Haim Gerber, *The Social Origins of the Modern Middle East* (Boulder, Colo.: L. Rienner, 1987).

14. Blackburn, *The Vampire of Reason,* 271.

15. Yves Lacoste, *Ibn Khaldun: The Birth of History and the Past of the Third* (London: Verso, 1984), 109.

16. As noted, there were many conflicts and challenges, not to the caliphate, but to particular claims of descent.

17. This is not to ignore the change in governance that did occur, rather none of the states spontaneously gave rise to modernization or industrialization, nor like Asian states, did they gain much investment to do so.

18. Theda Skocpol, *States and Social Revolutions: A Comparative Analysis of France, Russia, and China* (Cambridge: Cambridge University Press, 1979); Gerber, *The Social Origins of the Modern Middle East.*

19. Lewis, *Islam and the West.*

20. Schluchter, "Hindrances to Modernity, Max Weber and Islam," 108.

21. Gerber, *The Social Origins of the Modern Middle East.*

22. Timur Kuran, *The Islamic Commercial Crisis: Institutional Roots of the Delay in the Middle East's Economic Modernization* (Los Angeles, California, 2001): USC Center for Law, Economics, and Organization, Research paper, CO01–12, http://papers.srn.com/abstract _id+276377.

23. For Weber, rational commerce, together with a "methodological orientation to everyday life," required clear records; double entry bookkeeping, a running record of income, costs, and expenses, became a central moment in the growth of capitalism. Similarly, Kuran (2001) contrasted the operations of the Medici, Bardi, Peruzzi, or Fugger enterprises with Islamic partnerships to indicate how and why the former led to intergenerational growth while the latter were unlikely to endure.

24. Kuran, *The Islamic Commercial Crisis.*

25. Kuran, *The Islamic Commercial Crisis.*

26. Kuran, *The Islamic Commercial Crisis.*

27. Downing, *The Military Revolution and Political Change.*

28. Max Weber, *From Max Weber: Essay in Sociology,* H. H. Gerth and C. Wright Mills, trans. and eds. (New York: Oxford University Press, 1946).

29. Schluchter, "Hindrances to Modernity, Max Weber and Islam," 85.

30. Nehemia Levtzion, "Aspects of Islamization: Weber's Observations on Islam Reconsidered," in Toby E. Huff and Wolfgang Schluchter, eds., *Max Weber and Islam* (New Brunswick, N.J.: Transaction, 1999).

31. Downing, *The Military Revolution and Political Change.*

32. Downing, *The Military Revolution and Political Change.*

33. Downing, *The Military Revolution and Political Change,* 65.

34. This resurrection of the fundamentalist as "holy warrior" was evident in Algeria and the Afghan *mujahadeen* sponsored by the CIA to battle the Russians.

35. Gerber, *The Social Origins of the Modern Middle East.*

36. For example, many of the Southeast Asian countries have prospered in the last decades while Islamic countries, especially in the Middle East have remained poor.

37. Gerber, *The Social Origins of the Modern Middle East.*

38. This needs to be qualified since at certain times, there were a number of centers of power.

39. Besides orthodoxy we might also note the role of Sufic mysticism, moving subjectivity to a trance-induced other worldliness, served to sustain the status quo.

40. There are of course wide variations, Turkey, as a result of geography and history has large factories and encourages nationalism, its own, not that of its Kurdish population. The UAE has a successful and growing airline.

41. Lewis, *Islam and the West,* 79.

42. Lacoste, *Ibn Khaldun,* 109.

43. We might note a similarity with China, in the fifteenth century the emperor cut off foreign trade and halted emerging industrialism, understanding that a powerful merchant class would challenge his authority.

44. Gerber, *The Social Origins of the Modern Middle East.*

45. Support for the House of Saud actually began in the 1920s. In 1953, the CIA and MI6 jointly overthrew the democratically elected prime minister of Iran, Mossadeq, who wanted to put oil royalties into schools and hospitals. The despotism of the Shaw led to Khomenie's Islamic revolution.

46. This needs qualification, countries like Turkey, Lebanon, and Malaysia have worked out accommodations with globalization and while none approach the affluence and toleration of the Danes these are not the hotbeds of fundamentalism found in Saudi Arabia, Iran, or Algeria.

47. Paul Lubeck and Bryana Britts, "Muslim Civil Society in Urban Public Spaces: Globalization, Discursive Shifts, and Social Movements," in J. John Eade and Christopher Mele, eds., *Understanding the City: Contemporary and Future Perspectives* (Malden, Mass.: Blackwell, 2002).

48. Fundamentalism has generally failed to achieve its goals, and terrorism can be seen as last stands of desperation. As Giles Kepel (2002) has argued, fundamentalism is under assault, as generations removed from village life mature, it will exit the current stage of world history.

49. Erich Fromm, *The Anatomy of Human Destructiveness* (New York: Holt, Rinehart, and Winston, 1973).

50. Douglas Kellner, "Nietzsche's Critique of Mass Culture," www.gseis.ucla.edu/faculty/kellner/Illumina%20Folder/kell22.htm.

51. We do need to note that there have been wide variations in receptivity to western ideas and technologies, Turkey was relatively open within the limits of being an Islamic Sultanate. Moreover, the technologies have often been introduced, indeed quickly absorbed while values have been rejected. So much for theories of technological determinism and cultural lag.

52. Robert W. Hefner, *Civil Islam: Muslims and Democratization in Indonesia* (Princeton, N.J.: Princeton University Press, 2000).

53. Lubeck and Britts, "Muslim Civil Society in Urban Public Spaces," have noted the importance of mosques as "public spheres."

54. Paul M. Lubeck, "The Islamic Revival: Antinomies of Islamic Movements under Globalization," Robin Cohen and Shirin M. Rai, eds., *Global Social Movements* (New Brunswick, N.J.: Athlone Press, 2000).

55. Frantz Fanon, *The Wretched of the Earth,* Constance Farrington, trans. (New York: Grove Press, 1965); Friedrich Nietzsche, *On the Genealogy of Morals*, Walter Kaufmann and R. J. Hollingdale, trans. (New York: Vintage Books, 1967).

56. Fromm, *The Anatomy of Human Destructiveness.*

57. Lauren Langman and Valerie Scatamburlo, "Fanon Speaks to the Subaltern," *Current Perspectives in Social Theory* 20 (2001): 237–54.

58. Some recent commentators have claimed this was a mistranslation; they would receive seven delicious raisins.

59. Caleb Carr, *The Lessons of Terror: A History of Warfare Against Civilians: Why It Has Always Failed and Why It Will Fail Again* (New York: Random House, 2002).

60. By the end of 2002, a number of Palestinian elites have publicly argued that the Intifada and its martyrdom operations have been a failure.

61. Of the forty-nine states with Muslim majorities, only one, Mali, has a genuinely free press. *The Al Jazeera* television network does represent a major step in providing otherwise restricted information such as interviews with Israeli politicians.

62. The theocrats argue that a spiritual revolution did not promise prosperity—though many of the mullahs and ayatollahs live quite lavishly. Growing numbers of youth, most of whom care less about spiritual riches and have consistently voted for progress parties that dominate the Majlis.

63. In these ways, there is a great similarity between the conservative lower-middle classes that supported Fascism in the 1920s, and the class of small merchants and lower echelon civil servants who have supported Islamisms since the 1980s. But much like

Fascism, certain segments of the elites, impelled by ideological factors, opt for Islamisms—Bin Laden and Zawahari being prime examples. But further, a large number of supporters are young men trained only in Quran by radical clerics embrace various Islamisms.

64. Carr, *The Lessons of Terror.*

65. Gilles Kepel, *Jihad: The Trail of Political Islam,* Anthony F. Robert, trans. (Cambridge, Mass.: Harvard University Press, 2002).

Europe in the Mirror of the Contemporary Middle East: Aspects of Modern European History Reconsidered

Sandra Halperin

INTRODUCTION

*H*ow the West traditionally views Islam, and how it continues to view developments in the Islamic world, is bound up with how it views itself. Any significant change in western views of Islam will likely depend, therefore, on the extent to which western scholars are willing to explore and transcend the conventional boundaries of western self-understanding. With that in mind, this chapter reflects on some of the ideas that have shaped our understanding of the West and of its development. It focuses, specifically, on conventional accounts of European historical development and, in particular, on a number of their central but, as will be argued below, profoundly erroneous assumptions.

Many assumptions of conventional European historiography were developed in association with the ideology of western superiority and progress that emerged during the age of European imperialism. The view of Europe and the nonwestern world that this ideology promoted inspired Europeans in the late nineteenth century to see their history as representing a chronicle of progress in the advance of reason and freedom. It was this view that formed the foundational underpinning of what William McNeill calls the "Victorian edifice" of conventional European historiography. Though the view ceased to be convincing after World War I, the edifice that had been built upon it, nonetheless, remained standing.[1] In fact, after World War II it was reinforced and refurbished—due, in large measure, to its compatibility with the aims of America's post–World War II "development project."

The central concern of America's "development project" was to shape the future of developing countries so as to ensure they would not be drawn into the Soviet Communist bloc. After World War II, the Communist pattern of organization had spread to much of Eastern Europe and to China. To prevent it from spreading still further and wider—to the newly independent countries of Africa and Asia—the United States enlisted its social scientists to study and devise ways of promoting capitalist economic development and political stability.

Through generous funding and institutional inducements, the "development project" attracted a steady and ever-expanding flow of research and writing from across the social sciences. Within a couple of decades, the work of its political scientists, economists, sociologists, psychologists, anthropologists, and demographers began to converge around a common set of analytic conventions and general themes. These eventually produced a common grounding for research and writing in all areas of social scientific inquiry. Though this has had a decisive impact on social science research, an equally notable achievement of the "development project" has been to restore the tottering "Victorian edifice" of conventional European historiography and to build up around it a radically revisionist account of European industrial capitalist development.

In the early and mid-nineteenth century, writing on European industrial development had focused on what at that time had been seen as its most characteristic aspects: domination, exploitation, uneven development, inequality, political instability, and authoritarianism. These had been the principal foci of the narratives and analyses of countless social scientists and reformers; the speeches, official documents and reports, and other writings of European statesmen; and the work of the century's greatest literary figures.

But in the accounts of modern European history produced in America after World War II, all these aspects of industrial capitalist development, all the elements that for nineteenth-century social scientists had revealed its intrinsic costs and engendered pessimism and doubt about it,[2] recede into the background. Instead, the emergence of industrial capitalism and democracy in Europe is depicted as resulting from a gradual, evolutionary change: slowly but steadily wealth diffuses; gradually, but inevitably, equality and liberty spread into increasingly wider domains. It is a reassuring and inspiring tale of progress, a story devoid of bloody conflict, power, and privilege, of suffering, division, and struggle. Thus, while the ideological fervor and politics of the Cold War were suppressing communism, as well as socialist and other reformist and progressive elements in the "developing world," it was also working through the "development project" to suppress, in history, the role of these elements in achieving social democracy and prosperity in Europe.

Most accounts of modern European history focus on dynamic (but actually limited and scattered) focal points of growth found throughout Europe in the nineteenth century. They tend to emphasize processes of urbanization, industrialization, liberalization, urban working-class movements, and democratization, and to ignore or downplay the persistence of rural, preindustrial, feudal, and autocratic structures of power and authority. European societies were, in fact, characterized by all the features associated with contemporary Third World dependent development: enclave economies oriented to foreign markets; weak middle classes; alliances between the state, traditional landowning elites, and new industrial classes; unstable and partial democracy, sharp inequalities, and increasing poverty. On the eve of World War I, all of these features were as characteristic of Europe as they are of the developing world today.

In sum, a highly idealized account of modern European development has been constructed and widely disseminated and, in general, uncritically accepted. Most researchers and writers use this account of the European experience as a starting point and basis of comparison for analyzing the contemporary developing world. Since, for example, the problem of achieving industrial development and democracy in the contemporary developing world is usually analyzed, explicitly or implicitly, on the basis of assumptions about how industrialization and democracy were achieved in Europe, a distorted understanding of the European past undermines our ability to understand the problems of developing countries today. It is in this way that western views of the nonwestern world and western self-understanding are interconnected.

The next section investigates what for generations of students has represented the critical turning point in the development of industrial capitalism and democracy in Europe: the nearly simultaneous industrial and French revolutions. As section I will argue, these events did not represent a revolutionary break with the past, but only the beginning of a process that was slow, bloody, and had many setbacks. A vast frontier lay between the "industrial revolution" and the achievement of industrial capitalism in Europe. On the eve of World War I, Europe was urbanizing, but not urban; industrializing, but not industrial; liberalizing, but neither liberal nor bourgeois. In 1914, the bulk of Europe's population still lived and worked in rural areas and it was there, where in nearly every country, the seat of national political power and the dominant social ethos were found.

The French Revolution is widely seen as a turning point in the democratization and secularization of Europe. However, nearly a century and a half after the French Revolution, lower classes and ethnic minorities in Europe were still effectively excluded from political life and from opportunities for economic advancement. Moreover, as section II shows, contrary to a widely held assumption, the Revolution did not set in motion a process of accelerated secularization in Europe. In fact, one of the largely forgotten but crucial aspects of the nineteenth century was the resurgence of religion in Europe. This resurgence was fueled and sustained by politically powerful, militant, and fundamentalist religious movements that, in many respects, are closely analogous to the movements associated with the Islamic revival in the contemporary Middle East. In light of these aspects of modern western history, section III reflects on the socioeconomic and political topography of the contemporary Middle East and the current Islamic revival there.

I. EUROPE'S NINETEENTH-CENTURY ECONOMIC AND POLITICAL DEVELOPMENT: A RECONSIDERATION

The division between the advanced industrial world and the Third World has become conventional for social science. It is generally assumed that this division is a further evolution of processes that defined the separation of Europe from the non-European world: chief among these were the advances achieved in Europe during what has been called "the long sixteenth century," the Industrial Revolution, and the French Revolution. None of these events marked the decisive period of the European advance. In fact, European economic history diverged decisively from that of the rest of the world only after 1945.

It is certainly true that Europe experienced enormous growth during its "long sixteenth century."[3] But the assumption that, as a consequence, Western Europe had become rich compared to other parts of the world by the start of the Industrial Revolution[4] is erroneous. In the seventeenth century, European growth was halted and, in some areas, reversed. Thus, on the eve of the Industrial Revolution the level of GNP per capita in Europe was, in fact, about even with that of the non-European world.[5]

Scholars have argued for over a century that the period we call the Industrial Revolution was not the radical break with the past that the term suggests; and recent research confirms this.[6] However, with the publication in 1884 of Arnold Toynbee's *Lectures on the "Industrial Revolution,"* the expression was adopted by the purveyors of European triumphalism and, despite objections, incorporated into historical terminology.[7] During the classic Industrial Revolution, Britain actually experienced only gradual industrialization.[8] However, Europeans in the late nineteenth century, impressed by the technological advances of the time, accepted the idea that Europe's level of economic well-being and its rate of progress were incomparably superior to anything that had gone before.[9] Such beliefs became deeply embedded in the historical consciousness of that and subsequent generations. They did so, most likely, because they helped to shape the identity of Europe in relation to areas of the world being exploited by European governments and peoples and were used, in fact, as a rationale for that exploitation.

However, despite the general acceptance of these beliefs, the incomparable advance of Europe was more myth than reality. The level of income in

Britain by the middle of the nineteenth century and in Germany or France in 1870 was comparable with that of classical Greece. Colin Clark calculates that the real earnings of a typical British factory worker in 1850, and those of an Italian worker in 1928, were approximately equivalent to those of a free artisan in Rome in the first century A.D.[10] Europe's rate of growth, though faster than it had been, was not spectacular in the nineteenth century; compared to European rates after World War II (4.5 percent), its annual growth (0.9–1.0 percent) was slow.[11] Nor was Europe's growth spectacular relative to the rest of the globe.[12] Between 1870 and 1913, per capita national income in Britain and France and in much of Central and Southeast Europe was growing slower than in Colombia, Brazil, and Mexico.[13] On the eve of World War I, Europe as a whole had achieved a level of economic well-being about equal with that of Latin America.[14] Europe was still "preeminently preindustrial," as Arno Mayer has argued.[15] In all of Europe except England, agriculture was still the single largest and weightiest economic sector. Even after World War I, France still drew its wealth principally from agriculture, and approximately half of the population was engaged in agricultural pursuits.[16] Central Europe had not yet begun its industrial takeoff; Eastern and Southern Europe had neither developed industrially nor moved significantly into agricultural exports; in fact, on the eve of World War I, these areas of Europe were exporting less primary products than Latin America.[17] In 1914, most of Europe was still rural,[18] and most of rural Europe had not changed substantially since the Middle Ages.

The "Capitalist Bourgeoisie"

According to conventional accounts, industrial development in Britain was "promoted and led by an independent capitalist middle class which fought against the old aristocracy as well as against the restrictive power of the state."[19] These accounts assume that "bourgeois revolutions" occurred in Britain and France when middle-class elements (the Independents in the English Revolution, the Montagnards in the French Revolution) fought and won a struggle for state power against merchant and financial monopolists that had originated in the feudal land aristocracy (the Royalists and Monarchists of the English and French Revolutions).[20] Barrington Moore argued that, as a result, Britain had a "fully capitalist bourgeoisie" in the nineteenth century that, with "minimum help from the state, was able to convert a large part of the globe into [its] trading area."[21]

This is largely a fiction. It was the aristocracy that led and won the revolt against absolutism, both in Britain and elsewhere in Europe; and, though concessions were granted to wealthy nonaristocratic industrialists after the 1848 revolutions, the aristocracy remained the dominant faction of the bourgeoisie throughout the nineteenth and early twentieth centuries. In consequence, it was traditional elites that led capitalist development in Europe and formed the basis of its "capitalist class."[22]

Many have argued that this elite had become bourgeosified by the eighteenth or nineteenth century. However, throughout the nineteenth century, the most effective elites were traditional and aristocratic, landowning, and rent receiving as well as oligarchic. This elite dominated the state apparatus and used it to channel industrial expansion into noncompetitive, ascriptive, monopolistic forms that ensured the continuity of rural, preindustrial, feudal, and autocratic structures of power and authority. Thus, despite the claim that the establishment of nation-states in Europe represented the emergence of rationalized, "autonomous" state institutions that operated to advance "state" or "national" interests; and the large and influential body of writing concerning the "new" liberal age, the end of absolutism, and the creation of the bourgeois state and bourgeois law did not bring about the separation of economic (class) power from political (state) power but, rather a structure of power that fused both for extraction of surplus, locally and abroad, by extra economic compulsion.[23]

Europe's Dualistic Economic Expansion

With the so-called industrial revolution, traditional elites in Europe used the wealth and privileges that they had acquired in the past to ensure that processes of industrialization would not adversely affect their interests.

Throughout the nineteenth and early twentieth centuries, various forms of economic protection and monopoly, as well as restrictions on labor organization and on political participation, enabled Europe's small elite of landowners and wealthy industrialists to monopolize land, as well as the entire field of industry and trade. This produced a "dual" pattern of development that, in all aspects, resembles the dual economies described by theories of contemporary Third World development.[24]

Dual economy models were developed to explain the economies of colonial countries and, in particular, their most characteristic feature: the existence of an island of western economic institutions and organizations surrounded by traditional communities and institutions and an underdeveloped economy. Many developing countries today are characterized by a sharp division between a dynamic foreign-oriented, "corporate" sector and the larger traditional economy and society. There is no investment beyond this sector: profits are either reinvested there or exported. Improvements in technology do not diffuse outward to agriculture or to cottage industry. What income distribution takes place is confined to the corporate sector and does not occur between it and the noncorporate sector. Thus, the economy as a whole is characterized by a lack of internal structural integration and dependency on outside capital, labor, and markets. Most perspectives on development, whether Liberal or Marxist, assume that this kind of dualism is unique to the contemporary developing world and that, in the industrializing countries of the West there were "leading sectors" (e.g., cotton textiles in the British "take-off" from 1783 to 1803, railroads in France from 1830 to 1860) that were essentially indigenous and closely interwoven with the other sectors of the economy.

But European countries were also characterized by a lack of internal structural integration and dependency on outside capital, labor, and/or markets. Great Britain, France, Italy, Germany, Spain, Portugal, the Austro-Hungarian Empire, Russia, Belgium, and much of the Balkans all had dynamic, foreign-oriented economic sectors that failed to transform the rest of their economies and societies. Some European countries experienced widespread growth, though less widespread and much later than is usually supposed; but in most, modern industrial sectors oriented to and dependent on international markets, formed enclaves within nonindustrial, mainly agricultural and backward hinterlands linked, not to other sectors of the domestic economy, but to similar industrial enclaves in other countries. Production was largely for external markets; trade was external; capital was invested abroad. Concerned to consolidate and maintain their control of labor while, at the same time, mobilizing it for the expansion of production, elites sought to increase profits through a dualistic system of internal restriction and external expansion.

Europe's economic expansion was based on the use of production methods that deskilled labor and kept it fragmented and impoverished. Profits increased, not through increasing the productivity of labor in wage goods industries, but by applying large quantities of unskilled or semiskilled labor to producton, as is typical of primary export production in the contemporary Third World. In Britain, whole families (women and children) were put to work to earn, together, the same wage that once had been paid to a single "head of household." By making it necessary for the whole family to contribute to its reproduction rather than a single "head of household," the employer got more workers for no additional cost. Profits increased also by increasing the duration or the normal intensity of labor, by making workers work longer and with fewer and shorter breaks, and faster. Cheap food was imported from abroad to further decrease the cost of labor. Workers were also forced to consume poorer quality food, either by dismantling regulations prohibiting the adulteration of basic foodstuffs or, as in Ireland, making them dependent on the potato crop for sustenance.[25]

Because the workforce was, by these means, rendered too poor to function as a factor of consumption, the dynamic sectors of European economies were dependent on the development of exogenous demand and consumption.

The export of British goods and capital played a leading role in creating an international circuit of investment and exchange for this purpose.

Europe's dualistic economic system expanded production and increased profits for a transnational landowning and industrial elite while at the same time limiting the geographic and sectoral spread of industrialization, mass mobilization for industrial production, and the rise of new classes at home. A generally low level of industrialization and the production of high-cost goods for export avoided the need for both redistribution of the national income—the need to provide workers with the purchasing power to consume the goods that they produced, and a significant factory proletariat. This ensured that the benefits of expanding production would be retained solely by the property-owning classes.

The property-owning classes of European states were part of a single transregional elite whose broadly similar characteristics, interests, capabilities, and policies were constituted and reproduced through relations of interaction, connection, and interdependence. These relations of connection had for centuries created similarities and interdependencies among states. As the various economies of Europe began to expand in the nineteenth century, their advanced sectors became tied more closely to those within the economies of other European countries than to the more backward sectors within their own. As a result, and as time went on, economic development in Europe took place within, and was crucially shaped by, an increasingly interdependent industrial system.

Britain increased its industrial production by expanding its shipbuilding, boilermaking, gun, and ammunition industries. This enabled it to penetrate and defend markets overseas. British exports of capital provided purchasing power among foreign governments and elites for British-built railways, canals, and other public works; banks, telegraphs, and other public services; factories, and mines. All of this helped to fund the development and transport of food and raw materials exports to Britain, thus creating additional foreign purchasing power and demand for British goods, and also decreasing the price of food, and thereby the value of labor, in Britain.[26]

In the nineteenth century, Britain devoted a substantially smaller proportion of her national output and savings to home investment than did any of her major competitors. In some respects London institutions were more highly organized to provide capital to foreign investors than to British industry.[27] As Charles Kindleberger has shown,

> A limited number of firms in a limited number of industries could get access to the London new-issues market—railroads, shipping, steel, cotton (after 1868), along with banks and insurance companies. And some

attention was devoted to refinancing existing private companies. For the most part, however, the flow of savings was aimed abroad and not to domestic industries.[28]

At the same time that British investors were investing abroad, British industry was, relative to that of its nearest competitors, slow to mechanize and to introduce new technologies. As a result, Britain's "Industrial Revolution" was both sectorally and geographically limited.[29] Its industrial breakthrough in the 1780s and 1790s involved the mechanization of only one branch (spinning) of one industry (cotton). The other branch, weaving, remained unmechanized for forty years.[30] There was no mechanization outside the cotton industry. By 1850, the total number of factory workers amounted to not much more than 5 percent in England.[31] There was no mechanized transport for fifty years. Before World War II, less than a third of those employed in the transport sector were employed by the railways (28 percent in 1931).[32] There was no mass-produced machinery for sixty years and no large steel production for seventy.[33] Despite the British origins of the machines and machine tools industry, it was not until the 1890s that automatic machine-tools production was introduced in Britain. The impetus came from the United States, and the desire on the part of employers "to break down the hold of the skilled craftsmen in the industry."[34]

The building industries grew by expanding employment, rather than by introducing innovations either in organization or technology.[35] Though Britain had pioneered electrotechnics, by 1913 the output of the British electrical industry was little more than a third of Germany's.[36] Gas manufacture was mechanized late, and as a result of pressure from trade unions. Even Britain's export industries were slow to adopt new techniques or improvements, not only in textiles, but in coal, iron, steel, railways, and shipbuilding. The supply of coal increased,[37] not by the introduction of labor-saving techniques, but by increasing the number of coalminers.[38] In the 1930s, "more than 40% of British coal was cut, and practically 50% conveyed, without the aid of machinery."[39]

As is typical throughout the contemporary Third World today, in Britain during the nineteenth century, the structure of landholding and the low productivity of the labor force engaged in growing food for home consumption continued to limit industrial production for the home market.

Throughout the nineteenth century, the larger landowners continued to enlarge and consolidate their holdings. In 1897, 175,000 people owned ten-elevenths of the land of England, and forty million people the remaining one-eleventh.[40] The landless rural population subsisted on low wages; the rest subsisted on small plots of land. The majority of farms in England

and Wales did not possess either a tractor or a milking machine until World
War II, despite their having been available for some thirty years or more.
They remained relatively small and investment in them relatively low. As late
as 1935, 18 percent of all agricultural holdings comprised less than 5 acres,
and a further 45 percent less than 50 acres.[41] On the eve of World War I,
more than 60 percent of the adult agricultural laborers of the kingdom received less than the amount necessary for the maintenance of a laborer and
his family on workhouse.[42]

Like its agriculture, Britain's financial and industrial sectors were
bound by monopoly and restriction. The regulative, protective system of
mercantilism was only selectively dismantled; and by the end of the nineteenth century, there was a full-blown return to monopoly and regulation.
The City of London, in which greater fortunes were made than in the
whole of industry, remained "enmeshed in a pseudo baronial network of
gentlemanly non-competition."[43] One of the key concerns of the national
states that emerged with the defeat of absolutism was to deprive foreigners
and minorities of their economic power and position, and reduce their
role in finance, commerce, and trade. Thus, despite its reputation for cos-
mopolitanism, in the last decades before 1914, "the rare dynamic entre-
preneurs of Edwardian Britain were, more often than not, foreigners or minority groups"—Jews, Quakers, Germans, Americans.[44] In the industrial
sphere, traditional corporatist structures—guilds, patronage, and clientelist
networks—survived in some places and grew stronger; elsewhere, new corporatist structures were created. As the nineteenth century progressed, industry became increasingly penetrated by monopoly and protection. The
modern cartel movement began to develop in the crisis of 1873 and during
the subsequent depression years. In Britain and France industry maintained
tacit limits on competition that were about as effective as formal contracts.
However, despite the strong tendency in Britain to the kind of gentleman's
agreement that makes cartels unnecessary, cartels did appear there in metal-
lurgy, milling, chemicals, and glassmaking. In what David Landes aptly calls
"a commercial version of the enclosure movement,"[45] Britain's answered the
cartel movement with the "combine," which grouped sizeable fractions of
the productive units in a given trade in various degrees of amalgamation.
Combines, like cartels, were designed to control the market by eliminating
competition, fixing prices, sharing out supplies, buying raw materials en
bloc, and cutting out middlemen. By 1900, there were no German enterprises of any consequence, except shipbuilding, which were not affected
profoundly by the cartel movement.[46] But, by 1914, cartelization pervaded
industry everywhere in Europe.[47]

Autocracy

It is frequently claimed that, in contrast to the political evolution of societies in the contemporary Third World, "In the early part of the twentieth century," most western European societies "were either political democracies, or well on the way toward becoming so."[48] The French Revolution is thought to have introduced "the first experience of democracy"[49] and, thus, to have begun a "democratic revolution" that, following the Revolution, spread equality and liberty into increasingly wider domains. However, the actual impact of the Revolution, in terms of inaugurating change, was far more limited. Because restrictions in sites of production and throughout economies were reproduced by maintaining them throughout the polity, political participation in Europe remained highly restricted until the era of the world wars.

Before 1945, what has uncritically been accepted as "democracy" in Europe was a severely limited form of representative government that was everywhere constructed on the basis of a highly restrictive, means-tested suffrage that excluded the majority of the population from participation in the political process. Like democracy in the ancient world, it was really an "egalitarian oligarchy," in which "a ruling class of citizens shared the rights and spoils of political control."[50] The great majority of adults were excluded from participation: men below the age of twenty-five or thirty-five, and women (see table 5.1). Given that the life expectancy in Europe before World War I was between forty-one (e.g., in Austria, Spain) and fifty-five years of age, this meant that those who had the vote were men in the last third of their life. If the same system prevailed in the West today, the vote would be restricted to men over fifty-four years of age.

Table 5.1.   Europe in 1910

Country	Life Expectancy	Voting Age
Belgium	47	25
Germany	47	25
Denmark	55	35
Norway	55	25

Source: R. J. Goldstein, *Political Repression in Nineteenth Century Europe* (London: Croom Helm, 1983).

Universal adult suffrage would have enfranchised 40–50 percent of each country's population. In 1910, only some 14–22 percent of the population was enfranchised in Sweden, Switzerland, Great Britain, Belgium, Denmark, the Netherlands, and Germany (see table 5.2).

Table 5.2.   Percent of European Population Enfranchised, 1910

Country	%	Country	%
Finland	45	Austria	21
Norway	33	Sweden	19
France	29	U.K.	18
Spain	24	Denmark	17
Bulgaria	23	Portugal	12
Greece	23	Romania	16
Serbia	23	Russia	15
Germany	22	Netherlands	14
Belgium	22	Italy	8
Switzerland	22	Hungary	6

Source: R. J. Goldstein, *Political Repression in Nineteenth Century Europe* (London: Croom Helm, 1983), 241.

While, in some places, the suffrage included members of the poorer classes, three-class and other weighted and plural voting systems, as well as open balloting, restrictions on and biases against working-class organizations and parties made it futile for poor people to vote. Thus, the figures in tables 5.1 and 5.2 do not reflect the actual number of people who were permitted to vote under the systems existing at the time.

Though the tendency to equate the existence of parliaments with democracy is no longer a feature of studies of contemporary developing countries, it continues to be accepted in studies of European political development. The development of parliamentary institutions in nineteenth-century Europe did not affect the character of popular representation in Europe. In fact, before World War I, parliaments in Europe functioned rather more like royal courts than the parliaments and other legislative bodies that exist today in the West. On the eve of World War I, hereditary transmission of sociopolitical status was still widespread. The British House of Lords, a purely hereditary body monopolized by the great landowning families, had absolute veto power over legislation proposed by the House of Commons until 1911.

It was not until the middle of the twentieth century that stable, full democracy was established in western European societies. Until then, Europe, in common with parts of the contemporary Third World, experienced partial democratization and reversals of democratic rule. On the eve of World War I, Norway was the only country in Europe with universal and equal suffrage. Everywhere else, democracy was partial and unstable. Constitutions and democratic civil liberties were continually thwarted by extralegal patronage systems and by corruption. Great Britain had still not enfranchised the whole male working class and its electoral system was corrupted further by plural voting. Only after the Second World War did universal, equal, direct, and secret suffrage become the norm throughout western Europe.

In sum, political institutions in nineteenth-century Europe were established by elites for the purpose of preserving and extending their social and economic power and, as a result, were continually compromised and undermined by efforts to preserve privilege and to forestall the acquisition of power by subordinate groups and classes. Political participation was severely limited. Where liberal electoral politics were introduced, governments had difficulty in maintaining them for sustained periods of time. Parliaments were dissolved, election results were disregarded. To preserve privilege and to forestall the rise of socialism, constitutions and democratic civil liberties were continually thwarted by conservative restorations and reaction, by extralegal patronage systems, corruption, and violence. Thus, despite the massive population movements within and outside of Europe, and the appearance of great flux and change over the entire surface of European life, traditional bases of social and political power remained intact. In fact, a battle between traditional and religious authority and new secular forces dominated the history of nineteenth-century Europe.

II. RELIGIOUS REVIVALISM
IN NINETEENTH-CENTURY EUROPE

A common assumption concerning western historical development is that by the end of the eighteenth century, the path from religious to secular society in Europe had largely been traversed. But during the nineteenth-century secularization[51] battled a revival of militant, literal, old-fashioned religion, of "religion in its most uncompromising, irrationalist, and emotionally compulsive forms."[52] This war dominated the history of nineteenth-century Europe. In much of Europe—in France, Switzerland, Italy, Spain, Portugal, Russia, and elsewhere—the separation of church and state did not become law until the twentieth century.

While the unity of religion and politics that existed in the early years of Islam has no parallel in the early years of Christianity, later in its history, the ecclesiastical and political realms in Christianity became closely associated. Between the tenth and seventeenth centuries, the Popes claimed and exercised exclusive sovereignty in temporal affairs in Europe as God's representative on earth. Kings and princes were accountable to the religious authorities, and their control of political and economic affairs within their realms was circumscribed or limited, in various ways, by the church. Popes exercised direct authority over political and class struggles, economic life, education, social welfare, and the whole of the intellectual life of Europe. They raised large armies, organized crusades, dethroned monarchs, distributed kingdoms, raised funds by direct taxation, and brought offenders to justice. Throughout Europe, their legates watched over the execution of his orders and the maintenance of discipline. Though there were rebellions against papal authority, e.g., at the end of the thirteenth century, it was only in the seventeenth century that the church-dominated international political order came to an end.

Even after the Peace of Westphalia in 1648 marked the end of the Church's exclusive sovereignty over European political life, the church refused to recognize any distinction between ecclesiastical and political domains.[53] When the French Revolution led to an attempt throughout continental Europe to subject the church completely to the authority of the state, there ensued a great war between religious and secular authority in Europe.

The Catholic Church—the greatest international organization of that or any other day, as a historian wrote in 1944—forcefully condemned the separation of church and state, freedom of conscience, freedom of books, liberalism and the liberal state, industrialization, capitalism, republicanism, democracy, and socialism, and called for a return to medieval Christian principles.[54] It showed no willingness for compromise. In the course of the century, the breach between the church and the dominant secular forces of the time "approached the dimensions of a schism in civilization."[55] As this breach widened, European societies became increasingly polarized and politically volatile.

A revitalized, more militant and monolithic "Ultramontane" Catholicism emerged in Europe after the French Revolution. Its principal exponents were the Jesuits, who were reconstituted after the Revolution, as well as a host of new orders, like the assumptionists. In France, where the movement began, ultramontane clergy led revivalist meetings in public squares, held mass to purge the sins of Jacobinism, and imposed on Catholics weekly attendance at mass. The movement spread to other Catholic countries and to Catholic communities within predominantly Protestant states. Everywhere in Catholic Europe, there was a phenomenal revival of pilgrimages, processions, and venerations of saints. New saints, and accordingly new places of pilgrimage, were continually being born, as living men and women won a local reputation for holiness. There was also a steady increase in the number of churches, a phenomenal revival of religious orders,[56] and a revival of Catholic missionary activity throughout and outside Europe.

There was a revival, also, within the established Protestant churches. After the French Revolution, there was an explosion of Protestant missionary activity[57] and an astonishing mass conversion to Protestantism. Protestant sects that had been large and influential in the revolutionary seventeenth century but had lost considerable ground in the course of the eighteenth, grew into mass religions.[58] The Free Kirk movement in Scotland (which initiated a religious awakening in defense of the "Crown Rights of the Redeemer"), Germany's "Awakening," and the revival of orthodox Calvinism in the Netherlands were part of the revival that took place within the established churches. Other, new Protestant movements arose whose harsh puritanism and literalist understanding of Scripture became the foundation of modern fundamentalism.

The Politics of Religious Revival

The religious revival in Europe was initiated by the clergy largely in defense of church interests. However, during the subsequent century and a half it was sustained by a variety of groups, and in pursuit of political ends not solely or directly related to the church or the defense of corporate church interests. After 1815, much of Europe saw the development of religious-political parties and connections opposed to the secularization of European society and concerned to make the machinery of the state serve the interests of the church. As a result of these parties, church issues—particularly conflict over education—occupied a large place in European politics throughout the century.

The church sought to defend a number of interests in the political arena. Chief among them was the preservation of itself as the state religion. The introduction of religious toleration at various times, in France, Britain, Germany, Scandinavia, and elsewhere, threatened the character of the church as the state religion and, thus, its status as the sole religion enjoying the privilege of public worship. In France, the Catholic ultramontane clergy condemned the state for allowing Protestants, Jews, and freethinkers to exercise equal rights with Catholics. The issues of Catholic emancipation and disestablishment occupied a large place in British politics throughout the century. When the German government began to dismantle its anti-Catholic legislation in 1866, the Evangelical League was formed "for the defense of German Protestant interests" against "false parity and tolerance concepts," and took an active part in election campaigns and other aspects of public life both under the Empire and in the Weimar Republic.[59]

Measures to introduce civil marriage and divorce became a leading grievance of the church, and these reforms were fiercely contested. When states set about creating new systems of mass schooling, the church condemned the idea that "Catholics may approve of the system of educating youth unconnected with the Catholic faith and the power of the church" (in Pius IX's *Syllabus of Errors*) and encouraged the political involvement of the faithful in defense of confessional education. Conflict over education erupted in 1847, and remained a central issue in Belgian politics for the rest of the century. Militant Calvinists and the large Roman Catholic minority in the Netherlands organized themselves politically in the 1870s to fight for state support for their own schools.

In Austria, the church involved itself more directly in politics and moved into a closer alignment with the political right to fight against the introduction of civil marriage and state-controlled education. In England, vested religious interests in education were a constant obstacle to the development of general education throughout the century; England, in fact, was the last of the western European states to establish a national school system.

The ranks of politically active religious parties and movements were swelled by groups who found in these parties and movements a means of pursuing political ends relating, not to the defense of church interests, but to the class conflicts that emerged after the French Revolution and that increasingly worked to polarize European society in the course of the nineteenth century.

The French Revolution's attack on traditional society had involved not only the church but the traditional landowning elite as well. During the Revolution, these two pillars of traditional society joined forces to defend the institutions upon which their power and privileges depended.[60] The church was a highly desirable ally, as its symbolism, emotionalism, wealth, and organizational power made it an ideal instrument for offensive political operations. The aristocracy as a class remained committed to the defense of the church as a social and political institution throughout the century. Religious control over education became one of their most ardent causes.

In France and most other west European countries, the state joined forces with the church after 1815 to suppress the revolutionary forces sweeping through the region. From time to time and in various places the alliance dissolved when the state failed to uphold church interests.[61] In Greece, Serbia, Romania, and Bulgaria, churches joined in or led uprisings against the state (Hapsburg or Ottoman) when reforms designed to centralize administration and lighten the burdens of the peasantry threatened traditional privileges. Churches also helped to bring down governments in Portugal (1933), Austria (1934), and Spain (1936). However, by and large, the alliance between altar and throne endured until the world wars of the twentieth century.

Religious-political parties and connections were powerful elements in national politics. Catholics had a powerful voice in French politics after 1815 and it became more powerful as the century progressed: in 1871, French Catholics won their greatest electoral victory since 1789. Germany's Catholic Center Party, which became almost totally identified with the defense of church interests, was the largest party in the national and Prussian legislatures from the 1870s until 1912. In 1870, Belgium's Catholic Party won the greatest electoral victory of any Catholic party up to that time. The Calvinist Anti-Revolutionary Party in the Netherlands, formed in 1878, successfully secured state-sponsorship for religious schools and became an important source of support for forces on the right. The Catholic Church in Austria was a powerful force in Austrian political life and directly involved itself in national politics through its Social Christian Party. Britain's Conservative Party identified itself with the Anglican Church and was committed to the defense of its interests throughout the century. In Tsarist Russia, the Eastern Church was an extension and branch of state power, and its clergy took an active part in party, electoral, and parliamentary politics.[62]

Religion provided a fundamental basis for national identity and nation building during the nineteenth century. French Catholics believed that France's special mission was a Christian one, and that a return to faith was a means of preserving its national unity and reviving its greatness.[63] There was a total fusion of religion and nationality in Spain and Poland. The national independence movements of Greece, Serbia, Bulgaria, and Rumania fused religion and nationalism; and Catholic Croatia and Orthodox Serbia represented unions of religion and nationhood within the state of Yugoslavia established after World War I. A bishop led Cyprus in its independence struggle, as well as after it. Being Russian and being Orthodox was the same thing in the nineteenth century. The main organ of Scottish identity was its church. In Croatia, Ireland, Cyprus, Greece, Poland, Belgium, and Slovakia, bishops spoke for nations. The earliest nation-wide movements in Ireland—the campaigns for Catholic emancipation in the 1820s and for repeal of the union in the 1840s—depended heavily on the work of the clergy.[64] In 1939, an independent Slovakia emerged with a Catholic priest as president.

As traditional elites increasingly monopolized gains from economic development, tensions increased between the upper and middle classes. As these tensions increased, dissident, "nonconformist," or radical religious movements emerged. In an era in which electoral systems severely restricted the political participation of all but the most wealthy, these movements provided a means by which the middle and professional classes could express political opposition to the existing order and attract support from the multitude of urban poor, particularly in cities like London and in the port towns where vast accumulations of immigrants lived in crowded slums.

The church attracted mass support in Europe primarily through a vast and growing network of charitable organizations that offered the poor social services not provided by the state. The Societé de Saint Paul, which was founded in France in 1833, was among the most successful of these. It supplied the poor with soup kitchens, cheap food, old clothes, help with rent, warm public rooms in winter, cheap housing, employment agencies, free medical and legal advice, holiday camps, old people's homes, catechist teaching, orphanages, apprenticeships, adult classes, clubs, allotments, libraries, and pilgrimages. As was typical of church-sponsored charitable organizations throughout the century, the Society's attitude toward the poor was paternalistic and traditional; it was primarily concerned, not with curing the causes of poverty, but with "resisting liberal ideas" and preserving Catholics from compromise in religion and politics.[65]

The new Protestant movements were largely middle class in character.[66] However, they were essentially conservative and, like the established churches, hostile to religious minorities. They sought to impose totalitarian controls over those who they brought within their sphere. They isolated them from over-close contact with an unbelieving world,[67] and attacked all forms of behavior that appeared idle, irresponsible, undisciplined, and wasteful. Alcohol consumption, above all, was the symbol of everything they opposed, and by the end of the century, total abstinence became a basic tenet of popular Protestantism both in Britain and in Scandinavia.[68]

There was intense conflict between the state churches and these new movements, particularly after the 1830s. Then, in the 1880s, as the upper and middle classes closed ranks against the rising tide of socialism, conflict within the church abated. In England, wealthier members of the nonconformist churches defected to Anglicanism, and the membership of the nonconformist churches began to decline.[69] In France, there was a "return toward faith and toward those who profess it" on the part of both upper and middle classes. De Tocqueville noted two causes for this: (1) the contribution of religion "to the government of the masses," which for the moment at least gave back to the church and the landowners "an influence which they ha[d] not had for sixty years;" and (2) "the fear of socialism" which affected the middle classes in much the same way as the French Revolution had affected the traditional landowners.[70]

Throughout the nineteenth and early twentieth centuries, the church and the traditional nobility worked together to preserve traditional structures and institutions. Even where, early in the century, traditional elites and the church were at odds with one another—for instance, in Italy, where the existence of rival secular and Papal governments split the aristocracy from the church; or in Spain, where popular hostility to the church made it a poor vehicle for preserving traditional society—the nobility and the church eventually closed ranks. Later, divisions within the church and between the upper and middle classes dissolved or were submerged as the threat of socialism increased. The tensions engendered by the rise of socialism increasingly polarized European society and led, eventually, to the world wars. Religion was thoroughly interconnected with these conflicts and integral to their development.

After the 1880s, as socialist activity became more violent, frequent, and widespread, the church throughout Europe moved further to the right. During the interwar years, in Germany, France, Austria, Portugal, Spain, Poland, Belgium, Holland, Italy, Norway, and Sweden, corporatist regimes or structures were established whose organizational basis was the clerico-corporatist social order defined by the church in *Rerum Novarum* and, which in a variety of forms, embodied all of the themes that the church had used throughout the century to oppose the breakdown of traditional society.[71] The church relaxed its ban on Catholic participation in Italian politics in the hope of stemming the tide of socialism in Italy; and, in 1929, it formalized its support of fascism in the Lateran Treaty. A clerico-fascist regime came to power in Austria in 1934 and ruled until the country united with the German Reich in 1938. As socialist forces grew stronger in Spain, its most widely read religious periodical, the *Messenger*, called for a "crusade" to make Spain fully Catholic again.[72] The constitution of Spain's Second Republic (1931–1936), which declared a separation between church and state, the confiscation of some church properties, and the exclusion of the religious orders from education, set the stage for a bloody civil war between Left and Right. The victory of Fascism over the Republic in that war was regarded by most Catholics as a Christian triumph.[73] The church helped to bring about the collapse of Portugal's Republic and the establishment, in 1933, of an authoritarian regime under Salazar. In Germany, despite the overt atheism of Nazism, only a small minority of Protestants and Catholics opposed Adolf Hitler's rise to power. The Catholic Center Party voted to pass the Enabling Act granting Hitler dictatorial powers, and then officially dissolved itself. After 1933, many Catholic organizations were merged with Nazi organizations.[74] In France, authoritarian movements, particularly Charles Maurras's monarchist *Action Française*, were supported by the vast majority of French bishops;[75] and in the 1940s, the church supported the Vichy regime. Clerico-fascist regimes were established in the 1940s in Croatia and Slovakia.

III. THE CONTEMPORARY MIDDLE EAST IN HISTORICAL COMPARATIVE PERSPECTIVE: A RECONSIDERATION

Culturally, racially, even religiously, the Middle East and Europe have had more in common with each other than with the civilizations of Asia and Africa. The peoples of the two regions shared the heritage of a Greco-Roman and Judeo-Christian past, as well as of a remoter antiquity. Most of Europe and of the older Islamic lands had at one time formed part of the Roman Empire, and the organization, ideas, and evolution of the medieval social estates of Europe and of the classical four estates in the Middle East resembled each other.[76]

The ideological, political, and organizational power of Catholicism and Protestantism in Europe and of Islam in the Middle East—unlike Latin America,

Asia, and Africa—predated the nation-state system in both regions and limited its power from the start. In both regions, the religious establishment was a vital constituent and pillar of the old traditional classes. By enhancing the organizational capacities of these classes, the "church"[77] in both regions played a critical role in the class struggles that emerged in the course of "nation-building" and industrial development.

Traditional elites both in Europe and in the Middle East survived the transition from empires and absolutist states to nation-states; national movements in both regions were, in most cases, led by traditional elites in reaction to the leveling effects of the bureaucratic rationalization and liberalization undertaken by absolutist states. Nationalist movements ensured that civil servants would be drawn from local privileged groups; it deprived foreigners and minorities of their economic power and position, and reduced their role in finance, commerce, and trade. It enabled traditional elites to gain control of capitalist development and channeled it into noncompetitive, ascriptive, monopolistic forms.

Thus, both in Europe and in the contemporary Middle East, the end of empires and absolutist states marked the beginning of the rule of traditional landowning and urban elites. It did not bring a liberal, capitalist bourgeoisie to power in either region. Rather than losing power to a rising, secular, capitalist bourgeoisie, traditional elites, with the help of the "church," of a dependent middle class and, frequently, of a military or petite bourgeois governing group, was able to retain its wealth and power and to play the dominant role in industrial capitalist development. As a result, the overall pattern of economic and political development in pre-1945 Europe and in the contemporary Middle East was broadly similar. Development in both regions was dualistic and retarded by traditional forces. Traditional elites in both regions maintained their power by means of a highly restricted franchise and other restrictions on political participation. In both regions, these elites were able to effectively block the spread of liberalism and the establishment of liberal institutions.

The construction of the contemporary Middle East state system out of the Ottoman Empire changed only the political structure of the region: the old Ottoman social structure dominated by the traditional aristocracy of landowners and nobles survived the transition from empire to state system intact. While army officers, technocrats, and professionals have acquired political power in some countries, this supposedly "new" governing elite of party, bureaucratic, and military personnel does not differ substantially from the Ottoman petite bourgeois and military governing elite. Under the Ottoman Empire traditional elites exercised local, not central, power. They continue to do so under current regimes. Where they do not directly control the political and military apparatus of the state, their continued control of traditional local power bases has enabled them to block far-reaching reforms in economic and social structures.

Religious elites in alliance with landowners, members of the salaried middle class, and the professional upper class have successfully thwarted government efforts to effect meaningful economic reform. Thus, despite independence movements, coups d'etat, insurrections, and rebellions, the social structure of the region has remained essentially the same.

Despite all that has been written about rapid development in the Middle East, the most salient feature of the region is its lack of development. As in Europe, in the Middle East dominant classes have sought to take advantage of new opportunities of increasing their wealth in ways that would allow them to avoid transforming their societies. As a result, in most Arab countries, dual economic structures exclude the mass of the population from the economic life of the country; most are dependent on a narrow range of export goods and a few trading partners and are characterized by highly unequal land tenure structures and highly unequal distributions of income. A small elite of landowners and wealthy industrialists in the region has monopolized the agricultural, mineral, and industrial wealth of the region. Both land and industry are highly concentrated. In some countries, traditional corporatist structures have survived and been strengthened (e.g., Lebanon and Iran); elsewhere, corporate structures have been constructed to limit competition and to control or repress labor organization (e.g., Egypt and Iraq). Nowhere in the region has industrialization acquired a sustained momentum: manufacturing's share of production in 1990 was only 13 percent, which is precisely what it was in the mid-1950s.

In the Middle East, as in Europe, the religious establishment is linked to the traditional landowning elite and urban notability; and, as in Europe during an earlier period, in the Middle East there was a resurgence of religion and of religious fundamentalist movements that reversed a centuries-long trend in which religion had become increasingly separate from and subordinate to state power. In both regions, religious elements occupy the most powerful, most privileged position in the old order being challenged by processes of industrial development and social change. In Syria, Egypt, and Iran, the Muslim clergy led popular movements against land reform and the redistribution of other resources. States in the region have been generally unable to withstand the antireform pressure either of the right-wing religious and traditionalist establishment or of new "Islamist" groups. Thus, in many matters of personal status Egypt is still governed by laws enacted under the monarchy. In Iran, where the most vigorous efforts were made to dismantle traditional institutions and structures, these efforts were met by an equally powerful reaction from clerical, traditional landowning, and urban elites and culminated, after sixteen years of ceaseless effort on their part, in the revolution of 1979.

The current Islamic revival in the Middle East exhibits a similar pattern of relations between state, "church," and social classes as that which sustained the Christian revival in Europe during the nineteenth century. As in Europe during the nineteenth century, in the Middle East the alliance between traditional landowning and religious elites was joined by the state as social forces began to threaten the structures of traditional society on which, in varying ways, the power of all three depended.

After the emergence of independent states in the region, the first project of this alliance was the elimination of the foreign and minority elements that, in the nineteenth century, had performed the functions of an entrepreneurial bourgeois class in trade, finance, industry and, to a large extent, even the professions. Following the demise of the Ottoman Empire, there had been large-scale French migration to Morocco, Italian to Libya, and Jewish to Palestine.[78] The large emigration of Jews to Palestine became a particular concern of religious and traditional elites. Concerned that Jewish capital, technical know-how, and contacts with the West would deprive it of its hoped-for Middle Eastern markets, Egyptian industrialists and landowners, Palestinian notables, and the Egyptian Muslim Brotherhood, worked together to oppose further Jewish immigration and to make the preservation of Palestine as an Arab country the preeminent Islamic and Arab cause.[79]

The second project of this alliance between states and religious and other traditional elites, was to stem the rising tide of socialism and communism in the region.

The explosive rise of communist, socialist, and other leftist political organizations, and the intense social conflicts that emerged throughout the region as a result of them, had a profound impact on the subsequent economic and political development of the region.

Parties and movements of the Left that emerged after World War I in Iran, Egypt, Syria, Lebanon, Iraq, and elsewhere in the region, were suppressed by local security forces with the help of Britain and France. The resurgence of these groups and parties after World War II triggered a campaign in the 1950s and 1960s to eradicate not only communists and socialists, but *any* element in the region calling for democratic government or for land reform. The campaign against liberal, left-of-center, and reformist elements, along with communists and socialists, was carried out by local elites, by means of violent conflict, bloody police action, expulsion, and incarceration, and with the help, initially, of the British and later with that of the United States, as well. Communist activity and the increasingly militant worker's movement were important elements in bringing about a revolution in Egypt and the demise of its monarchy in 1952. Labor conflicts had erupted more or less continuously throughout the 1940s and 1950s. There were communist-inspired strikes and vast demonstrations in every major Egyptian city,[80] and widespread rebellions among the rural poor.[81]

The "Free Officers" who overthrew the monarchy and came to power in the 1952 Revolution did not represent class interests fundamentally divergent from those of the traditional ruling class.[82] The Egyptian propertied classes and foreign economic interests in the country viewed the new elites, not as enemies of the ruling class, but as a replacement within the established structure that offered a stronger guarantee of social stability. In alliance with the Muslim Brotherhood and other traditional elites, the new regime acted swiftly to suppress communism and labor militancy in Egypt. It outlawed strikes and trade-union activity and all political organizations, except for the Muslim Brotherhood.[83] It enacted an Agrarian Reform soon after the Revolution; but this was conceived principally as a means of preventing the restoration of the monarchy (it confiscated the land of the "royal" family) and of forestalling Communist revolution.[84]

However, by 1955 the Communists were the most strongly organized political group in the universities, and were gaining strength in the trade unions.[85] The high level of labor conflict continued unabated.[86] Nasser attempted to halt these conflicts by introducing, among other reforms, the abolition of the *sharia* courts and nationalization of the religious endowments (*awqaf*). This set the Muslim Brotherhood against the regime. Though the government dissolved the organization, antireform pressure from the religious and traditionalist establishment continued to thwart attempts at reform.[87] Nasser's successor, Anwar al-Sadat, also attempted to use the Muslim Brothers as a counterweight to the Left; but ultimately, like Nasser, came into conflict with the organization.

In Jordan the government suppressed all political parties but permitted the Muslim Brotherhood to continue to operate throughout the 1950s and 1960s. Jordan (before 1967) and Israel (after 1967) also allowed Islamic groups to operate in the West Bank as a counterweight to Leftist, secular nationalist forces. Eventually, Islamic groups came into direct conflict with these states and began to organize against them.

Later, religious and other traditional elites broke with the state and closed ranks with middle-class elements to oppose government-imposed socialist policies. State governments and wealthy elites throughout the region had actively aided the growth of the religious far right as a bulwark against communism and revolution. However, as in Europe, attempts to liberalize economies, rationalize legal systems, and attract foreign investment and expertise, eventually brought about a rupture between states and religious elites. Dissident religious movements fed on the ambition and frustration of middle and professional classes who sought a means by which to increase their power. As in Europe, these movements were able to gain mass support through the provision of social services not provided by the government. In the 1960s and 1970s, in Syria, Lebanon, and Iran, Islamic radicalism began to emerge and to oppose land reform and other socialist policies that threatened the traditional patron-age system and other structures of traditional society from which traditional elites had benefited. The revolution in Iran in 1979 was the culmination of six-teen years of effort on the part of the clergy and other traditional elites to dis-mantle land and liberal reform instituted under the government of the Shah. In the 1980s, dissident religious movements of largely middle-class character emerged in Egypt, Lebanon, Saudi Arabia, Algeria, and Jordan.

The overall pattern of relationships that has emerged in the Middle East is broadly similar to that which emerged in Europe in the course of the nine-teenth century: (1) an alliance between state "churches," traditional elites, and states seeking to preserve elements of the traditional order upon which, in varying ways, their privileges depend; and (2) largely middle class and essen-tially conservative dissident or radical religious sects that seek to challenge the power of traditional elites but preserve traditional structures that keep the lower classes in check; but also (3) an alliance between upper and middle classes where socialism or socialist reforms threaten to undermine the tradi-tional order.

CONCLUSION

The dominant social and political system of Europe up until 1945 paralleled that which exists in the contemporary Middle East: a social structure in which the most effective elites are traditional and aristocratic and not bourgeois; land-owning and rent-receiving, not capitalist or entrepreneurial; religious, not sec-ular; oligarchic, not democratic. No secular, independent capitalist bourgeoisie came to power in nineteenth-century Europe, and there established democ-racy. On the contrary, in nineteenth-century Europe, as in the contemporary Middle East, the bourgeoisie was conservative and autocratic, religion a pow-erful political force, and democracy late and restricted in its arrival. Both re-gions, in fact, saw a return to militant, literal, old-fashioned religion as processes of economic expansion began to threaten traditional structures. In both re-gions, religion was used by politically motivated social groups seeking to de-fend or extend their power by excluding other classes and groups from partic-ipation in political and economic life.

While there are some differences between European historical and con-temporary Third World development, these differences have been greatly ex-aggerated. Contrary to the "European model" that has served, implicitly or ex-plicitly, as a point of departure and basis of comparison for studying contemporary Third World development, actual social, economic, and political development in Europe followed a path that is similar to the one being followed by contemporary Third World countries. External dependence, dualism, inequality, political instability, authoritarianism, and other well-documented aspects of contemporary Third World development are constitutive of a pattern of development that is equally applicable to the recent European past. Thus, we should not continue to use frameworks, concepts, categories of analysis, and theories that define contemporary Third World development as sharply different from the European experience. While the West and the Islamic world cannot be understood wholly through comparisons with each other, the comparison is a useful one, nonetheless. It suggests to students of Europe and of the Islamic world that insight into those parts of the globe may be found, not within the narrow terrain marked out for us by conventional historiography and by the architects of contemporary movements and events, but within the broader arena of human history and experience.

NOTES

1. W. H. McNeill, *The Shape of European History* (London: Oxford University Press, 1974), 3–4.

2. Pessimism and doubt about whether the ever-expanding productive capacity of society leads to human happiness was expressed by the classical theoreticians of liberalism as, for instance, David Ricardo, in this reflection:

> Happiness is the object to be desired, and we cannot be quite sure that, provided he is equally well-fed, a man may not be happier in the enjoyment of the luxury of idleness than in the enjoyment of a neat cottage and good clothes. And after all we do not know if these would fall to his share. His labour might only increase the enjoyment of his employer.

Letters of David Ricardo to Thomas Robert Malthus, 1810–1823, James Bonaro, ed. (Oxford: Clarendon Press, 1887), 138.

3. Fernand Braudel, *The Mediterranean and the Mediterranean World in the Age of Philip II* (New York: Collins, 1972); Immanuel Wallerstein, *The Modern World System I* (New York: Academic Press, 1974).

4. See for example, David Landes, *The Unbound Prometheus* (Cambridge: Cambridge University Press, 1969).

5. Bairoch (1981) estimates the level of GNP per capita of future developed countries around 1750 at $182. For the future Third World he estimates the figure to be $188, a level of income some 3–4 percent above that of the future developed countries. Thus, he concludes that the differential in level of income was 1 to 1.02 percent, or parity. More recently, Angus Maddison has taken up the question in a series of papers (1983, 1989, 1990). Using Maddison's most recent data for 1913, 1870, and 1830, Bairoch calculates the weighted average GNP per capita income for the Third World in 1750 as $170–$190, which is similar to his own 1981 estimate. Maddison's figures for the future developed world can lead to a level expressed in 1980 dollars of

$550–$600 for Europe (including Russia) around 1750, which in 1960 dollars and prices translates to $180–$215. Therefore, Bairoch can claim, according to Maddison's most recent effort, the differential between future developed countries and the future developed countries in 1750 of the order of 1 to 1.1–1.3 percent, compared to his own 1981 estimate of 1 to 1–1.1 percent. Paul Bairoch, "The Main Trends in National Income Disparities since the Industrial Revolution," in P. Bairoch and M. Levy-Leboyer, eds., *Disparities in Economic Development since the Industrial Revolution* (London: Macmillan, 1981); *Economics and World History: Myths and Paradoxes* (London: Harvester, 1993), 105–6; Angus Maddison, "A Comparison of Levels of GDP Per Capita in Developed and Developing Countries, 1700–1980," *Journal of Economic History* 43 (1983): 27–41; "Measuring European Growth: The Core and the Periphery," in E. Aerts and N. Valerio, eds., *Growth and Stagnation in the Mediterranean World in the 19th and 20th Centuries* (Leuven, Belgium: University of Leuven Press, 1989); *The World Economy in the Twentieth Century* (Paris: Development Centre Studies, 1990).

6. D. C. North, *Structure and Change in Economic History* (New York: W. W. Norton, 1981), 162; Rondo Cameron, "The Industrial Revolution: A Misnomer," in Jurgen Schneider, ed., *Wirtschaftskrafte und Wirtschaftwege: festschrift für Hermann Kellenbenz* 5 (Stuttgart: in Komission bei Klett-Cotta, 1981); and Rondo Cameron, "A New View of European Industrialization," *Economic History Review* 38, no. 1 (February 1985): 1–23; Fores, "The Myth of a British Industrial Revolution."

7. For a brief survey of the scholarly objections voiced at the time, see Cameron, "A New View of European Industrialization," 1–23.

8. N.F.R. Crafts, "British Economic Growth, 1700–1813: A Review of the Evidence," *Economic History Review* 2, no. 36 (1983).

9. Colin Clark, *The Conditions of Economic Progress*, 3d ed. (London: Macmillan, 1957), 652.

10. Clark, *The Conditions of Economic Progress*, 652, 654.

11. The figure for the nineteenth century comes from Paul Bairoch, "Europe's Gross National Product 1800–1975," *Journal of European Economic History* 5, no. 2 (fall 1976): 309. The latter figure is for the period 1950–1970 and comes from Bairoch, *Economics and World History*, 142.

12. See Sandra Halperin, *In the Mirror of the Third World: Capitalist Development in Modern Europe* (Ithaca, N.Y.: Cornell University Press, 1997), statistical appendix, tables 10 and 11.

13. W. Arthur Lewis, *Growth and Fluctuation, 1870–1913* (London: George Allen & Unwin, 1978), 216; Celso Furtado, *The Economic Growth of Brazil* (Berkeley: University of California Press, 1965), 162–65.

14. See Halperin, *In the Mirror of the Third World*, statistical appendix, tables 1 and 2.

15. Arno Mayer, *The Persistence of the Ancien Regime* (New York: Pantheon Books, 1980), 187, 301.

16. F. A. Ogg, *Economic Development of Modern Europe* (New York: Macmillan, 1930), 185.

17. Lewis, *Growth and Fluctuation*, 166.

18. See Halperin, *In the Mirror of the Third World*, statistical appendix, table 4.

19. Daniel Chirot, *Social Change in the Twentieth Century* (New York: Harcourt, Brace, and Jovanovich, 1977), 223.

20. In England, the upper class closed ranks during the Napoleonic Wars against the menace of radicalism and revolution. Moore argues, however, that this reactionary phase was relatively brief, and "movement towards a freer society commenced anew during the nineteenth century." Barrington Moore Jr., *Social Origins of Dictatorship and Democracy* (Boston: Beacon, 1966), 31.

21. Moore, *Social Origins of Dictatorship and Democracy,* 32.

22. The position remains true, however, for the United States, New Zealand, Canada, Australia, and perhaps for South Africa, as well.

23. Locally, the state-controlled system of paramilitary and police forces, and concentrations of regular troops on permanent garrison duty, in the working-class areas of industrial towns; elsewhere, the opening up and control of territories for exploitation by armed aggression.

24. And erroneously restricted in their application to that world. The argument is more fully developed in Halperin, *In the Mirror of the Third World.*

25. British overseas investment and, in particular British railway and harbor and ship building for Baltic and, later, North American grain, produced a backflow of cheaply produced/regulated raw materials and foodstuffs that did not compete with domestic English agriculture and drove domestic working-class wages down. Britain imported a third of its food after 1870, including nearly half of its bread grains. M. Barratt Brown, *After Imperialism,* rev. ed. (London: Merlin Press, 1970), 66.

26. Britain's industrial wage-earners realized 55–60 percent of their wage in the form of food; the steady fall in prices of staple food imports after 1874 (grain, tea, sugar, lard, cheese, ham, and bacon), allowed real wages in Britain to rise until World War I. Peter Mathias, *The First Industrial Nation: An Economic History of Britain, 1700–1914.* 2d ed. (New York: Methuen, 1983), 345.

27. Committee on Finance and Industry, *Macmillan Report* (1931), 171.

28. Charles Kindleberger, *Economic Growth in France and Britain, 1851–1950* (Cambridge, Mass.: Harvard University Press, 1964), 62.

29. Geographically, the industrial revolution was limited to the great centers of the export industry in the North and "Celtic Fringe" (Manchester was the capital of the basic export industries).

30. The introduction of the factory system in spinning, in fact, actually *increased* the number of domestic weavers (to handle the expanded production in yarn). Traditional manufacturing organized around the putting-out system continued to make profits of as much as 1,000 percent; and, as long as it did, there was little incentive to introduce new techniques having the capacity to produce social externalities. J. R. Gillis, *The Development of European Society, 1770–1870* (Boston: Houghton Mifflin, 1983), 41, 159.

31. C. Lis and H. Soly, *Poverty and Capitalism in Pre-Industrial Europe* (Sussex, U.K.: Harvestor Press, 1979), 159.

32. A majority of those engaged in transport worked for a small employer or were self-employed. John Benson, *The Working Class in Britain, 1850–1839* (London: Longman Press, 1989), 22–23.

33. J. Foster, *Class Struggle and the Industrial Revolution* (London: Weidenfeld, 1974), 20.

34. Eric Hobsbawm, *Industry and Empire* (London: Weidenfeld and Nicolson, 1968), 181.

35. New techniques were introduced "slowly and with considerable reluctance." In the 1930s, half the industry's workforce still practiced "their traditional handicrafts, especially in house-building, largely untouched by mechanization." Benson, *The Working Class in Britain,* 20.

36. Hobsbawm, *Industry and Empire,* 180.

37. From 49 million tons in 1850 to 147 million in 1880.

38. There were 200,000 coal miners in Britain in 1850, half a million in 1880, and 1.2 million in 1914. Hobsbawm, *Industry and Empire,* 116.

39. Benson, *The Working Class in Britain,* 16.

40. J. Romein, *The Watershed of Two Eras* (Middletown: Wesleyan University Press, 1978), 195. In 1900, less than 1 percent of the population owned more than 40 percent of the land of Austria, Hungary, Romania, Germany, and Poland; less than 4 percent of the population owned 25 percent of the land of Denmark and France. Ten percent of landowners held 85 percent of Italy; less than 1 percent of the landowners controlled over 40 percent of the land of southern and central Spain. Goldstein, *Political Repression in Nineteenth Century Europe,* 240.

41. Benson, *The Working Class in Britain,* 19.

42. According to a semiofficial Land Enquiry Committee report in 1912; cited in Ogg, *Economic Development of Modern Europe,* 174.

43. Hobsbawm, *Industry and Empire,* 169. The City of London was operated by men of English or Scottish stock and members of the established church. "Anti-Semitism was as widespread in the city as elsewhere in the country." R. W. D. Boyce, *British Capitalism at the Crossroads, 1919–1932* (Cambridge: Cambridge University Press, 1987), 20.

44. Hobsbawm, *Industry and Empire,* 169.

45. Landes, *Prometheus Unbound,* 247.

46. Thus in the weaving industry, whereas in 1882 there were no fewer than 255,000 separate undertakings, of which 157,000 were carried on by single individuals, in 1907 the number of separate undertakings had fallen to 67,000 and the number carried on by separate individuals to 31,000. This was the general trend throughout German industry. Shipbuilding was probably the only major exception to it. Ogg, *Economic Development of Modern Europe,* 222.

47. The table leaves out Romania, Poland, Bulgaria, and other countries with cartelized industry. For a fuller discussion, see Halperin, *In the Mirror of the Third World,* chapter 7.

48. Chirot, *Social Change in the Twentieth Century,* 222.

49. Françoise Furet, *Penser La Révolution Française* (Paris: Gallimard, 1978), 109.

50. Robert MacIver, *The Modern State* (London: Oxford University Press, 1932), 352.

51. Defined as the "process whereby religious thinking, practice, and institutions lose social significance" and are increasingly restricted to the domain of private faith. Ernest Krausz, "Religion and Secularization: A Matter of Definitions," *Social Compass* 18 (1971–1972).

52. Eric Hobsbawm, *The Age of Revolution 1789–1848* (New York: Mentor, 1962), 271.

53. This was true, too, of the Eastern Orthodox Church and of Protestantism: the Anglican Church (established in the sixteenth century) holds that the religious and political

domains are inseparable, and assert that church and crown, while distinct in function, are inseparable in substance and subject to the same law; Puritanism (which emerged in the seventeenth century) maintains that the administration of men are directly subject to divine law, and that the state will ultimately be a single church/state entity.

54. See for example, Mirari Vos, 1832; Quanta Cura and the Syllabus of Errors, 1864; Immortale Dei, 1878; Quadrigesimo Anno, 1931; Divini Redemptoris, 1937; and Rerum Novarum, 1891.

55. R. Brinkley, *Realism and Nationalism, 1852–1871* (New York: Harper, 1935), 67.

56. The number of religious orders rose in France from 37,000 to 162,000 between 1851 and 1901; in Belgium, from 770 to 1,643 between 1846 and 1890; in Spain from 15,000 to 68,000 between 1861 and 1920. Demetrius Boulger, *Belgian Life in Town and Country* (New York: G. P. Putnam, 1904), 167; Hugh McLeod, *Religion and the People of Western Europe, 1789–1970* (Oxford: Oxford University Press, 1981), 49.

57. The Baptist Missionary Society (1792), the Netherlands Missionary Society (1797), the interdenominational London Society (1799), the British and Foreign Bible Society (1804), Wesleyans (1813–1818), the Basel Missionaries, the Berlin and Rhenish societies (1820s), the Church of Scotland (1824), the United Presbyterians (1835), the Swedish, Leipzig, and Bremen societies (1830s), and the Norwegian society (1842).

58. The Methodist movement in England, which had less than 60,000 adherents before the French Revolution, increased its membership to 143,000 in 1811, and 600,000 in 1850. McLeod, *Religion and the People of Western Europe,* 37; Eric Hobsbawm, *Primitive Rebels* (New York: W. W. Norton, 1959), 129.

59. Ellen Lovell Evans, *The German Center Party, 1870–1933* (Carbondale: Southern Illinois University Press, 1981), 93.

60. The church was a natural ally of the traditional landowning elite since it was, itself, a major property owner. On the eve of the French Revolution, the Catholic Church owned outright roughly 10 percent of the surface of France. Claude Geffre and Jean-Pierre Jossua, eds., *1789: The French Revolution and the Church* (Edinburgh: T. & T. Clark, 1989). In England, the clergy were among the chief beneficiaries of the enclosure acts (between 1760 and 1850) and, for the most part, identified with wealthy landowners throughout the nineteenth century.

61. When Louis Napoleon assisted Piedmont in its struggle against the papal states in 1859, the ultramontane clergy declared war on him and exhorted French Catholics to unseat him and restore Henry V to power. The Societé de Saint Paul was found to be involved in plans to assassinate him, and one of its clandestine presses printed instructions for the home manufacture of gunpowder. See Zeldin, *Conflicts in French Society,* 150.

62. Anatole Mazour, *Russia Past and Present* (New York: D. Van Nostrand, 1951), 44–74.

63. Zeldin, *Conflicts in French Society.*

64. J. Newsinger, "Revolution and Catholicism in Ireland, 1848–1923," *European Studies Review* (October 1979): 463. Even at times when relations between the clergy and the revolutionary wing of Irish nationalism became strained (e.g., during the Fenian risings and conspiracies in the 1860s), Catholicism remained associated with the nationalist cause.

65. Theodore Zeldin, *Conflicts in French Society* (London: George Allen & Unwin, 1970), 108.

66. Sheridan Gilley, "Christianity in Europe: Reformation to Today," in Stewart Sutherland et al., eds., *The World's Religions* (London: G. K. Hall, 1988), 236.

67. McLeod, *Religion and the People of Western Europe*, 36.

68. McLeod, *Religion and the People of Western Europe*, 40.

69. McLeod, *Religion and the People of Western Europe*, 12, 69.

70. Alexis de Tocqueville, *Oeuvres Completes*, vol. 6 (Paris: Gallimard, 1866), 178.

71. V. R. Berghahn, "Corporatism in Germany in Historical Perspective," in Andrew Cox and Noel O'Sullivan, eds., *The Corporate State: Corporatism and State Tradition in Western Europe* (Aldershot, U.K.: Edward Elgar, 1988); M. Sutton, *Nationalism, Positivism and Catholicism* (Cambridge: Cambridge University Press, 1982); Matthew H. Elbow, *French Corporative Theory, 1789–1948* (New York: Columbia University Press, 1953); Ralph Bowen, *German Theories of the Corporative State* (New York: McGraw-Hill, 1947); Charles A. Gulick, *Austria from Hapsburg to Hitler*, vol. 2 (Berkeley: University of California Press, 1940).

72. McLeod, *Religion and the People of Western Europe*, 52.

73. Raymond Carr, *Spain, 1808–1939* (Oxford: Clarendon Press, 1966).

74. Evans, *The German Center Party*, 395.

75. William Buthman, *The Rise of Integral Nationalism in France* (New York: Columbia University Press, 1939); Robert Soucy, *Fascism in France: The Case of Maurice Barrès* (Berkeley: University of California Press, 1972). Although the Church condemned the *Action Française* in 1926, it later relaxed its ban against Catholics joining it.

76. Many scholars have held the view that Islamic society was not divided into classes. Yet, the idea of social stratification appears in early religious writings as well as in the sociopolitical treatises of the Muslim rationalist philosophers. See Maxime Rodinson, "Histoire économique et histoire des classes sociales dans le monde Muselman," in M. A. Cook, ed., *Studies in the Economic History of the Middle East: From the Rise of Islam to the Present Day* (London: Oxford University Press, 1970), 139–55; and S. D. Goitein, *Studies in Islamic History and Institutions* (Leiden: E. J. Brill, 1966), 219–22.

77. Three forms of the word "church" will be used here: (1) "church," used in statements meant to apply to both Christian and Islamic religious establishments; (2) Church, used to refer to the Catholic Church in Europe; and (3) church, used when referring to both the Protestant and Catholic churches in Europe.

78. Eric Davis, *Challenging Colonialism: Bank Misr and Egyptian Industrialization, 1920–1941* (Princeton, N.J.: Princeton University Press, 1983).

79. The Muslim Brotherhood played an active role in encouraging anti-Zionist and anti-Jewish demonstrations (as well as attacks on Catholic, Armenian, and Greek Orthodox churches), and took the lead in mobilizing mass support for the Palestinian Arabs. Walid Kazziha, *Palestine in the Arab Dilemma* (London: Croom Helm, 1969), 43–44; Davis, *Challenging Colonialism,* 171–72, 182, 191.

80. M. T. Audsley, "Labour and Social Affairs in Egypt," *Middle East Affairs* 4, no. 1 (1958): 99–102.

81. Gabriel Baer, "Egyptian Attitudes Towards Land Reform, 1922–1955," in Walter Z. Laqueur, ed., *The Middle East in Transition* (London: Routledge & Kegan Paul, 1958), 97.

82. Mahmoud Hussein, *Class Conflict in Egypt: 1945–1971* (New York: Monthly Review Press, 1975), 95.

83. Joel Beinin, "Labor, Capital, and the State in Nassirist Egypt, 1951–1961," *International Journal of Middle East Studies* 21 (1989): 71–90.

84. Baer, "Egyptian Attitudes Towards Land Reform." It ultimately involved at most about 16 percent of Egypt's cultivated land, leading to the actual redistribution of 13 percent of that land to about 10 percent of Egypt's rural families. See John Waterbury, *The Egypt of Nasser and Sadat* (Princeton, N.J.: Princeton University Press, 1983), 266–67.

85. Walter Z. Laqueur, *Communism and Nationalism in the Middle East* (London: Routledge & Kegan Paul, 1956), 50–51.

86. The average number of labor disputes in the years 1952–1958 was three times the average during the preceding seven years. See "Labour and Social Affairs in Egypt;" Beinin, "Labor, Capital, and the State in Nassirist Egypt."

87. Mohammed al-Nowaihi, "Changing the Law on Personal Status in Egypt Within a Liberal Interpretation of the Shari'a," *Middle East Review* (summer 1979): 11, 4; Baer, "Egyptian Attitudes Towards Land Reform."

· 6 ·

Deconstructing Arab-Islamic History:
A Discussion of its
Evolutionary Dynamics

Wadood Hamad

$\mathcal{I}$t behooves all intellectuals, political theorists, and activists to delve deeply into the historical formation of religion, not only to understand its impact on culture, and vice versa, but to provide—particularly that nowadays many are experiencing fervent bouts of ideological fluctuations—a cogent analysis of the principal conditions that brought it to existence, and the influence of these conditions on the masses. The aim of this essay is basically threefold. First, to expose the origins, historical trajectory, and the impact of Islam on the masses; secondly, to shed some light on the materialist aspects of Arab-Islamic philosophy and thus refute the orientalist mindset of the sole spiritual basis of eastern cultures; and, thirdly, to examine how to objectively explain the current rise in Islamic tendencies in the Middle East and how this rise influences Middle Eastern politics. From this point forward, I will principally focus on culture and religion and strive to expound the pertinent interconnections and, indeed, contradictions therein. Needless to say, this contribution is neither the first nor the last; nor is it the most comprehensive—for volumes might still not do justice to such an involved and contentious topic.[1]

In order to embark on a serious discussion to explicate social change, one must be sincere in painting a picture of what has actually taken place—negative aspects included, not a mythological interpretation of events, or what one wishes would have happened. Obvious perhaps, yet preordained (mis)conceptions have taken hold of any treatment, particularly in the aftermath of the September 11 terror attacks, of (most of) the debate on the region, its inhabitants, their very existence, and the trajectory of their future. It is therefore imperative to probe the historical, cultural, and social formations that gave rise to (whatever) movements so as to better understand various developments as they occur and, as a result, be better equipped to effectively deal with them in order to ultimately provide a logical basis for effecting the necessary conditions for genuinely progressive social change. The task is neither paltry nor trite. Indeed, prevalent socioeconomic conditions (or rather upheavals) demand a sincere commitment to adopting a modality based on scientific analysis.

Basing analysis on the materialist conception of history—i.e., the consistent continuation and extension of materialism into the domain of social phenomena—removes two shortcomings. First, examining only the ideological motives in the historical activities of human beings without investigating the origins of those motives, or ascertaining the objective laws governing the system of social relations, or seeing the roots of these relations in the degree of development reached by material production; secondly, no other social theory has embraced the activities of history's principal agents—people—as objectively and critically. However, it is important to enunciate that dogmatism and generally rigid interpretations of social circumstances are not only unwarranted, but are antithetical to the very essence of historical materialism. The latter is a powerful tool, a *methodology* that itself must continually reevaluate (microscopic) details without losing sight of (macroscopic) realities. That is, to infer progress with time—as more facts are unraveled—necessarily requires the adroit rearrangement and, indeed, apt abandonment, of hypothetical assumptions that have been proven inadequate—afar from the mechanical application of powerful theories, thus realizing the dynamic universality of historical materialism.

THE DIALECTICS OF CULTURE AND RELIGION: ORIENT VERSUS OCCIDENT

The turbid understanding of not-so-few leftist intellectuals, western or otherwise, as to why Islam still appeals to a huge portion of the masses has created a situation not dissimilar to the prejudices propagated by Eurocentric orientalists who view Islamic superstition as being mystically pervasive in the entire region of the Middle East. It has become formulaic to label oriental cultures as merely being of a spiritual nature and lacking any materialist basis at all, with respect to philosophy. Thus, peoples of the orient are branded as a bunch of emotional fanatics, devoid of any rational thinking or cognitive analysis. To all intents and purposes, omissions of historical events and facts, on the part of these pundits, and attempts to smear realities are all but clear and, inter alia, are not due merely to an incorrect approach in analysis, nor incoherent information; they are rather committed intentionally. The Eurocentric vision of philosophical thought has helped, and still does, provide the driving force and legitimacy for western powers to colonize and monopolize the natural re-sources and wealth—and also wreak havoc among peoples—of the East under the pretext of democratizing and developing them.

Analyzing the rise and fall of civilizations must be governed by carefully examining the prevalent social and economic forces of the particular era in question. Any development or advancement must also be seen in global terms, i.e., in relation to the whole of human activity. Any parochial view, albeit claiming cultural advances at any one period, which maintains seclusion and isolation from the past, or even present culture—nay takes an antagonistic view toward them—is doomed to fail due to the insurmountable inconsistencies and contradictions inherent within them. Why, then, is such an approach not al-lowed to prevail in much of the (mainstream scholarly) research on Arab and Islamic culture and history? The answer essentially lies in the very nature of the predominant capitalist system: one that can only thrive on (ferocious) com-petition; a necessary consequence of the latter is the need to dominate re-sources, uphold the upper hand on the means of production, and, in turn, the distribution of wealth, which will subsequently determine the scope and ex-tent of exercising power and control deemed necessary, locally and globally.

Any civilization, which is essentially a function of both time and social formation cannot flourish, much less survive, unless it is dynamic and main-tains a close-knit relation with other civilizations. For colonized countries, the colonial/imperial condition has effected a polarized situation: A seg-ment of the colonized society becomes subservient to the colonial powers, another—the larger one—hostile, but (generally) lacks the concrete founda-tion, theoretically and practically, for advancing its proposed struggle for lib-eration, freedom, and progress. A case in point: attempts by some liberal modernists in the Arab world to unequivocally abdicate the Arab culture of today from any links with the past since they promulgate that the sole rea-son for existing problems is nothing other than the very rudiments of Arab-Islamic heritage. Subsequently, they seek to forcefully impose upon the peo-ple any semblance of western culture (since it is the dominant one, albeit itself nonuniform) without an in-depth analysis of the parameters involved. Equally pernicious is the Islamist fundamentalist approach (*al-Ussuliyoon*), which takes a diametrically opposing view and proclaims that it is the "evils" of western culture that have eroded the Arab-Islamic heritage and they therefore call for the complete elimination of anything modern or re-motely western so as to preserve a mythological "good of the past." Both views are seriously flawed and, indeed, nefarious, for they perceive culture as being static and isolated—a fatal error. Let me elaborate.

The technological revolution of the twentieth century is the direct consequence of the industrial revolution that preceded it a century earlier.

But could the latter have been realized without the invention of the wheel? Mesopotamian astronomy, accurate and based on rigorous observations, was rediscovered in the Hellenistic period, only to be developed later— notably by the Arabs and then of course in modern times. The Chaldeans also produced a general mythology of the universe—in which the stars were situated with respect to (and above) what was later called the sublunary world. After Mesopotamian astronomy and Egyptian calculus, Greek mathematics constituted a qualitative leap forward, which enriched by the Arabs, would only be surpassed in modern times. Is not, then, the western culture of today the legitimate offspring of the ancient cultures of Babylon and Sumar of Mesopotamia? Could Copernicus or Galileo have ever been able to advance scientific knowledge without the conscious use and understanding of the scientific and philosophical discoveries of Ibn-Sina (Avicenna), Ibn-Haythem, Jaber ibn-Hayyan, etc.? Moreover, was Arab culture itself not directly influenced by Indian, Chinese, and Greek civilizations; and did it not tremendously influence European culture and civilization? Ibn-Rushd (Averroes), for example, would not have been able to advance an iota in his philosophical endeavors without thoroughly and clearly comprehending the works of his predecessors from past times and from different geographical localities. Patently, Islamic civilization, in itself, epitomizes the very climactic cohesion of Arab, Indian, and Persian cultures.

What I have endeavored tersely to emphasize is the very intricate link, and continuity—albeit, to a varying extent, unconscious and spontaneous—among cultures and civilizations. This is not to conclude that civilizations fuse into one another; on the contrary, particular features nurture the development and characterize the distinct structure and formation of each. This should be clear to the serious observer/intellectual/researcher; however, ideological undertones deliberately obfuscate this clarity and perpetuate a campaign of disinformation and falsification. In what follows I shall delve through the underlying concepts of religion, philosophically and socially; then focus the discussion on the underpinnings of Islam and its apparent rise among a wide portion of the populace.

FROM A CRITICAL VIEW
OF RELIGION TO A CRITIQUE OF THE STATUS QUO

"*Religious* suffering," Marx wrote some 150 years ago, "is at one and the same time the *expression* of real suffering and a protest against real suffering. Religion is the sigh of the oppressed creature, the heart of a heartless world and the soul of soulless conditions. It is the *opium* of the people" [emphasis in original].[2]

The well-known phrase, "opium of the people," purports a poignant dichotomy, which requires some elaboration. Opium is indeed a drug under whose effect one experiences a notable change in control and awareness over physical and mental actions; but it clearly possesses medicinal attributes, as with a litany of other drugs used nowadays. Thus the analogy between religion and opium is not merely that the former robs people of their cognitive and mental faculties, it actually functions as a tranquilizer, a pain reliever to the suffering of the masses.[3] This fact is of crucial importance to understanding the appeal of religion to people, all and sundry. As such, the material value of religion stems from what religion unveils through the pain it strives to express and the spiritual transcendence of this pain. This is done through ruptures of real life and contradictions of the world in which people live. They feel these ruptures and contradictions via their noxious effects on society, which become manifestations of a religious form. A truly genuine critique of religion should be based on transforming the world through the eradication of the very ills that cause the suffering and destitution of the masses. Abandoning religion as the fictitious happiness of the people demands seeking their real happiness. It further demands forsaking the perceived misconceptions of people's conditions, and renouncing a situation that requires illusions. Therefore, to be content with limiting belief and appealing to people to fight religion without changing the social conditions that essentially create their suffering would be to undertake an impudent course of action, devoid of any appreciation for human beings and lacking social conviction.

A systematic modality of analysis requires, on the one hand, the examination of the relation between the religious text and the relevant social conditions, which shed light on the former's formation, and, on the other, the realization why and in precisely what form this social experiment emerges to formulate religion. Between these two complementary tasks, the former is ostensibly easier to perform, whereas the latter comprises rather intricate complexities.

The world of religion is thus a reflection of the real world, underpinned by the evolving socioeconomic conditions that give rise to its founding. Religious beliefs essentially require a two-tiered set of conditions for their evolution. First, a *practical need* for people to believe that they have control over their personal lives; and second, a *theoretical need* to fathom their association with nature, other people, and society as a whole. Nevertheless, in reality, people have hitherto not succeeded in securing for themselves this theoretical and practical control over their lives. For the forces that are deemed uncontrollable appear to be foreign and external, and seemingly confront people in a threatening manner. This duality, being foreign and external, epitomizes the very contrary feeling it was meant to dispel, i.e., people's inability to exercise any notion of control whatsoever over the global running of temporal affairs.

In order to achieve a thorough understanding of the interdependence between the Islamic religion and Arab culture, this point must be examined in terms of its historical formulation. What constitutes the founding and the expansion of any religion cannot possibly be surmised solely by referring to the religion itself and the development of its thought. An endeavor must be made to discern why this religion found a spot of influence; why its message was/is accepted by the people. For after all, a religion is not really established unless a social group actually pronounces its affiliation with it and, subsequently, derives some rituals from its teachings. Hence, how does a religion come into existence? Why does it gain supporters? How does it develop?

The old school of materialist philosophy always considered religion as the negation of philosophy and science. It further perceived religion as a fallacious form of science, evil and dangerous. For adherents to this school of thought, religion was antithetical to reality and law, i.e., from a theoretical stance, it was a fabric of hallucinations, and from a practical viewpoint, deceptive. They further proclaimed that religion's social function was to reinforce the political hegemony of a coterie of charlatans benefiting from the simple-mindedness of the people—thus keeping them in a state of ignorance and fear. We are, therefore, poised with a significant peculiarity, namely, a comprehensive characteristic common to all religions. This proposition however eschews two fundamental aspects: (1) deception is not in the origin of religious faith, even though it might become a weapon for control afterwards; and (2) religion strives to satisfy theoretical and practical needs—as explained above. Therefore, the underlying historical aspects of religion may, by and large, be summarized in five points:

1. The material underpinnings of religion form the basis for its history, where, of course, these underpinnings are a product of the social relations among people and the underlying economic formations. With this in mind, it should become clear that the series of events leading to the formation of the material basis for religion does not coalesce in a haphazard fashion, nor indirectly. Consequently, the essence of Islam must be researched, and hence understood, within the political, national, cultural, and linguistic situations of the Middle East—i.e., its founding needs to be understood in terms of the prevalent circumstances in the seventh century A.D.

2. The circumstances or events that form the initial conditions for founding a religion cannot be explained through that religion and its teachings alone. By analyzing pertinent socioeconomic conditions, one can fathom how religion succeeds in winning followers among the populace.

3. Religion is not created from nothingness. On the contrary, much of its content already exists. However, what religion manages to do is to gather all the bits and pieces and reassemble them in accordance with a new modality.

4. No religion remains exactly as it first started. It acquires much from local surroundings and, possibly, revises some of its contextual substance with time.[4]

5. Finally, a religion does not remain alive unless it is continually buttressed by actual practice. But will it still survive after the historical (social, cultural, economic) conditions have ceased to exist?

ISLAM: CONDITIONS THAT LED TO A BURGEONING PROPENSITY

It seems appropriate at this stage to elaborate on the compelling reasons for choosing and adhering to the term, Arab-Islamic culture, throughout the text. The term is used to describe the subject matter historically and culturally, and, as such, it is applied in a humanistic context—and appears most precise. Specifically, the word Arab is not intended to indicate the belonging through the pure blood relation since this would obviate its historicity. To the contrary, it signifies the historical characteristics germane to the cultural formation resulting from the active interaction between the Arabs and other peoples who partook in the making of this history. Moreover, the term Islamic is used to describe this history as an expression of this multifarious participation and, within a global context, to pronounce the cultural rather than the religious aspects of this common history.

In order to resolve the interrelationship between the Arab culture at present—with all its national, social, and intellectual dimensions—and the heritage of the past, one must poignantly elucidate one aspect of paramount importance: the reality of the intrinsic interrelationship between the revolutionary contents of the heritage and the revolutionary outlook toward this heritage, i.e., the necessity to adopt a stance on the Arab-Islamic heritage that stems from the revolutionary considerations, or outlook, of the present.[5] The reality being considered here is not an illusion, nor a revelation, nor an opinion; it is the materialization of events/conditions. This is indeed the crux of the matter: the interrelationship that we seek to resolve is one that is essentially an objectively real one. In other words, it would be unrealistic, even inconceivable, for one to possess a progressive viewpoint of the present and yet be reactionary when studying cultural and intellectual heritage. Put bluntly, being progressive and revolutionary is a comprehensive state of affairs—indivisible. Anything short of this would constitute a parasitic and opportunistic claim, and will eventually bring the proposed idea to ruination.

Islam, from the viewpoint of historical materialism, must be seen as a revolutionary change over prevalent social relations some 1,400 years ago. A change that at the time brought valuable material gains to human beings in terms of proposing positive social, economic, and political formulae. Besides, the historic class struggle within it should not be ignored, nor slighted. The desire for practical equality among people, in this sense, could not take the form of an all-encompassing social or political struggle without the introduction of a new element: religion. People were far too divided along different lines. For, in spite of their unity in destitution, the peasants did not join force with the (trade and unskilled) laborers, and they could not contemplate, due to existing social conditions, uniting with the slaves. People, because of deeply intrinsic divisions, could therefore not strive to achieve their freedom and, hence, the desire for practical equality was no more than equality in hope and faith. This, in essence, is the conceptual dimension of Islam. It galvanized, on the one hand, negative equality—symbolized by equality in despair and submission—and, on the other, practical equality—signified by equality in struggle and, in turn, martyrdom for beliefs, and in salvation, too. Alas, both these forms of equality are only ideally reinforced, through faith, hope, and belief in more than just life after death.

Islam principally attempted from its inception to marry, albeit to a limiting degree (and subject to different interpretations), temporal and spiritual matters. It was, in its early days, a religion of the dispossessed, underprivileged, and oppressed against the usurious, opulent echelons of society. Supporters of Islam were ferociously fought by the privileged of the Arabian Peninsula. Concomitantly, we notice the staunch adherence to the ideals of Islam by its believers. It is worthwhile to note that the varying interpretations and apparent radicalization of Islam were direct consequences of the socioeconomic aspirations of the groups involved—regardless of the fact that for Muslims the basic reference was the Quran and the teachings of the prophet Muhammad.

In the aftermath of Muhammad's death, an evident schism was created between the masses as the merchant and more prosperous echelons of Arabian society strove to gain control and acquire absolute power over the entire burgeoning nation and, thus, alienate the portion of Muhammad's companions and followers swimming against the current. Indeed, during the reign of the caliphs (following Muhammad's death) and succeeding Islamic states, a metamorphosis of the interpretations of Islamic teachings took place. This subsequently effected stark, concrete changes in the action deemed necessary by one specific segment of the believers or another to achieve the desired goals.

Notwithstanding the emergence of the Islamic empire, which reached the out-skirts of China and secured a foothold in southern Europe, the bloody confla-grations between the "poor" and the "privileged" never ceased to exist. Many struggles took place seeking a more equitable existence for Muslims,[6] however, this effectively produced a situation where there existed what may be termed an *oligarchic* Islam, on the one hand, and an *insurgent* Islam, on the other. His-tory is replete with such examples; two will follow to elucidate the point.

Abu-thar al-Ghafari, a contemporary of Muhammad who survived the reign of the Ummayyads (Benu Ummayya), symbolized the genuine struggle of the wretched during those times to force the state into a more equitable form of distributing the wealth of the nation.[7] The ruling elites of Benu Um-mayya were notoriously truculent and led lavish lifestyles, while the over-whelming majority of the populace lived in literally squalid conditions. Atro-cious policies, political and thought suppression, as well as the widening gulf between the rich and poor were not due only to the avaricious appetite of the ruling clique. These policies actually signaled a deliberate response to any form of political agitation that might seek to undermine authority.

Another, from the tenth century during the reign of the Abbassids, is Hamdan ibn-al-Asha'ath. Al-Asha'ath, a peasant born in Kufa, Iraq, along with al-Hussayn al-Ahwazi,[8] led a large congregation of supporters that spread over an area from Kufa to Ahwaz[9] and founded an insurgent movement, *al-Quaramitta* (the Carmathians).[10] They recognized that the widening gap be-tween the haves and have-nots, and the former's utter disregard for the poor, could not possibly be addressed, let alone eradicated, through negotiations with the ruling elite, and could therefore see no solution other than armed struggle. Thereafter, they raised their slogan: *Collective ownership of land, land produce and arms*.[11] In fact, the struggle of *al-Quaramitta* galvanized the peasants of the countryside in unison with the (handicraft and semiskilled) laborers of the towns. Many of the movement's supporters were mercilessly annihilated and those who survived the genocide escaped to the marshes of southern Iraq, then to an island in the Arabian/Persian Gulf (modern-day Bahrain) where they formed a state that could not survive for long due to the severe blockade im-posed on it by its neighbors.

The aforesaid is testimony, in part, to the political mosaic of Islam. A di-mension that is incorporated both theoretically and practically in the real world: It is a dual manifestation that acclimatizes spiritual considerations into political struggle. The philosophy adhered to by *al-Quaramitta*, however, tran-scended the mere spiritual. They, as a matter of fact, strove to dissociate them-selves from the faith, which initially nurtured their ideals, once they recognized the impasse of utter reliance on the religious doctrine alone. They adroitly realized that the abominable situation (of the time) demanded means of comparable form and magnitude to combat the pugnacious state. The movement was, indeed, ahead of its time, organizationally, tactically, and in vision.[12]

THE REQUIREMENTS FOR LIBERATION AND PROGRESS

Is Islam a revolutionary or a conservative force? It is possible that it possesses some revolutionary characteristics at one time and the contrary at another. It is also possible that it is both at the same time, since there exist different social strata, which (dialectically) coexist and confront each other. Hence, Islam is clearly capable of alternatively being clad with a political guise, divested of any political fervor, or, even, denying and reneging any such affiliation in principle. And, similarly, it is capable of accepting or challenging the status quo as circumstance and interest dictate. However, the real question should be posed as follows: does Islam possess the theoretical and practical bases for effecting and maintaining progressive social change?

It is not a trivial matter to attempt to reach a conclusive verdict on the role of religion in a modern society, especially during tempestuous times such as we have been witnessing, and will be for some time, passing through. Orientalists, neoliberal academics and paraofficial propagandists have raged a vicious, degrading war against inhabitants of the East and their very being, especially in, but not limited to, the aftermath of the terror attacks of September 11, 2001, on New York and Washington.[13] A pause to ponder and reflect is deemed essential.[14] As a matter of fact, European colonizers have, for more than a century, found allies, from India to Morocco, in the conservative, religious elements of the orient—or wherever and whenever colonizers existed in time and space. This alliance was mutually beneficial and it particularly offered the colonizers an important trump card with which to stifle and suppress local opposition and proceed with its necessary plans to co-opt, starve, and/or enslave the ordinary local masses after which complete control over available (natural and/or geographical) resources, the principal target of colonization, may be exercized.

This situation, then as now, could not have been realized without the overwhelming power and influence religious leaders have over the impoverished, powerless masses. Religious beliefs have served to befuddle and intoxicate the masses and thus deepen their misery. But to be fair to history, that is not the whole story.[15] Islam, for many of the destitute in Asia and Africa, has not only been a source of (perceived) salvation but, also, a source for rebelling over the status quo. This paradox is not unique to Islam. Contrast the role of the reactionary Catholic Church to that of the revolutionary priests in parts of South America who took the appalling reality of poverty and destitution as

their frame of reference, and accordingly gauged their struggle against their oc-
cupiers, colonizers, and the multinational corporations.

However, one must not hastily deduce that religion loses its spiritual nature and dissolves completely into politics. It remains a religion in the sense
that political "evil" is considered an embodiment of spiritual evil; toppling the
polity would constitute a reflection of the aspects of faithful adherence to religious thought. Nevertheless, according to the aforesaid, the spiritual is dis-
tinctly unique: it supersedes politics and the apparent intercommunication is
merely opportune and, hence, temporary. It thus becomes necessary to analyze
not only the appeal, but also the power of religion. Indeed, it is this perspective that will have determined the modality of analysis, and, of equal import,
the (possible) interpretation(s) given to this analysis—and, consequently, one's
role in this complex posture of affairs.

In this light, while the organized religious establishment directly or indirectly serves the manipulative ends of bourgeois reaction—be it in the
Arabian peninsula or the Indian subcontinent or elsewhere—it is counter-
productive, if not ignorant, not to recognize the cycle of despair and submission that drives the populace of various parts of the region to espouse
varying manifestations of the religious doctrine. Pressed between the complex of sheer imperialist *puissance* intricately entwined with abject repression
practiced by local dictators—almost always clients of the former, on the one
hand, and worsening economic status (high inflation, soaring unemployment, and growing schism between the haves and have-nots)—organized religion, especially its marginal fundamentalist strand, incessantly and oppor-
tunistically pries over people's lives. Characteristically, it is not the private
practice of religious conviction that is in question here, but the organizational forms that utilize the theoretical appeal of beliefs in order to manip-
ulate people's practical circumstances: a situation whereby a mythological
past is presented to the powerless, hapless populace as their salvation. Organic to the growth of this phenomenon is the emotional manipulation of
a disillusioned, seemingly futureless youth. It is they who constitute the fod-
der for fundamentalist hyperbole, reaction, and violence; while the populace
at large is simply mesmerized by this and rankled by the state's counter-
violence and continued repression/oppression.

Sui generis, three principal, mutually nonexclusive factors serve to foster
this condition: (1) foreign occupation/settlement of local land and/or usurpa-
tion of resources; (2) persistent local-state oppression to primarily buttress the
hegemony of the few to prolong the interests of 1; and, (3) the diminution and
dilution of indigenous culture, folklore, and (the very) status of being and living. The absence of a progressive vision dialectically becomes both a cause and
effect of the coalescence of these factors. Palestinians, Iraqis, Lebanese, and

whoever else moved by their setting, are victims, not instigators of violence: to miss the obvious would only contribute to the perpetuation of a morass of hopelessness and despair. Consider the moral clarity of, for instance: Palestinian refugees deprived of their land and living in squalid camps under siege and bombardment by a vicious occupying force and subject to constant humiliation; Iraqis, who suffer the oppression of a ruthless, atrocious polity and the merciless, deliberate destruction of their society, culture, and their very livelihoods through genocidal economic sanctions; or Lebanese, from the south, who, on top of sectarian discrimination, abject poverty, and mind-boggling illiteracy, experienced the humiliation of occupation and inhumane shelling of the regional surrogate military and economic power. Thus, to explicate ad infinitum is not to condone violent actions by the victim; it is to endeavor to fathom the causes, so as—if serious solutions are genuinely sought—to offer hope for lasting progressive change. Violence and murder directed at the innocent—irrespective of the practitioner and target—is morally abhorrent, tactically inept, and strategically bankrupt; it is simply a testament to powerlessness and despair. However, there is no moral equivalency between state and individual acts of violence.

For now, rationality has ebbed, and there is a captivating and sweeping retreat into religious proselytizing and indoctrination. Conservative (fundamentalist) Islam among inhabitants of the East and a domineering laissez faire capitalism that impoverishes the majority and enriches the very few throughout the planet. Tragically, an alternative appears elusive: the implosion of the communist experiment, due to inherent contradictions and shortcomings of that particular historical epoch and practice; the resultant widely spread disillusionment; fear of the unknown; and, persistent incertitude/disgust with organizational practices of whatever tinge. Unabated, state-sponsored terror by the sole emporium of the twenty-first century and its surrogate, local thuggery cum polity will breed its mirror image: terroristic violence from fringe, religious fundamentalists of the East. Peoples of East and West will wade dazed throughout, victimized, and marginalized.

In the midst of all this, one need not acquiesce to a "stagist" vision of the evolution of society: namely, the idea that the non-western (developing) societies must "catch up," regardless of the means and road for change, with their advanced counterparts before they can face the contradictions of the prevalent capitalist system of today—in its corollary of core-periphery polarization. The commitment to effecting lasting change through comprehending the intricacies of indigenous culture is a necessary condition for progressive social change to occur from within. Furthermore, the applicability of historical materialism to analyzing Arab-Islamic heritage must not be perceived as exogenous: it is an essential critical methodology that endeavors to contribute to possible forms of praxis, forms necessitated not by mere intellectual interest but by concrete exigencies. A situation in which the critical moment demands the symphysis of genuine efforts to reread, reinterpret, and reevaluate. Evidently, this circumstance is intrinsically fueled by the pressing need to formulate a socially meaningful understanding, and by the urgency for liberation of the oppressed of the East, within the context of a truly universalist view: a mobilization of sincere efforts is of the essence, learning profound lessons from history an unavoidable prerequisite. In this light, as Marx presciently prescribed, in times seemingly less turbulent and dark than ours: Extremism in the defense of liberty is no vice, moderation in the pursuit of justice is no virtue.

NOTES

This essay is dedicated to the memory of Iraq's foremost Marxist historian, Hadi al-Alawi, an indefatigable educator, social critic, and activist, who departed us far too prematurely.

1. There have been major modern scholarly writings on multifarious aspects of Arab-Islamic history and philosophy, mostly in Arabic—alas almost unrecognized in the West. The following presents a critical sample:

a. Nasr Hamid Abu-Zaid, *al-Tafkeer fi-zaman al-Takfeer: Dhid al-Jahl wal-Zaif wal-Khurafa* [Free Thought in the Age of Thought Control: Against Ignorance, Sophistry, and Myth] (Cairo: Sina Publishing, 1995).

b. Leila Ahmed, *Women and Gender in Islam—Historical Roots of a Modern Debate* (New Haven, Conn.: Yale University Press, 1992).

c. Hadi al-Alawi, *Nadhariyatt al-Haraka al-Jawharriya 'ind al-Shirazi* [al-Shirazi: Theory of Intrinsic Motion] (Baghdad: Irshad Publishing, 1971).

d. ———, *Min Tarikh al-Ta'atheeb fil-Islam* [From the History of Torture in Islam] (Damascus: Center for Socialist Studies and Research in the Arab World, 1987).

e. ———, *al-Ightiyal al-Siyassi fil-Islam* [Political Assassination in Islam] (Damascus: Center for Socialist Studies and Research in the Arab World, 1987).

f. ———, *al-Muntakhab mina-Lizumiyaat: Naqd al-Dawla wal-Deen wal-Nas* [Selections from al-Ma'ari: A Critique of State, Religion, and People] (Damascus: Center for Socialist Studies and Research in the Arab World, 1990).

g. ———, *Fil-Siyassa al-Islamiya* [On Islamic Politics] (Budapest: Sahara Publishing, 1991).

h. ———, *Chapters from the History of Political Islam* (Cyprus: Center for Socialist Studies and Research in the Arab World, 1995), [in Arabic].

i. ———, *Shakhsiyatt ghair qaliqa fil-Islam* [Unperturbed Characters in Islam] (Beirut: Dar al-Kunooz al-Adabiya Publishing, 1995).

j. ———, *Chapters from the History of Women* (Beirut: Dar al-Kunooz al-Adabiya Publishing, 1996), [in Arabic].

k. ———, *Madarat sufiya: Turath al-Thawra al-Masha'aiya fil-Saharq* [On Sufism: The Heritage of Communalism in the East] (Beirut: Center for Socialist Studies and Research in the Arab World/Dar al-Mada Publishing, 1997).

l. Aziz al-Azmeh, *Islam and Modernities* (London: Verso, 1993).

m. Mohammed A. Bamyeh, *The Social Origins of Islam—Mind, Economy, and Discourse* (Minneapolis: University of Minnesota Press, 1999).

n. Mohammad Arkoun, *Lèctures du Coran* (Paris: Maisonneuve et Larose, 1982).

o. ———, *Pour une critique de la raison islamique* (Paris: Maisonneuve et Larose, 1984).

p. Ann Elizabeth Mayer, *Islam and Human Rights—Tradition and Politics* (Boulder, Colo.: Westview Press, 1999).

q. Hussayn M'rrwa, *al-Naza'at al-Maddiya fil-falsafa al-Aribiya al-Islamiya* [The Materialist Conception of Arab-Islamic Philosophy] 2 vols., 6th ed. (Beirut: al-Farabi Publishing, 1988). H. M'rrwa, M. A. al-Alim, M. Dekroub, and S. Sa'ad, eds., *Darasat Islamiya* [Studies in Islam] (Beirut: al-Farabi Publishing, 1987).

r. Maxime Rodinson, *Mohammed* (London: Penguin, 1991).

s. Georges Tarabichi, *al-Muthaqafoun al-Arab wal-Turath* [Arab Intellectuals and Their Heritage] (London: Riad el-Rayyes, 1991).

2. Karl Marx, "Contribution to the Critique of Hegel's Philosophy of Right, Introduction," in Karl Marx, *Early Writings* (London: Penguin, 1992), 244.

3. It has been commonplace for many to obscure the meaning of texts written by Marx, and Engels for that matter, by only extracting portions thereof, and out of context. In so doing, the totality of the meaning is distorted and the integrity of the work compromised.

4. Here are pressing questions that occupied the minds of many secular progressives: Why has Islam not had a reformation yet? Are there inherent factors keeping a reforming movement at bay? Or the trajectory of political events has caused the retardation of the emergence of a reforming movement? While no one has been able to provide completely satisfactory answers, serious attempts to rationally argue for the reasons, and prospects, for reformation have been made—see reading list in note 1. A recent contribution offers a fresh, critical assessment of this. See Ali Tariq, *The Clash of Fundamentalisms: Crusades, Jihads, and Modernity* (London: Verso, 2002), especially 13–68.

5. There is, for the sake of completeness, another important aspect. That is the reality of the revolutionary content of the present Arab irredentist movements. However, this is beyond the scope of this chapter.

6. It must be stated that, of course, not all uprisings had aims grounded in social justice. Many insurrections were for reasons far from that. I am not at all attempting to idealize the situation, rather provide few examples based on a thorough analysis of historical conditions/developments.

7. A chronological order of events, in brief, is: Death of Prophet Muhammad in 632 A.D.; first caliph was Abu-Bakr, then Omar, Uthman, and finally Ali. Thereafter, Benu Ummayya founded their state, whose capital was Damascus (661–750); succeeded by the Abbassids (moved the capital to Baghdad) who presided over the Islamic empire until the Mongol invasion of 1258.

8. al-Hussayn al-Ahwazi was a follower of Ismail, spiritual leader of the Ismaili sect (founded in 765), a splinter Shi'ite group. He severed links with the group to join Hamdan ibn-al-Asha'ath, having realized that genuine social change in Muslim society was not to be instituted through peaceful means, as the Ismailis, who opposed the Muslim leaders of the day, had professed.

9. Ahwaz, or Khuzistan, is Arab land, southeast of Iraq, which was divided by Britain and France in the aftermath of World War I and then appended to Iran.

10. The group's name is derived from the Arabic word *Quarmat*, which means the color red. This is indicative of the conscious association, and thus usage, on the part of the insurgent leaders.

11. For a good analysis of this period and of the shortcomings of the Carmathian struggle for social justice, see Hassan Bazzoun's excellent but brief study, *al-Quarmattiya baynal-Deen wal-Thawra* [The Carmathians: Between Religion and Revolution] (Beirut: Dar al-Haqiqa Publishing, 1988).

12. One may even argue, at a rudimentary level, that it truly represented the emergence of the *first* revolution in human history with clearly socialistic tendencies.

13. To glean a glimpse of such responses, see:

    a. Bernard Lewis, "The Revolt of Islam—When Did the Conflict with the West Begin, and How Could it End?" *The New Yorker*, November 19, 2001, pp. 50–63.

    b. ———, *What Went Wrong? Western Impact and Middle Eastern Response* (Oxford: Oxford University Press, 2002).

    c. Avishai Margalit and Ian Buruma, "Occidentalism," *The New York Review of Books*, January 17, 2002.

14. Several courageous counterresponses have emerged, principally amongst which are:

    a. Tariq, *The Clash of Fundamentalisms,* especially 13–68.

    b. Noam Chomsky, *9–11* (New York: Seven Stories Press, 2001), see especially 71–92.

    c. Edward Said, "Impossible Histories—Why the Many Islams Cannot Be Simplified," *Harper's Magazine*, July 2002, pp. 69–74.

15. In the morass of despair, a flicker of hope springs to being. An organic, vibrant civil movement is resolutely materializing now in Iran, which seeks to challenge societal organization—promulgated by a strict, self-serving interpretation for over two decades by the mullah oligarchy—using a progressive vision that espouses modernity and a fresher social analysis, still wedded in general terms to the tenets of Islam. Observing the evolution of this movement for social change will be of tremendous interest for those who believe that lasting progress can only originate from within—by challenging inherent inconsistencies and contradictions in existing social relations—not through externally imposed solutions whether by war or through restrictive, neoconservative economic restructuring approaches as practiced by the International Monetary Fund and World Bank. Historical evidence categorically indicates that these neoliberal measures can only lead to immiserization and ostracization of the indigenous populace, and consequently effect fertile ground for fundamentalist tendencies and sympathies—cf. the political and social situations in especially, but not exclusively, Egypt and North Africa.

· 7 ·

Critical Theory and the Islamic Encounter with Modernity

Farzin Vahdat

$\mathcal{I}$n his assessment of the global state of sociology, Immanuel Wallerstein has recently noted the predominant concern of sociologists from the Middle East with the place of Arab-Islamic civilization in the modern world (Wallerstein 1998, 325). In fact it would not be an exaggeration to claim that the question of modernity currently constitutes *the* central issue in many Middle Eastern and Islamic societies—be it its appropriation, its rejection, its transformation along more palatable lines—at the theoretical as well as the practical level. On the other hand, the studies of the Middle East and Islam in the West have been predominantly conducted by juxtaposition and opposition to western modernity. Contemporary scholarship on the Middle East and modernity is at a critical juncture. There is some spirited interest in this issue, and some important work is being done in this area (e.g., Boroujerdi 1996; Karimi-Hakkak 1995; Khuri 1998; Salvatore 1997; Lee 1997; Martin 1989; Rejali 1994), as these efforts attempt to discuss some aspects of the relationship between the Middle East, Islam, and modernity. Yet, an elaborate discussion of the phenomenon and a theory of modernity remain wanting. There are no comprehensive attempts to address the question of modernity and its various dimensions with respect to the Middle East. Moreover, the traditional "western" analysis of the region and its cultural modalities in terms of modernity is based on a notion of modernity, which suffers from an overly unilinear and unidimensional interpretation and conceptualization of the modern world.

One of the most complex and nuanced analyses of modernity is to be found in the body of thought known as Critical Theory. It is not only a profound source for a critical analysis of modernity, it also offers valuable insight enabling us to assess the normative content of modernity and its discontents. What I would like to propose is that studies of the contemporary Middle East

123

and its relation to modernity would vastly benefit by drawing on the insights derived from Critical Theory. In Critical Theory, from its Kantian and Hegelian foundations, to the Frankfurt School theorists and now to Jürgen Habermas, the issues associated with modernity have always constituted a central theme. Even so, very few attempts have been made to address the encounter of the civilizations of the Middle East with modernity from the perspective of Critical Theory. At least until recently, it has often been assumed that the process of development in Third World countries is primarily an economic issue, or alternatively a problem of political economy, and as such has traditionally been addressed from these perspectives first and foremost. As a result, cultural perspectives have lagged behind. Critical Theory itself has not been greatly interested in these issues and as a whole has refrained from any interest in Third World countries. This is more curious since the body of thought designated as Critical Theory has historically taken shape in response to the development of modernity in the West and the challenges involved in this process, which has had ineluctable global implications. Many of these Third World countries have been plunged into the modern situation and one way or another need to contend with it. Critical Theory has developed in response to similar processes in the West. Therefore, it has valuable lessons and insights for the countries that are now confronted by a similar process and face similar struggles and challenges. One of these insights, which has been stressed by more recent theorists of Critical Theory, is how close the interaction is between cultural development, economic development, and political democracy. This consciousness about the inseparability of these spheres is, in fact, an essential condition for the development of sociopolitical democracy in the context of the Middle East.

For critical theorists, the category of subjectivity has always been seen as constituting a key feature of modernity. Habermas has invoked Hegel to interpret the normative content of modernity principally in terms of subjectivity: "The principle of the modern world is freedom of subjectivity, the principle that all the essential factors present in the intellectual whole are now coming into their right in the course of their development" (Hegel 1967, 286; cited in Habermas 1990, 16). In *Philosophy of Right* (e.g., para. 124) and elsewhere, in his discussion of subjectivity, Hegel seems to be emphasizing not only human autonomy but also its beneficiary, the individual. In Hegelian thought subjectivity is considered the ontological foundation of the right-bearing individual. As a pillar of modernity, subjectivity in this sense can be viewed as the *property characterizing the autonomous, self-willing, self-defining, and self-conscious individual agent* (see Habermas 1990, 338). Subjectivity, very much rooted in the humanist tradition, tends to view the individual as the determinant of her or his own life processes and is closely related to notions such as human freedom, volition, consciousness, reason, individuality, etc.; but it is not reducible to any single one of these. An important aspect to keep in mind about subjectivity is that it is simultaneously the repository of emancipation as well as domination.[1] While the Cartesian cogito as the modern detached subject is the source of liberation (e.g., the philosophical foundations of the rights of citizenship), it is also responsible for the objectification of nature, the Other, such as the colonized and women, as well as of the subject itself.

From Hegel to Habermas many social thinkers and philosophers have attempted to reconcile this subject of modernity and its "other." Hegel conceptualized this synthesis primarily in terms of universality. As such, universality, a somewhat more elusive category to analyze, may be perceived as *the mutual recognition among the plurality of subjects of each other's subjectivity*. Expressed differently and in its bourgeois historical and political context, universality refers to elimination of restrictions based on privilege, status, and/or other essential considerations. In a more restricted sense, universality could be considered as bourgeois formal equality before the law. Hegel interpreted the two concepts of subjectivity and universality as epitomized in the notion of civil society, which according to him is comprised of "[a]n association of members as self-sufficient individuals in a universality, which because of their self-sufficiency is only formal" (Hegel 1967, 110).

In this passage Hegel expresses a concern about the "diremption" and the moral "chaos" that are the result of the process of subjectification and radical human autonomy associated with human subjectivity, which the principle of universality in civil society in the Kantian formulation is supposed to heal but that Hegel finds wanting because of the "vacuity" and formality of the bourgeois understanding of universality as mere equality before the law. In fact, Hegel was one of the first and most prominent to attempt to address and resolve the contradictions and the close affinity between subjectivity and universality in a substantive (as opposed to formal) synthesis of the two principles.[2]

Thus, the principle of subjectivity has given rise to freedom and the notion of individual and collective autonomy in modernity. But the unbridled subjectivity of modernity has also been responsible for the moral and political chaos and various types of the domination of the "others." And for this reason, much of the intellectual and political thought since Hegel has in one way or another attempted to address the abstract and monadic conception of the subject in modernity and has striven to embed it in a larger context.[3] The latest and most comprehensive effort at the synthesis between subjectivity and universality is elaborated in the works of Jürgen Habermas and his attempt at shifting the ontological foundation of modernity from mere subjectivity to that of intersubjectivity in his theory of communicative action. Habermas, following Hegel, is aware of the problems associated with "unchecked" subjectivity of the modern age and the associated problems of domination. Like Hegel, he sees the diremptions resulting from the expansion of the principle of modern subjectivity and attempts to "reconcile" those diremptions through a theory of intersubjectivity as opposed to mere subjectivity. But he criticizes Hegel for attempting to develop this intersubjectivity based on the principle of modern subjectivity itself and eventually failing to ground it in a communicative action theory (Habermas 1990, 30–31). Thus, Habermas seeks to continue the project of overcoming the problem of modernity, this time in its proper direction, which Hegel had failed to achieve, through the mediation of language: "Membership in the ideal communicative community is, in Hegelian terms, constitutive of both the I as universal and the I as individual" (Habermas 1984, 97).

THE EMERGENCE OF
HUMAN SUBJECTIVITY AND ALLAH'S WILL

At first glance it might seem that the principle of human subjectivity is diametrically opposed to monotheistic religions in general and to Islamic culture in particular. Indeed, Bassam Tibi, one of the most erudite scholars of Islam and modernity, has maintained just such a position. For Tibi, modernity as a cultural project, which has ushered in an anthropocentric view of the universe and the attendant knowing-agent (*Konnenbewusstsein*) engaged in changing the social and natural environment is contrary to Islam since, "the concept of *Konnenbewusstsein* runs counter to the Islamic belief that God is the Creator (*al-Khaliq*) and man is the *makhluq* (creature) unrestrictedly submitting to Allah's will and directed by it as it is revealed in the Koran" (Tibi 1995, 8). However, such a partial view distorts the reality of the emerging and current Islamic discourses, which in their diversity have addressed this issue in many subtle fashions. In many contemporary Islamic discourses, the theomorphic ontological foundations of modern subjectivity are being broached. The Islamic mystical tradition and philosophy are two sources for the construction of such notions of subjectivity with considerable potentials. The mystical/philosophical notion of the Perfect Human (*Insan Kamil*) according to which humans are viewed as individual microcosms incorporating the body, the spirit, and the synthesis between these, exhibiting certain attributes of God and having access to some of His knowledge, are being thematized (Khuri 1998, 195). The Islamic philosopher, Ibn 'Aarbi (1165–1240) is one of the founders of this Neoplatonic tradition in the Islamic world whose thought is being interpreted in the construction of modern subjectivity in some contemporary Islamic discourses.

As a soteriological religion, Islam also places much emphasis on the responsibility of the individual in his or her salvation, thereby containing the germ of individual subjectivity. Rooted in the Occidental Axial Civilization, the Islamic tradition of personal salvation is a crucial element in the long-term process of subjectification (Salvatore 1997, 28).[4] The notion of faith (*iman*) and its carrier, the individual, is taken as the precursor of Kantian moral autonomy as the foundation of individual subjectivity (Salvatore, 1997, 21). Such a course of subjectification would involve the transformation of religious faith into the notion that the individual as the member of a community is God's creature and therefore is naturally free and derives authority from Him, and His agent by virtue of submitting to His authority—a process parallel to the Calvinist path to modern subjectivity (Salvatore 1997, 27). This unfolding of human subjectivity involves a recognition that sovereignty belongs to the Divine Subject and it is only as a result of this recognition and submission to the Divine authority and no other authority, that the individual gains an in indirect subjectivity vis-à-vis other profane entities. Such a view is characteristic of some of the most influential Islamic discourse such as Sayyid Qutb's (1906–1966) in Egypt and some of his followers in the contemporary Arab Islamist movements (Salvatore 1997, 192–93).

The Quranic text itself provides another significant dimension of this vicarious subjectivity. The Quranic concept of the human as God's vice regent on earth (*Khalifat o'llah fi al-arz*), which explicitly informed the discourses of the architects of Islamic Revolution in Iran in the 1960s and 1970s, Ali Shariati and Ayatollah Motahhari (Ayatollah Khomeini does not seem to have referred to it explicitly), also constitutes an important path to modern subjectivity. In this discourse we encounter a simultaneous affirmation and negation of human subjectivity—and often individuality—in the metaphysical foundations of the thought of these vastly influential Iranian thinkers. The Islamic discourse that developed in intellectual, political, and social contexts of the post-1953 coup d'état in Iran, which overthrew the democratically elected government of Mossadeq and reinstituted the Pahlavi autocracy, was indeed variegated and nuanced. And the discourses of Ali Shariati, Ayatollah Khomeini, and Ayatollah Motahhari reflect this opalescence. However, the most basic element that connected the discourses of these three men was the phenomenon that may be designated as "mediated subjectivity." By mediated subjectivity I refer to the *notion of human subjectivity projected onto the attributes of a monotheistic deity— attributes such as omnipotence, omniscience, and volition—and then partially reappropriated by humans. In this scheme, human subjectivity is contingent on God's subjectivity. Thus while human subjectivity is not denied, it is never independent of God's subjectivity and in this sense it is "mediated."*[5] This situation is usually conducive to a great conflict between the Divine Subjectivity and human subjectivity, which gives rise to various other forms of conflict. One of the sharpest conflicts that results is the constant and schizophrenic shifting of ground between a confirmation and negation of human subjectivity in general, as well as a constant oscillation between individual and collectivity, but not their total denial.

The mechanism that Shariati, as well as Khomeini and Motahhari utilized to arrive at this indirect and tentative human subjectivity, was an interpretation of the metaphysics of monotheism, which viewed human existence in terms of a theomorphic and transcendental "journey" or "movement," which started at the level of "matter" and would carry and elevate humans to the level of God's spirit. However, the destination of this journey is never a modern individual subject as we know it, but nevertheless something close to it, especially in Motahhari's discourse. Hence the constant vacillation of the three figures between positing and negating subjectivity, each in their own way.[6]

In Shariati's discourse the tendency toward what theomorphic approach to subjectivity was at times quite explicit. He writes, "[i]n the language of religion, man is a divine essence, an essence superior to matter and dominant over nature. He originates from God's Spirit, which means he possesses God's attributes. But since the Fall unto earth, nature and society, man has forgotten his 'primal self-divinity' [*khud khodai nukhustin*] and merely allows his material and animal inclinations to develop. As a result, the sublime values invested in him die out and he considers himself merely as the highest life in the evolution of animals. He forgets that he is a spark from the divine realm, that his mission is to 'divinize' the world and that his being is God-like" (Shariati 1977, 19).

Shariati very explicitly uses God's attributes to proffer subjectivity to humans and to make them dominant over nature. In fact, he devoted a considerable portion of his rather vast corpus to the idea of human subjectivity, but as it is the nature of this mediated subjectivity, almost in all instances, as soon as he affirms human subjectivity he immediately negates it.

This simultaneous duality is reflected not only in the sociopolitical aspects and notions of citizenship in the discourses of these three figures of the Islamic Revolution, but to a large extent it also reverberates in the constitution and institutions of the Islamic Republic.[7] However, it is evident that the contradictions inherent in the discourse of mediated subjectivity render it a transitory but dynamic discourse with a large potential for transformation of itself and society because it, unlike "secular" discourses of modernity, which have had a limited and relatively shallow impact on the popular masses in the Middle East, has affected the majority of the Iranian population profoundly.

The Islamic discourse, owing to the contradictory nature of mediated subjectivity, *could* also *accommodate* and even *promote* a type of public engagement, especially in the political sphere, necessitated by mass mobilization and political participation. In his speeches and addresses during the Islamic revolution, Ayatollah

Khomeini often praised the participants in the demonstrations against the Pahlavi regime and encouraged them to remain "in the scene." He argued that if there were only one benefit deriving from the establishment of the Islamic Republic, it would be the presence of the people in social and political scenes, which was "tantamount to a miracle not realized elsewhere" (Khomeini 1985, 79). He even extrapolated the right of participation to women without whom, he admitted, the revolution would not have succeeded (Khomeini 1985, 99). At times he sounded as if the people by participating in the revolution have earned the rights to participate in the affairs of their own country.

In the Arab context too, the later writings of Sayyid Qutb on this element of subjectification found expression in an Islamic justification of citizenship (Salvatore 1997, 60). This type of public engagement assuming an Islamic mantle, can *in the long run*, be conducive to a form of universal subjectivity and ultimately a narrative of general citizenship and public discussion and deliberation (Salvatore 1997, 55).[8]

POSITIVIST SUBJECTIVITY
VERSUS UNIVERSALIZABLE SUBJECTIVITY

From the very beginning of the encounter of many of the Middle Eastern societies with the modern world in the nineteenth century, we can see a dual approach to modernity by secularists and Islamic reformists alike. On the one hand, there was a strong interest in the appropriation of modern western "technique" in general and bureaucracy and military knowledge in particular. On the other hand, there was some desire and curiosity for new ideas and institutions of civil society, albeit to a lesser extent and stunted in magnitude. To be sure, this duality in the appropriation of modernity in this part of the world reflected the very same duality that modernity had exhibited in its European birthplace. Therefore, in the Middle East as well, we observe a positivist interpretation of subjectivity side by side with what can be designated as a "universalizable subjectivity."

The notion of progress, for example, is of pivotal importance in both European and Middle Eastern contexts. But, in the positivist interpretation within the Middle East, progress is codified as the mere development of science and technology and their application to the social sphere, whereas in the trend that may be conceived in terms of universalizable subjectivity, the notion of progress refers more to the possibility of democratic change and transformation of the oppressive institutions where the concept of critique plays a central role. The same duality is expressed in the notion of law. According to the positivist interpretation, law is viewed primarily as order, regulation, and codification. In contrast, "positive law" manifests the universalizability of freedom and the rights and responsibilities of citizenship and the notion of government by consent and consensus.

At the institutional level, the same dichotomy is displayed in the difference between the interest in merely an efficient bureaucracy such as the creation of *Majlis Tanzimat* (Organization Assembly) on the one hand, and the setting up of parliamentary constitution and representative assembly on the other. Both of those tendencies inherent in the dual appropriation of modernity in the nineteenth-century Middle East had also adopted the idea of the modern nation-state and nationalism from the West. But while the positivist tendencies placed more emphasis on a notion of nationalism based on ethnic and historical identity (in this case of Iran, for example, the purported Aryan and pre-Islamic identity of the country as opposed to the "Semitic Arabs"), the universalizable approach leaned more toward a notion of nationalism based upon popular sovereignty within the confines of a nation-state. It is very important to bear in mind that both interpretations of modernity were simultaneously expressed in the discourses promulgated by Middle Eastern secular and Islamic reformist thinkers of the nineteenth and early twentieth centuries.

In contemporary Middle Eastern discourses on modernity we encounter a very close parallel dualism, where in reality there is a triumph of positivist subjectivity and the more emancipatory and universalizable moment of subjectivity has been eclipsed. The sentiment of humiliation as a result of the conflict with Israel, and recently more directly with the United States, has disposed the Arabs and Muslims more toward a technological and positivistic appropriation of modernity. As Khuri has observed, "in the contemporary Arab Muslim world, modernity itself is seen in mechanistic terms; for rather than grasp its rational and scientific components in their variety and richness, not to mention the moral values underlying it, urgency and haste reduce modernity to its most visible aspects: technological and economic advancement and democracy, themselves . . . reduced to mechanism" (Khuri 1998, 18–19). Moreover, because of its perceived cultural neutrality, the instrumental rationality of modernity, and what I have designated as positivist subjectivity, have been much more readily accepted by the religious forces and secular "modernizing" state elites in their encounter with modernity (Khuri 1998, 21–22).

AN EARLY ISLAMIC ENCOUNTER WITH MODERNITY: THE CASE OF JAMAL AL-DIN AFGHANI

The contemporary Islamic discourses and their relation to modernity have been much influenced by one nineteenth-century individual activist and thinker, namely, Jamal Al-din Asadabadi, better known as Afghani (1838–1897). For this reason an analysis of his thought in some detail is instructive in coming to terms with contemporary issues. In Afghani's discourse, the dual encounter with modernity takes a slightly different form. In reality, he created two discourses, one for what he considered to be the enlightened elite in Islamic societies, according to the principles of which individual subjectivity was affirmed in such concepts as critical thought. He also developed a parallel discourse, which appealed more to the "masses" motivated by his anti-imperialist goals, and which in many ways was in sharp contrast to his first critical discourse.

Underlying Afghani's discourse there is a strong assumption that the modern world necessitates a view of human agency expressed in, "activism, the freer use of human reason and political and military strength" (Keddie 1968, 3). It is interesting that in Afghani's case the critical component in his approach to modernity was weightier than the positivist component, which makes sense in the view of his commitment to the unorthodox "Islamic" philosophy.[9] "If someone looks deeply into the question," he wrote, "he will see that science rules the world. There was, is and will be no rule in the world but science" (Afghani 1968a, 102). But a few pages later in the same essay he qualified his statement by saying that,

A science is needed to be the comprehensive soul for all the sciences, so that it can preserve their existence, apply each of them in its proper place, and become the cause of progress of each one of those sciences. The science that has the position of a comprehensive soul and the rank of a preserving force is the science of *falsafa* or philosophy, because its subject is universal. It is philosophy that shows man human prerequisites. It shows the sciences what is necessary. It employs each of the sciences in its proper place. If a community did not have philosophy, and all the individuals of that community were learned in the sciences with particular subjects, those sciences could not last in that community for a century . . . that community without the spirit of philosophy could not deduce conclusions from these sciences. The Ottoman government and the Khedive of Egypt have opened up schools for the teaching of the new sciences for a period of sixty years and until now they have not received any benefits from those sciences (Afghani 1968a, 104).

What is of crucial importance is that Afghani grounded his conceptualization of philosophy in the idea of reasoning and critical argumentation since "the father and mother of knowledge [*elm*] is reasoning [*borhan*] and reasoning is neither Aristotle nor Galileo. The truth is where there is reasoning . . ." (Afghani 1968a, 107; translation slightly modified). In another essay entitled *Fawaid Falsafa* (*The Benefits of Philosophy*) Afghani took his argument one step further by contending that philosophy was even prior to revelation and the latter is but a preparatory stage for the achievement of philosophy. In other words, he argued that revelation was a base that would lead the way to a subjectivist epistemology based on philosophy. He first argued in favor of the centrality of critical faculties of thought:

> philosophy is the escape from the narrowness of animal sense impression into the wide area of human perception. It is the removal of darkness of bestial illusions with the light of natural intelligence; the transformation of blindness and lack of insight into clear-sightedness and insight (Afghani 1968b, 110).

He then discusses the role of Islam and the Quran in preparing the pre-Islamic "savage" Arabs to embrace the philosophical traditions developed by more civilized nations,

> In sum, in that Precious Book [The Quran] with solid verse, He planted the roots of philosophical sciences into purified souls, and *opened the road* for man to become man. When the Arab people came to believe in that Precious Book they were transferred from the sphere of ignorance to knowledge, from blindness to vision, from savagery to civilization, and from nomadism to settlement. They understood their needs for intellectual and spiritual accomplishment and for gaining a living (Afghani 1968b, 114; emphasis added).

These ideas later developed, Afghani argued, and Arabs realized that they could not develop further without the help of other nations. Therefore, notwithstanding the splendor and greatness of Islam and Muslims, in order to exact and elevate knowledge, the Arabs showed humility before the lowest of their subjects, i.e., the Christians, Jews, and Persians, until with their help, they translated the philosophical sciences from Persian, Syriac, and Greek into Arabic. "Hence it became clear that their Precious Book was the first teacher of philosophy to the Muslims" (Afghani 1968b, 114).

In the same essay, Afghani presented a view of human action that may seem very much to correspond to a Faustian view of subjectivity. He recognized the necessity of satisfaction of human material needs such as agriculture and animal husbandry, procurement of water, construction of shelter, preservation of health achieved through sciences and technology (Afghani 1968b, 110; Afghani 1958, 118). Yet, he considered critical philosophy to be the foundation of these sciences and technologies: "It [philosophy] is the foremost cause of the production of knowledge, the creation of sciences, the invention of industries and the initiation of crafts" (Afghani 1968b, 110; Afghani 1958, 118).

Afghani's most explicit statement of his critical thinking was given in an article published on May 18, 1883, in *Journal des Debats* in response to Ernest Renan's uncritical attack on Islam as being inherently against modern civilization. In this essay, Afghani demonstrated the baselessness of Renan's racist attitudes toward Arabs and yet praised the superiority of critical thought, i.e., "scientific" and philosophical thought, over revelation (Afghani 1968c, 81–87).[10]

Afghani's "second discourse" is most sharply expressed in a famous essay entitled "The Truth about the Neicheri Sect and Explanation of the Neicheris," written in 1881, even before he wrote the essays belonging to his critical discourse discussed above. In this essay, Afghani depicts a picture of an anti-imperialist collective subject, possessing political and military power incarnated in an Islamic nation that could stand up to western hegemony.[11] He identified the concept of "social solidarity" as the linchpin of this collective subject, which the West through its "agents" such as Sir Ahmad Khan was trying to subvert. Apparently drawing on Ibn Khaldun's parallel concept of *asabiyah* (solidarity), Afghani's concept of social solidarity explained the longevity of civilizations and nations in terms of sets of beliefs which bonded the members of a society together and protected that society from external invasion and internal disintegration.

The *Neicheris* or "materialists," as Afghani in his "second discourse" lumped together the unorthodox and critical thinkers, the socialists, communists, and nihilists, were in his view bent on destroying the social solidarity of nations, Islamic or otherwise, throughout history (Afghani 1968d, 140). What made social solidarity possible, in his analysis, was religious faith and specifically faith in a Transcendental Deity who would in the next world mete out reward and punishment as recompense to individual believers' deeds while living on earth (Afghani 1968d, 167). Afghani elaborated on components of religious faith that undergird the social order and social solidarity in society. These, which he termed as "Religion's Three Beliefs," consisted of: (1) the belief that "there is a terrestrial angel [human], and that he is the noblest of creatures"; (2) the certainty that one's community "is the noblest one, and that all outside . . . [one's] community are in error and deception"; and (3) the *belief* that, "man has come into the world in order to acquire accomplishments worthy of transferring him to a world more excellent, higher, vaster, and more perfect than this narrow and dark world" (Afghani 1968d, 141). As to the first and second components of the religious faith necessary for social solidarity and social order, Afghani reasoned that they were necessary for a sense of collective subjectivity vis-à-vis nature and other social collectivities (Afghani 1968d, 142). It was the third belief, however, which was, as Afghani put it:

> the best impulse towards civilization, whose foundations are true knowledge and refined morals. It is the best requisite for the *stability of the social order*, which is founded on each individual's knowledge of his proper rights, and his following the straight path of justice. . . . It is the best basis for the peace

and calm of the classes of humanity, because peace is the fruit of love and justice and love and justice result from admirable qualities and habits. It is the only belief that restrains man from all evils, saves him from vales of adversity and misfortune, and seats him in the virtuous city on the throne of happiness" (Afghani 1968d, 144).

In contrast to this collectivist notion of agency, Afghani argued, the most effective means by which the Neicheris and unorthodox attempted to undermine social solidarity was by the introduction of individual subjectivity rendered by Afghani as "egoism," which denies the beliefs in reward and punishment in the afterlife,

> And since, because of these corrupt opinions, each of them [people corrupted by disbelief] believed that there is no life but this one, the quality of *egoism* [in French transliteration] overcame them. The quality of *egoism* consists of self-love to the point that if a personal profit requires a man having that quality to let the whole world be harmed, he would not renounce that profit but would consent to the harm of everyone in the world (Afghani 1968d, 151).

The dual nature of Afghani's discourse is but an indication of the roots of the contemporary discourses of modernity in the Middle East and the Islamic world. Thus, while the element of individual subjectivity and its potential universalization exist in this part of the world, the collectivist interpretation of subjectivity and the notion of Islam as a historical subject is a close parallel to a positivist subjectivity that can impede the development of universalizable subjectivity and the development of democratic citizenship in the region.[12] The history of the twentieth century has shown how the notions of collectivist subjectivity and the historicism of an abstract subjectivity embodied in the idea of an ethnic group and a social class, or now a religious tradition, may lead to totalitarian ends. On the other hand, the work of Critical Theory has explained the reification and discontents associated with unsituated subjectivity.[13] The effort to sublate and reinsert the subject of modernity, whether in its atomistic incarnation in liberalism, or as the collectivist and historicist configuration, in a larger universality, is the task of contemporary critical theorists. Keeping this in mind, the relevance of Critical Theory to the current conditions of the Middle East and the Islamic world in general, where a notion of subjectivity in its various and complex dimensions is emerging, becomes clear—notwithstanding the misgivings of critical theorists themselves and other skeptics. In a similar vein, the power that Critical Theory possesses to expose the ideologies undergirding various types of domination based on class, gender, and religious affiliation, among others, which have been reinforced as a result of privileging the appropriation of dominative aspects of modernity in the Middle East, can potentially lend support to efforts in the creation of civil society and more democratic polities in the region.

NOTES

1. The thrust of Horkheimer and Adorno's argument in the *Dialectic of Enlightenment* was that modern subjectivity in order to enthrone itself has in the process objectified itself and thus annulled its own subjectivity: "Man's domination over himself, which grounds his selfhood, is almost always the destruction of the subject in whose service it is undertaken . . . ," 54.

2. On the dialectical relations between the two categories of subjectivity and universality and Hegel's attempt at a substantive synthesis between them see Taylor (1979). Also see Cahoone (1987); Kolb (1986); and Dallmayr (1993).

3. For a discussion of the contemporary debates regarding the efforts to embed the unbridled subject of modernity without compromising the freedom of subjectivity, see Benhabib (1986 and 1992).

4. For discussions of the Axial Civilization, see Shmuel Eisenstadt, ed. (1986).

5. For the notion of "mediated subjectivity" and discourse of the main architects of the Islamic Revolution in Iran, see Vahdat (2002).

6. In the case of Khomeini and Motahhari, this vacillation is discussed in terms of the problem of theodicy in which they struggle with the notions of Divine Justice, Will, and Sovereignty as opposed to notions of human volition, action, and sovereignty. The way they propose out of this aporia is a conceptualization of human subjectivity and sovereignty *subsumed* under Divine Subjectivity, notwithstanding the contradictions of such formulation.

7. Much in conformity with the characteristics of mediated subjectivity, i.e., contradiction, the Constitution of the Islamic Republic only allows "half-rights" for individuals as citizens, but never denies them in toto. Sovereignty does not belong to people even though they are assumed to be in charge of their own destiny (Articles 2 and 6). The right to legislate also exclusively belongs to God, while there are the provisions for a parliament whose members are the elected representatives of the people and legislation is approved by this body (Articles 2 and 58). In this constitution, the anti-democratic notion of the "Governance of the Jurist" is institutionalized. According to Article 107, the highest Jurist in the land is appointed as the Supreme Leader of the country. But the people elect an "Assembly of Experts," which in turn will *select* a jurist among the qualified jurists to be the Supreme Leader. Once the Supreme Leader is appointed he is only responsible to God, yet he could be dismissed by the same Assembly of Experts if he no longer fits the criteria for qualification. Moreover, while the Supreme Leader has vast powers under his command, there is a President who is elected by popular vote and responsible to the people (Article 24). Article 4 gives the power to run the affairs of the country to the Guardian Council, which consists of a body of twelve men appointed by the Supreme Leader and the head of the Judiciary who is himself appointed by the Supreme Leader. At the same time Article 6 recognizes people's rights to participate in the affairs of the country. Freedom of the press, publica-

tion, and unarmed gathering are guaranteed in this Constitution, provided they are not "detrimental to fundamental principles of Islam" (Articles 24 and 27).

8. The unfolding of the internal dynamism of mediated subjectivity in the revolutionary Islamic discourse has given rise to two mostly opposing discourses in the postrevolutionary Iran. The current intellectual milieu can be characterized as a bifurcation of the ambivalence associated with mediated subjectivity, resulting in a bipolar view of subjectivity and of citizenship in the postrevolutionary period. As it seems now, these two tendencies have adopted the opposite poles that were simultaneously present in the revolutionary Islamic discourse of 1970s and early 1980s and have brought them to their logical conclusions. The trend primarily articulated by Abdolkarim Sorush, drawing heavily on Karl Popper, represents the affirmative moment of mediated subjectivity and strives to posit human subjectivity—and eventually intersubjectivity and its political embodiment as universal citizenship—even though it takes a detour from the path pursued by its intellectual predecessors. The opposite trend, represented by Davari Ardakani, and influenced primarily by an antimodern interpretation of Heidegger, has elaborated on the negative side of the Islamic revolutionary discourse and attempted to eliminate the humanist element in contemporary Iran, while upholding the antidemocratic doctrine and the related institution of the "Governance of the Jurist." Of course, neither of these trends is confined to the theoretical level and both have engendered sociopolitical discourses of their own, taking truly opposite positions regarding the process of sociopolitical democratization in the postrevolutionary Iran. For a discussion of these postrevolutionary developments, see Boroujerdi (1994 and 1996).

9. In his private life and his intersts in "Islamic" learning, Afghani engaged in some quite unorthodox behavior, which caused much friction with the established religious figures. See Keddie (1968) for Afghani's biography and his interests in philosophy, which was frowned upon by the Islamic doctors.

10. Interestingly enough this essay has never been translated into Persian or other Islamic languages, thus veiling the heterodox and antireligious thoughts of Afghani from his Muslim audiences.

11. Neicheris were the followers of Sir Ahmad Khan (1817–1897) of India and the term "Neicheri" was derived from the English word "nature," which Afghani used as a generic term representing unorthodox views and atheism. See Keddie (1968) for more details.

12. For an analysis of Islam as a historical subject in the contemporary discourse of Islamists, or the so-called Islamic Fundamentalists, see Aziz Al-Azmeh (1993), chapters 1 and 2.

13. See Taylor (1979), especially 154–66.

REFERENCES

Afghani, Sayyid Jamal al-Din. 1958. *Ara' va Mu'taqedat Sayyid Jamal al-Din Afghani* [The Opinions and Beliefs of Sayyid Jamal al-Din Afghani]. Edited by Morteza Modaresi. Tehran: Eqbal.

———. 1968a. "Lecture on Teaching and Learning." In Nikki Keddie, trans., *An Islamic Response to Imperialism: Political and Religious Writings of Sayyid Jamal ad-Din "al-Afghani."* Los Angeles: University of California Press.

———. 1968b. "The Benefits of Philosophy." In Nikki Keddie, trans., *An Islamic Response to Imperialism: Political and Religious Writings of Sayyid Jamal ad-Din "al-Afghani."* Los Angeles: University of California Press.

———. 1968c. "Answer of Jamal ad-Din to Renan, *Journal des Debatas.* May 18, 1883." In Nikki Keddie, trans., *An Islamic Response to Imperialism: Political and Religious Writings of Sayyid Jamal ad-Din "al-Afghani."* Los Angeles: University of California Press.

———. 1968d. "The Truth about the Neicheri Sect and an Explanation of the Neicheris." In Nikki Keddie, trans., *An Islamic Response to Imperialism: Political and Religious Writings of Sayyid Jamal ad-Din "al-Afghani."* Los Angeles: University of California Press.

Al-Azmeh, Aziz. 1993. *Islams and Modernities.* London: Verso.

Benhabib, Seyla. 1986. *Critique, Norm, and Utopia: A Study on the Foundations of Critical Theory.* New York: Columbia University Press.

———. 1992. *Situating the Self: Gender, Community, and Postmodernism in Contemporary Ethics.* New York: Routledge.

Boroujerdi, Mehrzad. 1996. *Iranian Intellectuals and the West: The Tormented Triumph of Nativism.* Syracuse: Syracuse University Press.

———. 1994. "The Encounter of Post-Revolutionary Thought in Iran with Hegel, Heidegger, and Popper." In *Cultural Transitions in the Middle East.* Edited by Serif Mardin. Leiden: E. J. Brill.

Cahoone, Lawrence E. 1987. *The Dilemma of Modernity: Philosophy, Culture and Anti-Culture.* Albany: State University of New York Press.

Dallmayr, Fred R. 1993. *G.W.F Hegel: Modernity and Politics.* Newbury Park, Calif.: Sage.

Eisenstadt, Shmuel, ed. 1986. *The Origins and the Diversity of Axial Age Civilizations.* Albany: State University of New York Press.

Habermas, Jürgen. 1981. *The Theory of Communicative Action. Vol. 1. Reason and the Rationalization of the Society.* Boston: Beacon Press.

———. 1984. *The Theory of Communicative Action. Vol. 2. Lifeworld and System: A Critique of Functionalist Reason.* Boston: Beacon Press.

———. 1990. *The Philosophical Discourse of Modernity: Twelve Lectures.* Cambridge, Mass.: MIT Press.

Hegel, Georg Wilhelm Friedrich. 1967. *Hegel's Philosophy of Right.* Oxford: Oxford University Press.

Horkheimer, Max, and Theodor Adorno. 1997. *Dialectic of Enlightenment.* New York: Continuum.

Karimi-Hakkak, Ahmad. 1995. *Recasting Persian Poetry: Scenarios of Poetic Modernity in Iran.* Salt Lake City: University of Utah Press.

Keddie, Nikki. 1968. *An Islamic Response to Imperialism: Political and Religious Writings of Sayyid Jamal ad-Din "al-Afghani."* Los Angeles: University of California Press.

Khomeini, Ruhollah. 1985. *Simay-e Zan Dar Kalam-e Imam Khomeini* [The Image of Woman in the Discourse of Imam Khomeini]. Tehran: The Ministry of Islamic Guidance.

Khuri, Richard. 1998. *Freedom, Modernity, and Islam: Toward a Creative Synthesis.* Syracuse: Syracuse University Press.

Kolb, David. 1986. *The Critique of Pure Modernity: Hegel, Heidegger, and After.* Chicago: University of Chicago Press.

Lee, Robert Deemer. 1997. *Overcoming Tradition and Modernity: The Search for Islamic Authenticity.* Boulder, Colo.: Westview Press.

Martin, Vanessa. 1989. *Islam and Modernism: The Iranian Revolution of 1906.* Syracuse: Syracuse University Press.

Rejali, Darius. 1994. *Torture and Modernity: Self, Society, and State in Modern Iran.* Boulder, Colo.: Westview Press.

Salvatore, Armando. 1997. *Islam and the Political Discourse of Modernity.* Reading: Ithaca.

Shariati, Ali. 1977. *Bazgasht be Khish* [Return to the Self]. n.p.

Taylor, Charles. 1979. *Hegel and Modern Society.* Cambridge: Cambridge University Press.

Tibi, Bassam. 1995. "Culture and Knowledge: The Politics of Islamization of Knowledge as a Postmodern Project? The Fundamentalist Claim to De-westernization." *Theory, Culture, and Society,* vol. 12.

Vahdat, Farzin. 2002. *God and Juggernaut: Iran's Intellectual Encounter with Modernity.* Syracuse: Syracuse University Press.

Wallerstein, Immanuel. 1998. "Is Sociology a World Discipline?" *Contemporary Sociology* 127, no. 4 (July).

· 8 ·

Second Letter on Algeria

Alexis de Tocqueville

*S*uppose, Sir, for a moment that the emperor of China, landing on the shores of France and at the head of a powerful army, made himself master of our greatest cities and of our capital. And after having destroyed all of the public registers before even having given himself the pain of reading them, destroyed or dispersed all administrators without acquainting himself with their various attributes, he finally rids himself of all state officials from the head of the government to the *gardes champêtres,* the peers, the deputies, and in general of the entire ruling class; and that he exiled them all at once to some faraway country. Do you not think that this great prince, in spite of his powerful army, his fortresses, and his fortune, would soon find himself rather bothered in administering the conquered land; that his new subjects, bereft of all those who did or could manage political affairs, would be incapable of governing themselves, while he, coming from the opposite side of the Earth, knows neither the religion, nor the language, nor the laws, nor the customs, nor the administrative procedures of the country and who took care to send away all of those who could have instructed him in these matters, will be in no position to rule them? You will therefore have no difficulty in seeing, Sir, that if the regions of France that are effectively occupied by the conqueror were to obey him, the rest of the country would soon be left to an immense anarchy.[1]

You will see, Sir, that we have done in Algeria precisely what I supposed the emperor of China would do in France. In spite of the fact that the coast of Africa is separated from Provence by only about 160 leagues of sea, that there are published each year in Europe the accounts of several thousands of voyages

This selection was translated by Valery DeLame, Rutgers University. This translation is taken from volume III of the Écrits et Discours Politiques *from the* Oeuvres Complètes, *edited by André Jardin: Editions Gallimard, 1962, pp. 139–53.*

to all parts of the world, that here we study assiduously all of the languages of antiquity that are no longer spoken as well as several living languages that we never have the occasion of speaking, we could not meanwhile face the profound ignorance in which we lived, not more than seven years ago, on all that could concern Algeria: we had no clear notion of the different races that lived there, nor of their customs, we did not know a word of the languages that these people speak; the country itself, its resources, its rivers, its cities, its climate were unknown to us; one could have thought that the whole breadth of the world lay in between us. We know so little even of what regarded warfare, though this was the issue of greatest concern to us at this time, that our generals thought they would be attacked by a cavalry similar to that of the mameluks of Egypt, whereas our main enemy, the Turks of Algiers, have never fought on anything but on foot. It is in ignorance of all of these things that we set sail, which did not stop us from conquering, because on the battlefield victory is to the bravest and the strongest and not to the most knowledgeable. But, after the fighting, it did not take us long to see that to rule a nation it does not suffice to have conquered it.

You remember, Sir, that I had told you previously that the whole government, civil and military, of the Regency was in the hands of the Turks. Barely had we become the masters of Algiers that we hurried to gather all of the Turks without forgetting a single one, from the *Dey* to the last soldier of his militia, and we transported this crowd to the coast of Asia. In order to better eliminate the vestiges of the enemy domination, we took care earlier to tear up or burn all written documents, administrative registers, official or unofficial evidence, that could have kept alive a trace of what had been done before us.[2] The conquest was a new era, and from fear of mixing in an irrational way the past with the present, we even destroyed a great number of the streets of Algiers, with the purpose of rebuilding them according to our methods, and gave French names to all of those that we agreed to conserving. I think, in truth, Sir, that the Chinese of whom I spoke earlier could not have done better.

What is the result of all of this? You can guess without difficulty. The Turkish government owned in Algiers a great many houses and in the plains a multitude of domains; but its property titles disappeared in the universal wreck of the old order of things. It was found that the French administration, knowing neither what it owned nor what had remained in the legitimate possession of the conquered, was wanting of everything or thought itself reduced to appropriating haphazard what it needed, in spite of law and rights.

The Turkish government peacefully collected the fruit of certain taxes that out of ignorance we were not able to levy in its place, and we were forced to take the money that we needed from France or to extort it from our unfortunate subjects with methods much more Turkic than any the Turks had ever employed. If our ignorance was such that the French government became illegitimate and oppressor in Algiers, it also rendered all government outside of itself impossible.

The French had sent the *Caïds* of the *outans* back to Asia. They ignored completely the name, composition, and usage of that arab militia which, as composed of auxiliaries, was used as police and levied taxes under the Turks, and that was called, as I have said, the cavalry of the *Marzem*. They had no idea concerning the division of tribes. They did not know of the existence of the military aristocracy of the *Spahis*,[3] and, of the *marabouts*, it took them quite long to figure out, that when talking of them, one could mean a tomb[4] or a man.[5]

The French did not know any of these things, and to tell the truth, they hardly preoccupied themselves with learning them. In the place of an administration that they had destroyed down to its roots, they imagined they would substitute, in the districts we had occupied militarily, the French administration.

Try, Sir, I implore you, to picture these agile and untamable children of the desert ensnared in the thousand formalities of our bureaucracy and forced to submit themselves to the inertia, the formality, to the writings and the trifling details of our centralization. We conserved from the old government of the country only the usage of the yatagan and of the stick as ways to police. All of the rest became French. This applies to the cities and to the tribes that are tied to them. As far as the rest of the inhabitants of the Regency, we did not even try to administer them. After having destroyed their government, we gave them no other.

I would be leaving the framework that I had laid out if I took it upon myself to write the history of what has happened for the last seven years in Africa. I only wish to prepare the reader to understand it.

For the 300 years that the Arabs living in Algeria were submitted to the Turks, they had entirely lost the impulse to rule themselves. The leaders among them had been distanced from political affairs by the jealousy of the dominators; the *marabout* dismounted his horse to climb onto a donkey. The Turkish government was a detestable government, but after all it maintained a certain order and, though it tacitly authorized wars between the tribes, it reduced theft and made roads safe. It was furthermore the only link that existed between the diverse peoples, the center at which ended so many divergent rays.

The Turkish government destroyed, with nothing replacing it, the country that could not yet govern itself fell into a terrible anarchy. All of the tribes fell upon one another in an immense confusion, robbery organized everywhere. The very shadow of justice disappeared and each resorted to force.

This applies to the Arabs. As far as the Cabyles, since they were almost independent from the Turks, the fall of the Turks produced only few effects on them. They stayed vis-à-vis the new masters in an arrangement nearly analogous to the one that they had taken with the former. Only that they became even more inclusive, the inborn hate that they had for strangers coming to combine with the religious horror that they had for Christians whose language, laws, and customs were unknown to them. Men submit themselves sometimes to humiliation, to tyranny, to conquest, but never for long do they suffer anarchy. There is no people so barbarous as to escape this general law of humanity.

When the Arabs, whom we often looked to vanquish and submit to our will, but never to govern, were subjected for a while to savage intoxication given birth by individual independence, they began to search instinctively to remake what the French had destroyed. We quickly saw appear among them entrepreneurial and ambitious men. Great talents revealed themselves in some of their chieftains, and the multitudes began to herald certain names as symbols of order.

The Turks had pushed the religious aristocracy of the Arabs away from the use of arms and the direction of public affairs. The Turks destroyed, we saw it almost immediately once again become warlike and governing. The most rapid effect, and also the most certain, of our conquest was to give back to the *marabouts* the political existence that they had lost. They again took up Mohamed's scimitar to fight the infidels and soon used it to govern their fellow citizens: this is a great fact and one which must draw the attention of all those who concern themselves with Algeria.

We have let the national aristocracy of the Arabs be reborn, it is only left to us to use it. To the west of the province of Algiers, near the frontiers of the empire of Morocco, was living since long ago a family of very famous *marabouts*. Its lineage led straight back to Mohamed himself, and its name was venerated throughout the Regency. At the time when the French took possession of the country, the head of this family was an old man named Mahidin. In addition to his illustrious birth, Mahidin joined the advantage of having been to Mecca and a long history of being energetically opposed to the Turks. His saintliness was greatly venerated and his abilities well known. Once the tribes of the surrounding area began to feel the intolerable malaise which the absence of power causes in men, they went to find Mahidin and proposed to him that he take charge of their affairs. The old man had them gather in a large plain; there, he told them that at his age one had to concern himself with the sky and not the Earth, that he refused their offer, but he urged them to bring their suffrage to one of his youngest sons, which he brought before them. At length he enumerated the qualifications of this one to govern his compatriots; his precocious piety, his pilgrimage to the Holy Lands, his descendance from the Prophet; he made known several striking signs of which the sky had made use to designate him among his brothers and he proved that all the ancient prophecies that announced a liberator to the Arabs manifestly applied to him. The tribes proclaimed by unanimous agreement the son of *Mahidin emir-el-mouminin*, that is to say, leader of the believers.

This young man, who then was only twenty-five years old and of a frail appearance was named Abd-el-Kader.[6] Such is the origin of this unique leader; anarchy gave birth to his power, anarchy developed it without respite and, with the grace of God and our own,[7] after having given him the province of Oran and that of Tittery, it put Constantine in his hands and made him much more powerful than the Turkish government that he replaced had ever been.

While these events took place in the west of the Regency, the east offered another spectacle. In the time when the French took Algiers, Constantine Province was being governed by a bey named Achmet. This bey, contrary to all custom, was *coulougli*, meaning the son of a Turkish father and an Arab mother. It was a particular stroke of luck that allowed him, after the taking of Algiers, to stay in power in Constantine with the support of his father's compatriots and later to found his power on the surrounding tribes with the help of his mother's parents and friends.

While all the the rest of the Regency abandoned by the Turks and not occupied by the French fell into the greatest disorder, a certain quality of government therefore was maintained in the provinces of Constantine and Achmet by his courage, his cruelty, and his energy; there was founded the empire, solid enough, that we look to restrain or destroy today.[8]

Therefore, at this very moment, three powers are present on the soil of Algeria: In Algiers and on various points on the coast, are the French; in the west and to the south an Arab population that after three hundred years awakens and follows a national leader; in the east, the rump Turkish government, represented by Achmet, a stream that continues to run after the source has dried and will soon itself dry up or lose itself in the great flood of Arab nationality. Between these three forces and as though enveloped from all sides by them, meet an array of minor *Cabyles* peoples, who escape from any and all influences and play off of all governments. It would be pointless to extensively research what the French should have done in the time of conquest.

We can only say in a few words that we should have at first simply settled there, and as much as our civilization would permit it, in the place of the conquered; that, far from wanting from the beginning to substitute our administrative procedures for their own, we should have for awhile adapted our own, maintained political limitations, taken control of the agents of the defunct government, included its traditions and continued to use its procedures. Instead of exiling the Turks to the coast of Asia, it is obvious that we should have taken care to keep the greatest number of them among us; bereft of their leaders, incapable of governing on their own, and fearing the resentment of their former subjects, they would not have waited to become our most useful intermediaries and our most zealous friends, as were the *coulouglis* though they were much closer to the Arabs than were the Turks but nevertheless have almost always favored throwing themselves into our arms rather than theirs. Once we had known the language, prejudices, and the customs of the Arabs, after having inherited the respect that men always hold for an established government, it would have become possible for us to return little by little to our customs, and to galicize the country around us. But today that the mistakes are irrevocably committed, what is there left to do? And what reasonable hopes should we conceive?

We first distinguish with care between the two great races of which we have spoken further above, the *Cabyles* and the Arabs. When speaking of the *Cabyles*, it is visible that[9] there can be no question of conquering their country or colonizing it: their mountains are, as of now, impenetrable to our armies, and the inhospitable disposition of the inhabitants leaves no security to the isolated European who would there peacefully go to make himself a home. The country of the *Cabyles* is closed to us, but the soul of the *Cabyles* is open to us and it is not impossible for us to penetrate it.

I saw previously that the *Cabyle* was more positive, less religious, infinitely less enthusiastic than the Arab. In the life of the *Cabyles* the individual is nearly everything, the society nearly nothing, and they are just as far from bending themselves uniformly to the laws of a single government taken from their heart than to adopt our own.

The great passion of the *Cabyle* is the love of material joys, and it is through this that we can and must capture him. Though given that the *Cabyles* let us penetrate their society much less than do the Arabs, they show themselves much less inclined to make war on us. And even when a few of them raise arms against us, the others do not stop frequenting our markets and still come rent us their services. The cause of this is that they have already discovered the material profit that they can get out of our being neighbors. They find it greatly advantageous to come sell us their goods and to buy those of ours that can be useful to the kind of civilization that they possess. And, while they are not yet in a state to achieve our well-being, it is already easy to see that they admire it and that they would find it very sweet to enjoy it.

It is obvious that it is by our arts and not by our arms that we will tame such men. If frequent and peaceful relations continue to be established between us and the *Cabyles*; that the first do not have to fear our ambition and encounter among us a legislation that is simple, clear, and which they are sure will grant for their protection, it is certain that soon they will fear war more even than we do and that this almost invincible attraction that draws natives toward civilized man from the moment that they no longer fear for their liberty will be felt. We will see then that the habits and ideas of the *Cabyles* change without their realizing it, and the barriers closing their country off to us will fall on their own.

The role that we have to play vis-à-vis the Arabs is more complicated and more difficult. The Arabs are not solidly fixed in one place and their soul is even more nomadic than are their dwellings. Though they are passionately attached to their liberty, they adopted a strong government, and they are keen to form a great nation. And, though[10] they show themselves to be very sensual, immaterial joys are of great value in their eyes, and at every moment the imagination wisks them away toward some ideal good that she discovers for them.

With the *Cabyles*, it is most important to be concerned with questions of civil and commercial equity, with the Arabs of political and religious questions. There is a certain number of Arab tribes that we can and must govern directly from this moment on and a greater number upon which we must, for the time being, want to obtain only an indirect influence.

After three hundred years the power of the Turks established itself only incompletely over tribes remote from the cities. The Turks nevertheless were Islamic like the Arabs, had habits similar to theirs and had managed to remove the religious aristocracy from public affairs. It is easy to see that what with us not having any of these advantages and being faced with much greater difficulties, we cannot hope to obtain the level of influence on these tribes that the Turks had nor even approach it. On this point our immense military superiority is almost useless. It makes it possible for us to win, but not to keep under our laws nomadic populations that when the need arises will go deep into the desert where we cannot follow them, leaving us in the middle of the desert where we could not survive.

The object of all our present efforts must be to live in peace with those of the Arabs that we have no present hope of being able to govern, and to organize them in the manner least dangerous to our future gains.

The anarchy of the Arabs, which is so deleterious to these peoples, is vastly damaging to us, because having neither the will nor the power to submit them all at once by our arms, we can hope only to act on them indirectly through contact with our ideas and our arts; which can take place only to the extent that peace and a certain order reign among them. The anarchy pushes these tribes one on the other, throws them without end on us and robs our frontiers of all security.

We have then a great interest in recreating a government among these people and it is perhaps not impossible to succeed in making it so that this government depends partly on us. Today that the scepter has just left the hands that held it since three centuries ago, no one has an incontestable right to govern nor a good chance now at founding an uncontested power that will last. All of the powers that will establish themselves in Africa will therefore be unstable, and if our support is given with resolution, with justice, and with consistency, the new sovereigns will constantly be driven to resort to it. They will therefore depend in part on us.

We have to aim before anything else at accustoming these independent Arabs to seeing us meddle in their interior affairs and at making ourselves familiar to them. Because we must realize that a powerful and civilized people such as our own exercises solely by virtue of the superiority of its luminaries an almost invincible force on small, more or less barbarous peoples; and that, to force these to incorporate themselves with it, it only needs to be able to establish sutainable relations with them.

But if we have an interest in creating a government with the Arabs of the Regency, we have a much more visible interest in not letting only one government establish itself there. For then the peril would be far greater than the advantage. It is without a doubt very important for us not to leave the Arabs subject to anarchy, but it is even more important for us to not expose ourselves to seeing them aligned all at once against us.

It is with this point of view that the last treaty with Abd-el-Kader and the expedition planned for Constantine are of a nature to arouse certain fears. Nothing is more desirable than to establish and legitimize the power of the new emir in the province of Oran where his power was already strong. But the treaty concedes to him in addition the government of the *beylik* of Tittery and I cannot stop myself from believing that the expedition that is in preparation will have for a final result of delivering to him the greater part of the province of Constantine.

We can be sure that with the extent of power that Abd-el-Kader has achieved, all of the Arab populations that find themselves without a leader will go to him of their own volition. It is therefore imprudent to destroy or even undermine the Arab powers independent of Abd-el-Kader; it would be better to think of bringing some about if there are not some already. In opposition to all of this, if our campaign in Constantine succeeds, as we have every reason to believe it will, it can only result in destroying Achmet without putting anything in his place. We will overthrow the *coulougli* and we will not be able to succeed him nor give him an Arab successor. Our victory will therefore deliver the tribes that are under Achmet to an independence that they will not wait long to sacrifice in the hands of the emir who neighbors them. We will make anarchy and anarchy will make the power of Abd-el-Kader.

This is what we can foresee from a distance and with our ignorance of the details. What it is possible to affirm from now with certitude is that we cannot suffer that all of the Arab tribes of the Regency ever recognize the same leader. It is already far too little with two. Our present security, and the care for our future, demands that we have at least three or four.

Independently of the tribes over which it is in our interest to look only to exercise, for now, an indirect influence, there is also a considerable part of the country that our security as well as our honor oblige us to keep under our immediate forces and to govern without an intermediary.

This is the case where we find a French population and an Arab population that must be made to live peacefully in the same region. The difficulty is great. I am far from believing it, however, to be insurmountable. I do not pretend to engage here, Sir, with you in a discussion on the specific means that we could use to reach this goal. It is enough for me to indicate in broad terms what appears to me to be the principal conditions of success. It is obvious for me that we will never succeed if we take it upon ourselves to submit our new Algerian subjects to the rules of the French administration.

We do not impose without consequences new concepts in the realm of political customs. We are more enlightened and more powerful than the Arabs, it is for us to bend at first to a certain point to their ways of life and prejudices. In Algeria as elsewhere, the main duty of a new government is not to create what does not exist, but to use what does. The Arabs lived in tribes two thousand years ago in Yemen; they traversed all of Africa and invaded Spain in tribes, they still live this way in our day. Tribal organization, which is the most tenacious of all human institutions, could not therefore be taken from them now nor long from now without sending a shock through all of their sentiments and ideas. The Arabs appoint their own chiefs, it is necessary to let them keep this privilege. They have a military and religious aristocracy, we should not look to destroy it, but to use it as had done the Turks. Not only is it useful to draw from among the political customs of the Arabs, but it is necessary to modify the rules regarding their civil rights only little by little. For you will know, Sir, that the majority of these rules are outlined in the Koran in such a way that with the Muslims civil and religious law are confused without end.

We must be careful most importantly of all in giving ourselves over to this taste for uniformity that torments us and acknowledge that to dissimilar beings it would be just as dangerous as it is absurd to apply the same legislation. In the time of the fall of the Roman Empire, we saw reign at the same time barbaric laws to which the Barbar was submitted and Roman laws to which the Roman was submitted. This model is a good one to follow, it is only in this way that we can hope to pass without perishing through the period of transition that takes place before two peoples of different civilizations can come to meld into a single whole.

Once Frenchmen and Arabs live in the same district, we must resolve to apply to each the legislation that he can understand and has learned to respect.

That the political leader be the same for both races, but that for long all of the rest differ, the fusion will come later on its own.

It would be quite necessary as well that the legislation that governs the French in Africa not be exactly the same as the one operating in France. An emerging people can hardly tolerate the same administrative hassles as an old people, and the same slow and multiplied formalities that guarantee at times the security of the latter prevent the former from developing and nearly from being born.

We need in Africa as much as in France, and more than in France, fundamental guarantees for the man who lives in society; there is not a country where it is more necessary to establish individual liberty, respect for property, and the guarantee of all rights than in a colony. But on the other hand a colony needs a simpler administration, more expeditious and more independent from the central power than the one that governs the continental provinces of the empire.

It is therefore necessary to retain with care in Algeria the substance of our political state, but to not hold on too superstitiously to its form; and to show more respect for the spirit than for the letter. Those who have visited Algeria claim the opposite is happening: they say that the smallest details of the administrative methods of the mother country are there scrupulously observed and that often are forgotten the great principles that serve as a foundation for our laws. In acting like this we can hope to increase the number of public officials, but not of colonists.

I imagine, Sir, that now that I reach the end of this too-long letter, you are tempted to ask me, after all, my hopes for the future of our new colony.

This future appears to me to be in our hands, and I will tell you sincerely that with time, perseverance, ability and justice, I do not doubt that we could erect on the coast of Africa a great monument to the glory of our country. I have told you, Sir, that in the beginning the Arabs were both pastoralists and agriculturists, and that, though they possess all of the land, they only cultivate a negligable part of it. The Arab population is then widely dispersed, it occupies much more land than it can sow every year. The result of this is that the Arabs part with their land willingly and at a low price and that a foreign population can without difficulty settle at their side without their suffering from it.

You then understand from this, Sir, how easy it is for the French, who are richer and more industrious than the Arabs to occupy without violence a large part of the land and to introduce themselves peacefully and in great numbers all the way to the heart of the tribes that neighbor them. It is easy to see ahead to a time in the near future when the two races will be intermingled in this way in many parts of the Regency. But it is hardly enough for the French to place themselves at the side of the Arabs if they do not manage to establish a lasting bond with them and in the end form from these two races a single people.

Everything that I have learned of Algeria leads me to believe that this outcome is nowhere as chimerical as many people suppose.

The majority of Arabs still have a spirited faith in the religion of Mohamed; meanwhile it is easy to see in this Muslim part of the territory, as in all others, that religious beliefs constantly lose their vigor and become more and more powerless to fight against the interests of this world. Though religion has played a large role in the wars that we have made up to now in Africa, and that they have served as a pretext to the *marabouts* for taking up their arms once again, we can say that can only be attributed as a secondary cause for these wars. We have been attacked much more as foreigners and conquerors than as Christians and the ambition of leaders more than the faith of the people has put arms into hands against us.[11] Every time that patriotism or ambition does not carry the Arabs against us, experience has shown that religion did not stop them from becoming our most zealous auxiliaries, and, under our flag, they make as brutal of a war against others of their own religion as these make against us.

It is therefore possible to believe that if we prove more and more that under our domination or in our vicinity Islam is not in danger, religious passions will extinguish themselves, and we will only have political enemies in Africa. We would also be wrong to think that the Arab way of life would make them incapable of adapting to life in a community shared with us.

In Spain, the Arabs were sedentary and agricultural; in the areas surrounding the cities of Algeria, there is a great number among them who build houses and seriously devote themselves to agriculture. The Arabs are not naturally nor necessarily pastoralists. It is true that as one approaches the desert, one gradually sees houses disappear and the tents erected. But it is because as one moves away from the coasts security of property and person diminishes and that, for a people who fear for their existence and for their liberty, there is nothing more convenient than a nomadic way of life. I understand that Arabs like better to wander in the outside air than to stay exposed to the tyranny of a master, but everything tells me that if they could be free, respected, and sedentary, they would not wait to settle themselves. I do not doubt that they would soon take up our way of life if we gave them a lasting interest in doing so.

Nothing finally in the known facts indicates to me that there is incompatibility of sentiment between the Arabs and ourselves. I see on the contrary, that in times of peace, the two races mingle without difficulty, and that as they get to know one another, the distance between them lessens. Every day the

French develop clearer and more just notions on the inhabitants of Algeria. They learn their languages, familiarize themselves with their customs and we even see some who show a certain spontaneous enthusiasm for them. In addition, the whole of the younger generation of Arabs in Algiers speaks our language and has already in part adopted our customs.

When it was a question in the area surrounding Algiers of defense against robbery by a few enemy tribes, we saw form a national guard composed of Arabs and Frenchmen who joined the same units and who together shared the same exhaustions and dangers.[12]

There is therefore no reason to believe that time cannot succeed in amalgamating the two races. God does not prevent it; only the faults of men could put an obstacle in its way. Let us not therefore lose hope for the future, Sir. Let us not allow ourselves to be stopped by temporary sacrifices while an immense objective comes to light that with perseverant efforts can be reached.

NOTES

1. Tocqueville here seems to be paraphrasing the famous parable of St. Simon.

2. Gabriel Esquer, *Les commencement d'un Empire. La prise d'Alger.* Alger, 123, pp. 428–31. The author notes that the occupation of Algiers by French troops was achieved with great disorder, that they neglected to gather administrative, and that many soldiers lit their pipes with government papers. To establish the ownership of properties and of public revenue, it was necessary to take the word of claimants.

3. Originally, the term *spahi* (from the Persian *sipahi*, from which the word *cipaye* in India is also derived) simply designated a soldier. But, in the Ottoman Empire, the name was reserved for a corps of irregular cavalrymen, then for the elite cavalry. The Turks organized formations of these cavaliers in Northern Africa.

4. *Note Tocqueville.* The *Marabouts* give hospitality near the tomb of their direct ancestor, and this place bears the name of he who is buried there. From this came the error.

5. The notion of marabout is much more imprecise than thinks here Tocqueville: not only a tomb, but also a pile of rocks, and storks, etc., can be "marabout." Cf. Doutté, *Les Marabouts,* Paris, 1900.

6. Mahiedin, father of Abd-el-Kader, belonged to the *Hachem* tribe and was a *marabout* venerated by the powerful brotherhood of the *Kadria*. Once the tribes in the west of Algeria decided to fight against the French settled in Oran, they thought of putting him in command. But at the Essebieh Reunion near Mascara (November 22, 1832), he, enlightened by a dream, had his son Abd-el-Kader, who had just reached twenty-four years of age, nominated in his place.

7. The Treaty of Desmichels, February 26, 1834, named after the general commanding the forces in Oran, affirmed from the beginning the power of Abd-el-Kader by recognizing his title of emir, in not determining precisely the territorial limits of his

power nor the precise obligations of a vassal state; the treaty of Tafna signed by Bugeaut on May 20, 1837, ratified it by ceding him the province of Oran and the Tittery.

8. On El Hadj-Ahmed, bey of Constantine from 1826 to 1837, his tyranny and his cupidity, but also his qualities as a leader, see E. Mercier, *Histoire de Constantine,* Constantine, 1903, pp. 371–436. For his rapports with France in 1837, see above p. 129, n.2.

9. *Var.*: évident.

10. *Var.*: bien qu'ils.

11. In a study on the moral and intellectual state of Algeria in 1830 (*L'Etat intellectuel et moral de l'Algérie en 1830, Revue d'histoire moderne et contemporaine,* 1954, pp. 199–212), M. Marcel Emerit writes: "Many French and Arab witnesses tell us that the war did not have, at the beginning of French occupation, the character of a holy war. It was more a movement of resistance on the part of Arabs in the presence of soldiers from a foreign power to whom they had no reason of submitting."

12. Since December 24, 1830, Marshall (*Maréchal*) Clauzel had created in Algiers an urban guard to which could belong Frenchmen and those natives from twenty to sixty years old who owned property or industrial establishments. But from August 17, 1832, the Duke of Rovigo decided to admit to it only Frenchmen. On October 26, 1836, Clauzel, once again *directeur général,* went back on this decision by creating an African militia to which natives could be admitted with special permission.

·9·

A Wild Goose Chase:
To Cope, Must Islam "westernize"?

Nissim Rejwan

WHAT WESTERNIZATION INVOLVES

*I*n a rather jeering passage in *Life's Handicap*, published in 1891, Rudyard Kipling speaks of a certain type of Russian he had seemingly encountered in real life. "The Russian," Kipling observes, "is a delightful person till he tucks in his shirt. As an Oriental he is charming. It is only when he insists on being treated as the most easterly of western peoples instead of the most westerly of easterns that he becomes a racial anomaly extremely difficult to handle."

And one cannot help but wonder what, precisely, was Kipling's otherwise delightful Russian trying to do in so tucking in his shirt? Look more "modern"? Dress, walk, talk, and generally conduct himself like a westerner? In other words, what does it take, in Kipling's perception, to be "western"? Ceasing to be "eastern" ("the most easterly of western peoples instead of [pretending to be] the most westerly of easterners")?

Again, in terms of culture as the concept is understood today—namely, as the sum total of a people's way of life, comprising their modes of thinking, acting, and feeling as expressed, among other things, in religion, law, language, art, and custom, as well as in material products such as residences, clothes, and tools— was our modernizing-westernizing Russian friend trying—unsuccessfully, to be sure—to go through some sort of self-imposed culture cleansing? And how, if anything, can this help us in trying to appraise what is generally seen as the plight of the contemporary East in general and the world of Islam in particular? Much has been written on this and on related questions with regard to the state of Islam today, not least by Muslims themselves. What follows is a brief but comprehensive survey of theses and ideas on what I will call the modernization/ westernization controversy.

Muslims have always been aware of the fact that Islam is in some need of being "modernized." Some of the most prominent Muslim scholars and theologians began voicing their complaints and laments about the sorry state of their faith as far back as the last two decades of the eighteenth century. "With Muslims, determinism has come to stay and has gradually suppressed action," wrote Sheikh Rashid Rida, Egypt's leading theologian of his time, in the 1920s. "They call indolence trust in God," he added, "and the search for truth heresy. For them this is religion, and anyone who holds different views is exposed to abuse. Unquestioning acceptance of everything old is the heart of wisdom."[1]

One of Rida's contemporaries, Fat'hi Zaghlul, a leading thinker, writer, and translator, lamented: "We are weak compared to the nations of the West—weak in agriculture, commerce, industry, and science; in will and determination. . . . There is no chivalry among us any longer. Religious solidarity has gone and so have racial bonds. Our feet are too feeble for us to stand on our rights or do our duty. We are so weak that we do nothing ourselves; we ask the government instead."[2]

Despite these and a host of similar sentiments voiced throughout the past century, no significant changes or reforms have been made by way of coping with the problems posed by the modern world and its ways. The result has been, as Professor Bernard Lewis has put it in his recent, much-acclaimed book, *What Went Wrong?: Western Impact and Middle Eastern Response*, that, whatever the form and manner of the question of the title and of the answers that it evokes, "there is no mistaking the growing anguish, the mounting urgency, and of late the seething anger with which both question and answers are expressed."

And there is indeed good reason for questioning and concern, "even for anger;" for in the course of the last hundred years or so "it became abundantly clear in the Middle East and indeed in the lands of Islam that things had indeed gone badly wrong." The primacy and dominance of the West became clear for all to see, "invading the Muslim in every aspect of his public and—more painfully—even his private life."

Not that Muslims failed to make an effort, Lewis notes. There were indeed serious attempts, through reforms and, more recently, through revolution. All these efforts concentrated in three main areas—military, economic, and political—and all failed. As he puts it, "The quest for prosperity through development brought, in some countries, impoverished and corrupt economies in recurring need of external aid, in others an unhealthy dependence on a single resource—fossil fuels . . . doomed, sooner or later, to be exhausted or superceded."

Worst of all was the political result. "The long quest for freedom has left a string of shabby tyrannies, ranging from traditional autocracies to new style dictatorships, modern only in their apparatus of repression and indoctrination." Again, many remedies have been tried—weapons and factories, schools and parliaments—"but none achieved the desired results." Here and there they brought some alleviation, but "they failed to remedy or even to halt the deteriorating imbalance between Islam and the western world."[3]

One aspect of the subject that Lewis emphasizes is the distinction he draws between modernization and westernization, pointing out that, while "even the most extreme and most anti-western fundamentalists nowadays accept the need to modernize and indeed to make the fullest use of modern technology, especially the technologies of warfare and propaganda," they shun westernization. According to him, the difference between modernization and westernization is most pronounced in the subject of the emancipation of women. Whereas the introduction of such western innovations as modern technology, economic reforms, education, and political organization are seen as aspects of modernity, "the emancipation of women is westernization; both for traditional conservatives and radical fundamentalists it is neither necessary nor useful but noxious, a betrayal of true Islamic values. It must be kept from entering the body of Islam, and where it has already entered, it must be ruthlessly excised."[4]

This is an interesting distinction though obviously it needs some elaboration. I myself find that, generally speaking, the difference between modernization and westernization is seldom clear-cut. The proof Professor Lewis provides here is related to the subject of attire. "While the dividing line between westernization and modernization is difficult to establish in the attire of men," he writes, "it is very clear in that of women. Unlike soldiers and civil servants, women were never compelled to adopt western dress or to abandon traditional attire. . . . For men to wear western clothes, it would seem, is modernization; for women to wear them is westernization, to be welcomed or punished accordingly." Yet surely using the headscarf and the veil does not necessarily rule out the adoption of other aspects of westernization. Fully "westernized" Iranian women nowadays use them.

The whole subject of modernization and westernization, and whether the former cannot be accomplished without the latter, has been a point of discussion and controversy for some time now. To elaborate a little further on the argument made by the author of *What Went Wrong?*, however, it would be useful to turn to the explanations offered by David Pryce-Jones, author of *The Closed Circle: An Interpretation of the Arabs.*

In a long and comprehensive review of Lewis's book, in which he amplifies some of the points made there, Pryce-Jones agrees with the author's diagnosis, namely that "what has happened to most Muslim societies . . . is modernization without westernization." The sense of these two abstract nouns, he adds, must be carefully distinguished. "Modernization in the Muslim world has resulted in national armies, all ranks equipped with European-style uniforms and weaponry, and such other features as high-rise buildings and oil wells and paved roads and flyovers—in short, the outward appearances that are observed in any non-Muslim country. The novel and the theater and film-making are cultural forms successfully transplanted across the cultural divide, as are clocks and timetables and calendars. Voltaire at his estate of Ferney, it turns out, had men making watches for the Turkish market. But also in the package of imports are filing systems, computers, surveillance devices and other instruments of the tyrannical government which is the curse of the Muslim world at present. For the unfortunate man and woman in the Muslim street, modernization has no necessary connection with such integral features of the West as freedom, civil rights, or equality of opportunity." And he adds:

> Going beyond the mimicry of externals, westernization involves a change of thinking profound enough to shift the basic institutions and assumptions of social and political life. Westernization would replace autocracy and one-party rule with democracy and the rule of law; it would replace civil war and the secret police with power-sharing. Westernization means respect for the rights of others, in particular the acceptance of women on juridically equal terms with men. In a society in which the conduct of women is held to be the source of honor or shame for men, this latter reform is not merely an upturning of long-held values but a crude invasion of Muslim private life. In an aside, Lewis draws an analogy between soccer and parliamentary politics, both of which stem from the English genius for drawing up rules. The adoption of soccer in the Middle East is modernization. The adoption of parliamentary politics would be westernization. In another inspired aside, he takes the plot of Verdi's "Aida," commissioned by the khedive of Egypt in 1871, which turns on the choice tormenting the opera's hero between two women he loves. This would have been meaningless in the Egypt of the day, or in Saudi Arabia today, where the hero could have had both ladies legally.[5]

Pryce-Jones also has some thoughts of his own to offer on the question of what went wrong with the Muslim world. "Lack of intellectual curiosity is in itself a fatal flaw," he writes, "and in this case it had been conditioned, and then consummated, by misplaced pride. Continuous defeat in war at the hands of despised unbelievers began 'to shake the very structure of Muslim society.' This danger imposed the question: What was the secret of European success? As the Japanese were to do when they found themselves in the same predicament, Ottoman and Iranian and Moroccan rulers began in the early part of the nineteenth century to send envoys to the capitals of the West with the mission of studying what should be done. As Lewis puts it, knowledge was something to be acquired, rather than grown or developed."

In his concluding remarks, the reviewer offers some more thoughts, with some hints at what can be done. "In both its religious and its secular nationalist forms," he writes, "Muslim rage looks to provide for some time to come an organizing principle for mobilizing against the United States and western civilization in general. In short, we may be facing another variant of cold war, or worse. But there must be Muslims who will read Lewis and agree that catastrophe lies down this road." What is required, he adds, is "reinvention, and this in turn requires a philosopher, the equivalent of a Muslim Locke or Montesquieu, to provide new definitions of the role and purpose of Islam in the state and society, and so recover a properly-working Muslim identity in the contemporary context." There seem to be no such persons, he concludes—and adds: "In that case, the suicide bomber may become a metaphor for the whole region, or else some outside power might conquer the Muslim world once and for all. There are not enough civilizations for mankind to so heedlessly write off any one of them. We should all hope, therefore, along with Professor Lewis, for the true victory of Islam—not against the West, but for itself."[6]

To go back to the case as Lewis presents it. Women's attire, of course, is not the only aspect of westernization that he says today's Muslims failed to adopt. He lists a number of others, though only at random and without making it sufficiently clear what, in reality, westernization entails. He starts with the subject of the emancipation of women, as we have seen above. The difference between modernization and westernization, he continues, particularly but not exclusively in relation to men and women, can be vividly seen in the dress reforms that began at the end of the eighteenth century and have continued, with occasional interruptions, ever since.[7]

Again, on the subject of scientific achievements Lewis relates that the relationship between Christendom and Islam in the sciences has now been reversed. "Those who had been disciples now became teachers; those who had been masters became pupils, often reluctant and resentful pupils. They were willing enough to accept the products of infidel science in warfare and medicine, where they could make the difference between victory and defeat, between life and death. But the underlying philosophy and the sociopolitical context of these scientific achievements proved more difficult to accept or even to recognize."

Lewis considers this rejection one of the more striking differences between the Middle East and other parts of the non-western world that have in one way or another endured the impact of western civilization. "At the present time," he writes, "scientists in many Asian countries make important contributions to what is no longer a western but a worldwide scientific movement. Except for some westernized enclaves in the Middle East and some scientists of Middle Eastern origin working in the West, the Middle Eastern contribution—as reflected for example in the internationally recognized journals that are at the cutting edge of scientific progress—compares poorly with that of other non-western regions or, even more dramatically, with its own past record."[8]

On the subject of the response to western music, and the larger question of cultural change that it raises, Lewis devotes quite a few pages, his conclusion being that, except for Turkey and Israel, "western art music falls on deaf ears" in the Muslim world. Many Middle Eastern Muslims as well as students of the contemporary Muslim world would take strong exception to this depiction of the situation.[9]

Some aspects of western culture that Lewis says Middle Easterners did manage to adopt, even if partially, are:

Team sports. "A really significant cultural change may be seen in the arena of sport. Sport was not unknown of course; there were large-scale enterprises like hunting, and individual competitions like wrestling. There appears to have been only one team sport: polo, and that was rare and aristocratic. The practice of team sports like football and basketball and the rest is purely western, mostly English in origin. It was the English who invented football and its analogue—parliamentary politics. There are remarkable resemblances between the two and both obviously come from the same national genius. The adoption of competitive team games has so far been more successful in the Middle East than the adoption of parliamentary government."

Dining. "As distinct from merely eating—is another western 'cultural' influence. We have fascinating descriptions of dinner parties at various stages in the process of acculturation; dining and partying and of course the very shocking business of gentlemen and ladies dining together, even dancing together. This brings expressions of shock and outrage from many nineteenth-century and early-twentieth-century travelers from East to West."

Verbal culture. "During the centuries of western impact on the Middle East, western verbal culture was completely accepted and internalized. One would have thought that the verbal culture would be the most difficult since it requires either knowledge of a language or the mediation of a translator. Yet for some reason, it has been the most successful and the most accepted."

Other, nonverbal cultural influences "show a contrast between the visual, including physical, which have been on the whole successful; and the musical, which has been remarkably unsuccessful, and indeed to this day western musical influence is minimal in this region. It seems that science and music remain the last citadels of western civilization that some non-westerners have managed to penetrate but others, particularly in the Middle East, have not."

It must be pointed out here, however, that, as far as the subject of music is concerned, conservatories of western music are to be found in many Arab capitals—Beirut, Cairo, Baghdad, Damascus, Tunis, Rabat, and Amman.

Throughout the decades, these institutions produced thousands of western-style musicians who have staffed the numerous symphony orchestras and opera companies all over the Arab world.

Many regions, Lewis notes, have undergone the impact of the West, and suffered a similar loss of economic self-sufficiency, of cultural authenticity, and in some parts also of political independence. "But some time has passed since western domination ended in all these regions, including the Middle East. In some of them, notably in East and South Asia, the resurgent peoples of the region have begun to meet and beat the West on its own terms—in commerce and industry, in the projection of political and even military power, and, in many ways most remarkable of all, in the acceptance and internalization of western achievement, notably in science. The Middle East still lags behind."

In the arts, Lewis finds an even more dramatic contrast—not just between the Middle East and other regions, but even between different arts within the Middle East. "The impact of European painting and architecture (though not of course sculpture, which is excluded for religious reasons) goes back a long way. In the course of the eighteenth century, and even more in the nineteenth century, European visual culture, architecture, and interior decoration, even painting, became not only accepted but even dominant. In the late nineteenth and still more in the twentieth century even sculpture was sometimes used for the glorification of rulers. The more traditional forms have virtually disappeared, except for an occasional rather self-conscious burst of neoclassicism."

European literary influence, facing the barrier of language and the interposition of translators, took somewhat longer to penetrate. By now, however, western literary forms and fashions are thoroughly assimilated. Such distinctively European vehicles as the novel and the play have become normal forms of literary self-expression in all the literary languages of the Middle East. "The ready acceptance of the visual and verbal arts," Lewis adds, "makes the rejection of music the more remarkable. It was not for lack of trying. Sultan Mahmud II was not alone in his experiment with a brass band. Other rulers saw the relevance of western music to western drill, and hence to western warfare. Even the Ayatollah Khomeini . . . was willing to make exception for marches and anthems."

In Turkey, where westernization as distinct from modernization has made most progress, western music has won the widest acceptance and there are Turkish soloists, orchestras, and even composers in the western style. "But these address only a minority of the population, and elsewhere in the Middle East—except Israel—western music, that is of course western art music, falls on deaf ears. Recently there has been some interest in pop music and rock music. It is too early to say what this may portend. The contrast between visual and verbal acceptance and musical rejection is paralleled in other areas, as for example in the widespread cult, without the exercise of freedom, and the almost universal holding of elections, without choice."[10]

What went wrong, then—what the modernizers missed and thus rendered their work incomplete—was their failure to "westernize." Modernizers, by reform or revolution, concentrated their efforts in three main areas: military, economic, and political. The results achieved were disappointing. "The quest for victory by updated armies brought a series of humiliating defeats. The quest for prosperity through development brought, in some countries, impoverished and corrupt economies in recurring need of external aid, in others an unhealthy dependence on a single resource—fossil fuels. . . . Worst of all is the political result: The long quest for freedom has left a string of shabby tyrannies, ranging for traditional autocracies to new-style dictatorships, modern only in their apparatus of repression and indoctrination."

There was worse to come, however. "It was bad enough for Muslims to feel weak and poor after centuries of being rich and strong, to lose the leadership that they had come to regard as their right, and to be reduced to the role of followers of the West. The twentieth century, particularly the second half, brought further humiliations—the awareness that they were no longer even the first among the followers, but were falling even further back in the lengthening line of eager and more successful westernizers, notably in East Asia. . . . Following is bad enough; limping in the rear is far worse. By all the standards that matter in the modern world—economic development and job creation, literacy and educational and scientific achievement, political freedom and respect for human rights—what was once a mighty civilization has indeed fallen low."[11]

DOES MODERNIZATION ENTAIL WESTERNIZATION?

As is made clear from one of the passages quoted above from the book, the author of *What Went Wrong?* is well aware of the difficulty of fixing any clear dividing lines between modernization and westernization. More than once in the course of his analysis of the various aspects of the subject, Lewis himself seems undecided. In certain cases the distinction seems clear enough, in others it is practically nonexistent.

To be sure, many scholars and observers who dealt with the subject appear equally perplexed, and the seemingly unnecessarily large space given in this chapter to a summary of Lewis's thesis is provided here in the hope that the arguments and counterarguments to follow be equally comprehensive and based on a full coverage of the material.

The main question being asked here, and the real crux of the matter, is whether modernization, which can be said to mean acquisition by the aspiring party of certain skills and techniques, in order to be meaningful and give the desired results, entails westernization, which comprises a number of mainly cultural attributes. Scholars and commentators whose answer to this question is in the negative, like those who believe this to be the case, offer a variety of reasons and explanations. I will start by listing what is generally agreed to be the features of modernization and westernization.

In an essay published in 1996, "clash-of-civilizations" Professor Samuel Huntington offers two lists of the requirements, respectively, of modernization and westernization. The lists, although by no means either adequate or exhaustive, provides some useful guidelines. According to Huntington, modernization involves: industrialization, urbanization, increasing levels of literacy, education, wealth, social mobilization, and more complex and diverse occupational structures. Modernization, he adds, "is a revolutionary process comparable to the shift from primitive to civilized societies that began in the valleys of the Tigris and Euphrates, the Nile, and the Indus about 5000 B.C. The attitudes, values, knowledge, and culture of people in a modern society differ greatly from those in a traditional society. As the first civilization to modernize, the West is the first to have fully acquired the culture of modernity. As other societies take on similar patterns of education, work, wealth, and class structure, the modernization argument runs, this western culture will become the universal culture of the world."

The essential requirements of westernization, as Huntington sees it, seem all to relate to western values and institutions. What were the distinguishing characteristics of western civilization during the hundreds of years before it modernized, he asks. The various scholars who have answered this question, he writes, differ on some specifics but agree on a number of institutions, practices, and beliefs that may be legitimately identified as the core of western civilization. These include:

> *The Classical legacy.* As a third-generation civilization, the West inherited much from earlier civilizations, including most notably Classical civilization: Greek philosophy and rationalism, Roman law, Latin, and Christianity. Islamic and Orthodox civilizations also inherited from Classical civilization, but to nowhere near the same degree as the West.
>
> *Western Christianity.* Western Christianity, first Catholicism and then Protestantism, is the single most important historical characteristic of western civilization. Indeed, during most of its first millennium, what is now known as western civilization was called western Christendom. . . . When westerners went out to conquer the world in the sixteenth century, they did so for God as well as gold.

European languages. Language is second only to religion as a factor distinguishing people of one culture from those of another. The West differs from most other civilizations in its multiplicity of languages.

Separation of spiritual and temporal authority. Throughout western history, first the church, and then many churches existed separate from the state. God and Caesar, church and state, spiritual authority and temporal authority had been a prevailing dualism in western culture.

Rule of law. The concept of the centrality of law to civilized existence was inherited from the Romans. . . . The tradition of the rule of law laid the basis for constitutionalism and the protection of human rights, including property rights, against the arbitrary exercise of power.

Social pluralism and civil society. Western society historically has been highly pluralistic. What is distinctive about the West . . . is the rise and persistence of diverse autonomous groups not based on blood relationship or marriage.

Representative bodies. Social pluralism gave rise at an early date to estates, parliaments, and other institutions that represented the interests of the aristocracy, clergy, merchants, and other groups. These bodies provided forms of representation that in the course of modernization evolved into the institutions of modern democracy.

Individualism. Many of the above features of western civilization contributed to the emergence of a sense of individualism and a tradition of individual rights and liberties unique among civilized societies.

Huntington admits that the above list is not an exhaustive enumeration of the distinctive characteristics of western civilization. Nor is it meant to imply that those characteristics were always and everywhere present in western society. "They obviously were not; the many despots in western history regularly ignored the rule of law and suspended representative bodies. Nor is it meant to suggest that none of the characteristics have appeared in other civilizations. They obviously have: the Quran and the *sharia* constitute basic law for Islamic societies; Japan and India had class systems paralleling that of the West (and perhaps as a result are the only two major non-western societies to sustain democratic governments for any length of time). Individually, almost none of these factors is unique to the West. But the combination of them is, and has given the West its distinctive quality. These concepts, practices, and institutions have been far more prevalent in the West than in other civilizations. They form the essential continuing core of western civilization. They are what is western, but not modern, about the West. They also generated the commitment to individual freedom that now distinguishes the West from other civilizations."[12]

Thus westernization, as Huntington sees it, involves the main culture and cultural traits. And here, of course, lies the difficulty. Culture counts. Each society, it has been pointed out by more than one social anthropologist, establishes a mode of existence, a distinct way of understanding itself, its activity, its history, and the world it inhabits, specific to it and all-embracing in its compass. Although variously defined, however, "culture" embraces the symbols, meanings, values, institutions, behaviors, and productions derived therefrom, which characterize a distinctive and identifiable human population group. The word carries its own weight of associations in different languages and intellectual traditions. Culture is therefore the living sum of meanings, norms, habits, and social artifacts that confers to individuals—identity as members of some visible community, standards for relating to the environment, for identifying fellow members and strangers, and for deciding what is important and what is not important to them.

If we accept this concept of culture and if we insist, as Lewis obviously does, that adoption of cultural features of the West are a necessary part of the modernization process, we face a gross contradiction. This is because westernization, often used as another term for "modernity," is, as one observer of the Japanese experiment has pointed out, a construct that "has certain attributes that are associated with western culture but that are not necessary for modernization." Citing the example of industrialization, the writer adds that Japan, "with its industrialization, with its rapid shift from a politically isolated and feudal nation to the second largest economy in the world, demonstrates that neither westernization nor modernity is necessary for modernization. It also suggests that modernization does not seem to foster the eventual development of modernity, even where the two are treated as complementary."[13]

Modernity refers to a set of related attributes that resulted from the Industrial Revolution and its social and economic ramifications. "Because the Industrial Revolution was the result of technological advances, in modernity scientific and rational thought are valued and economic efficiencies are promoted. This emphasis on rational thought and abstraction means that conscious states are considered more important than subconscious states; aesthetic or intuitive ways of thinking are considered peripheral to development."[14]

Modernity is also tied to Christianity through the Weberian proposition that Calvinism promoted an ethic of hard work and capital accumulation. "This is not to claim that modern nations are Christian (although many of Japan's modernizers were also encouraged by American supporters to embrace Christianity) but only that Christianity was to have established a set of values which fostered modernity. In fact, under modernity, tradition is rejected in favor of progress; development away from all traditions, including religion, is treated positively. Additionally, . . . the political and economic shifts which accompanied the Industrial Revolution and led to democracy or the privileging of the individual were implicit in modernity."[15]

Using this set of definitions, this writer concludes, it can be argued that modernization and modernity, while they appear to be a tautology, can be isolated. "Ironically, Japan proves this point through a complete disregard for many of the key concepts of modernity. The country did, however, deliberately set out to both modernize and westernize. That it has successfully modernized, while having been unsuccessful in its attempts to westernize, demonstrates where these issues diverge. While most of basic points of modernity simply do not apply to Japanese culture, the crucial differences in the field of architecture are probably the privileging of subconscious over rational thought and the acceptance of tradition in general, particularly religious traditions."[16]

"Does Modernization Require westernization?" In a paper under this title, Deepak Lal, professor of international development studies at the University of California, Los Angeles, writes in his concluding remarks: "Gregory VII's eleventh-century papal revolution played a crucial role in propagating the material beliefs that promoted the institutional changes required for the growth of the market economy. By now these beliefs have been embraced around the world. However, to promote the modernization sought worldwide, there is no need for the non-western world to accept the cosmological beliefs promoted by Gregory the Great's papal revolution of the sixth century. Societies can modernize without westernizing. Rather than heed the continuing western moral crusade in pursuit of its 'habits of the heart'—which, far from being universal, remain the culture-specific, proselytizing, and egalitarian ethic of what is still, at heart, western Christendom—the non-western world, observing the social decay that the West's cosmology has caused, might well invoke the ancient biblical injunction, 'Physician heal thyself.'"[17]

To the question as to whether to modernize, non-western societies must abandon their own cultures and adopt the core elements of western culture, Huntington has this to say: "From time to time leaders of such societies have thought [this] necessary. Peter the Great and Mustafa Kemal Ataturk were determined to modernize their countries and convinced that doing so meant adopting western culture, even to the point of replacing traditional headgear with its western equivalent. In the process, they created 'torn' countries, unsure of their cultural identity. Nor did western cultural imports significantly help them in their pursuit of modernization. More often, leaders of non-western societies have pursued modernization and rejected westernization . . . Japan, Singapore, Taiwan, Saudi Arabia, and, to a lesser degree, Iran have become modern societies without becoming western societies. China is clearly modernizing, but certainly not westernizing."[18]

A trenchant and rather fierce onslaught on westernization comes in a book by Jalal Ali Ahmad, an Iranian Islamist who died in 1969. The title of the book speaks for itself— *Occidentosis: A Plague from the West*, published posthumously by a Muslim publishing firm in Berkeley, California, as part of a series called "Contemporary Islamic Thought Persian Series." Following are excerpts from the book, cited here at some length as a fairly representative sample of what Muslim fundamentalists today generally feel:

> The occidentotic is a man totally without belief or conviction, to such an extent that he not only believes in nothing, but also does not actively disbelieve in anything. . . . He is a timeserver. Once he gets across the bridge, he doesn't care if it stands or falls. He has no faith, no direction, no aim, no belief, neither in God nor in humanity. He cares neither whether society is transformed or not nor whether religion or irreligion prevails. He is not even irreligious. He is indifferent. He even goes to the mosque at times, just as he goes to the club or the movies. But everywhere he is only a spectator. It is just as if he had gone to see a soccer game.
>
> The occidentotic normally has no specialty. He is jack-of-all-trades and master of none. . . . He is just like the old women in a household who in the course of lifetimes of experience have learned a little about everything, although their knowledge is limited by the perspective of illiterate women.
>
> The occidentotic has no character. He is a thing without authenticity. His person, his home, and his words convey nothing in particular, and everything in general. . . . [He] is effete. He is effeminate. He attends to his grooming a great deal. He spends much time sprucing himself up. Sometimes he even plucks his eyelashes. He attaches a great deal of importance to his shoes and his wardrobe, and to the furnishings of his home. It always seems he has been unwrapped from gold foil or come from some European "maison." He buys the latest prodigy in automotive engineering every year. His house, which once had a porch and a cellar, a pool, awnings, and a vestibule, now looks like something different every day. One day it resembles a seaside villa full of gaudy junk and bar stools. The next day all the walls are painted one color and triangles of all colors cover every surface. In one corner there is a hi-fi, in another a television, in another a piano for the young lady, in others stereo loudspeakers. The kitchen and other nooks and crannies are packed with gas stoves, electric washers, and other odds and ends.
>
> If perchance he is interested in politics, he is cognizant of the faintest right or left tendencies in the British Labour Party and is more familiar with the current U.S. senators than with the ministers in his own government. And he knows more about the staff of *Time* or the *News Chronicle* than about some nephew way off in Khurasan. And he supposes them more veracious than a prophet because all these have more influence on the affairs of his country than any domestic politician, commentator, or representative.[19]

Ahmad devotes a chapter to the pitfalls of the West-oriented educational system and its irrelevance to Iranian society and people. According to him, the educated class was a typical breed of occidentotics; all its activities and products lacked any sense of purpose and direction. Some passages from this chapter can be quoted to serve as an index for the study of the occidentotic elites of other similar countries, as Ahmad perceives it.

"With very few exceptions," he writes, "the sole output of these colleges over the last twenty or thirty years has consisted of distinguished scholars, all of whom know the language, know some biography, are scrupulous workers, write marginalia in others' books, resolve tough problems in language or history. . . . All these professors and their carefully trained pupils, with their ears stopped like Seven Sleepers', have retreated so far into the cave of texts, textual variants, and obscure expressions that even the roar of the machine cannot awaken them. . . . The encroachments of foreign tongues day by day are undermining the importance of the mother tongue and making a sound command of it less necessary."[20]

Reservations about modernity and its effects, however, are by no means confined to Muslims—or Confucians, or Buddhists, or any of the other non-western faiths and cultures. They come also from the Christian heartland. In a wide-ranging review essay on a number of books by leading Christian thinkers, Peter Leithart quotes from some of them. In a book titled *No Place for Truth*, David Wells writes: "the speed of technological and social change requires constant adaptation that produces anxiety and a sense of rootlessness. Modern society is mass society, which consists of a number of large, interlocking systems that form the structure of the society—the economy, for example, and the political world, state and federal government, the universities which manufacture and disseminate knowledge, and the mass media which manufacture and disseminate the images by which we largely understand ourselves. Each of these systems surrounds and envelops us, in the process intruding into our consciousness and carrying its values with it."

These features of modernity hold grave consequences for orthodox Christian faith. "Modernity relegates religion to a private sphere; the modern world is experimenting with the unprecedented project of erecting a civilization without religious assumptions. Public and private spheres are governed by different values and different languages. This social context encourages its inhabitants to become multilingual, speaking the language appropriate to each sphere in order to survive; the result is that truth becomes fractured. Modernity also produces pluralism, providing a plethora of choices in ideologies and religions as well as in clothing styles and flavors of coffee."

Wells, Leithart writes, distances himself from sociological determinism, arguing instead that there is a "dialectical" relationship between external sociological realities and the consciousness of the people who live in the midst of those realities. Social circumstances do not determine consciousness but they do exercise "a shaping influence." "Thus, Wells does not argue that modernization and modernity determine the response of evangelicals, but rather that modernity poses serious problems for Christian faith. The civilization of modernity does not reinforce Christian truth but instead tends to undermine the plausibility of the Christian worldview."

A similar diagnosis of the crisis of evangelicalism has recently been offered by Os Guinness and John Seel in their collections of essays, *No God But God: Breaking with the Idols of our Age.* The editors claim that many of the problems facing the American church "stem directly from modernization." Modernity, the great foe of contemporary Christianity, is defined as "the character and system of the world produced by the forces of development and modernization, especially capitalism, industrialized technology, and telecommunications." Modernity is the "first truly global culture in the world and the most powerful culture so far in history." As such, it is a "counterfeit of the kingdom of God." Like Wells, Guinness and Seel distinguish "modernism as a set of ideas built on the Enlightenment" from modernity; the former "has collapsed," while the latter is "stronger than ever." Elsewhere, the editors speak more precisely of the danger of uncritically adopting the "insight, tools, and general blessings of modernity," which leads to idolization of "modern approaches to life, such as politics, management, marketing, and psychology; we also have fallen prey to powerful modern myths, such as change, technique, relevance, and need."

The matter has been put most forcefully by James Davison Hunter, who asserts that "Modernity creates conditions in which 'immorality,' from the evangelical perspective, is structurally engendered. Bluntly put, modernity fosters 'sin' in the culture, jeopardizing the moral covenant widely believed to exist between God and America. In recent evangelical thought, in short, modernity has taken its place with the world, the flesh, and the devil as a threat to faith. It is obvious that the world civilization of the twentieth century has unique features, many of which are inimical to the Christian worldview and Christian morality. The global slaughter of unborn babies through abortion; the galloping statism that has characterized political life in the West, albeit to a lesser degree than in the East; the approval and celebration of sexual practices that Christianity has always condemned in the strongest terms; the growing intolerance for public expressions of Christian conviction; all these and many more features of contemporary life might be cited in support of the thesis outlined above. In this sense, the modern world poses serious threats and challenges to Christianity."[21]

From the detailed account given here, it becomes clear that "westernization," in the context of Lewis's thesis, amounts to nothing less than practically adopting another culture—something not too dissimilar to culture cleansing. This is because culture contains very nearly all the elements that westernization, as depicted by those who consider it an essential part of modernization, involves. For our culture, as one leading cultural anthropologist has put it, "is the way we eat and sleep, the way we wash and dress and go to work. It is the actions we perform at home and on the job. It is the language we speak and the values and beliefs we hold. It is the goods and services we buy and the way we buy them. It is the way we meet friends and strangers, the way we control our children and the way they respond. It is the transportation we use and the entertainment we enjoy. . . ."[22]

It is essential to remember, moreover, that a culture in this sense is more than just the sum total of its various parts. It is, in addition, the way in which those parts are organized to form a whole. "Just as several buildings can be made of the same materials yet differ in structure and function, so various cultures may share some similar elements yet each may organize them uniquely. Thus, to understand a culture we must grasp not only its parts but also the structure that holds them."[23]

The argument that westernization is a precondition of modernization, considered in light of the definition of culture quoted above, means quite plainly that for the present-day Muslim—or Jew, Buddhist, Confucian, African, Asian, Latin American, or Slav—to attain a degree of modernization that is considered adequate for him to cope with the demands of the modern world—this non-westerner ought to become practically someone he or she isn't.

Plainly, this is unattainable in any meaningful sense, unless, of course, this hypothetical person is to become someone like Kipling's luckless Russian—a "racial anomaly," an object of laughter and ridicule. Not that he or she would by then be more acceptable to your modernization-equal-westernization pundits though.

That there are significant differences between modern and traditional cultures is beyond dispute, Huntington writes. "A world in which some societies are highly modern and others still traditional will obviously be less homogeneous than a world in which all societies are relatively modern. It does not necessarily follow, however, that societies with modern cultures should be any more similar than are societies with traditional cultures. Only a few hundred years ago all societies were traditional. Was that world any less homogenous than a future world of universal modernity is likely to be? Probably not. 'Ming China . . . was assuredly closer to the France of the Valois,' Fernand Braudel observes, 'than the China of Mao Tse-tung is to the France of the Fifth Republic.'"

"Modern societies have much in common," Huntington concludes, "but they do not necessarily merge into homogeneity. The argument that they do rests on the assumption that modern society must approximate a single type, the western type; that modern civilization is western civilization, and western civilization is modern civilization. This, however, is a false identification. Virtually all scholars of civilization agree that western civilization emerged in the eighth and ninth centuries and developed its distinctive characteristics in the centuries that followed. It did not begin to modernize until the eighteenth century. The West, in short, was western long before it was modern."[24]

DEMOCRACY AND SECULARISM

Two other features commonly considered by the westernization school of thought as essential requirements of modernization if it is to be meaningful are democracy and secularism. One of the theses Lewis expounds in *What Went Wrong?* is that "Muslims developed no secularist movement of their own, and reacted sharply against attempts to introduce one from abroad. . . ." Some of them also considered that ideas of the French Revolutions "could threaten not only Christianity but also Islam, and . . . gave warning against them." Moreover, "Among the vast majority, the challenge of western secular ideas was not so much opposed as ignored. It is only in comparatively recent times that Muslim religious thinkers of stature have looked at secularism, understood its threat to what they regard as the highest values of religion, and responded with a decisive rejection."[25]

In an exhaustive, and generally critical, review of *What Went Wrong?* Michigan University Professor Juan Cole touches on this and on a few others of the points made in the book, among them the subject of secularism.

"Obviously," Cole writes, "if [Lewis] is referring to believing Muslims, they would not be secularists. If he means persons of Muslim background, then the secularist wing of Iran's National Front in the 1940s and 1950s was developed by Muslims; the secularist policies of Mohammad Reza Pahlavi, the Shah of Iran, were developed by his circle of Muslim technocrats; Turkey's secularist movement was developed and promoted by Muslims; and although the Baath Party was initially the brainchild of Christian Arabs, its secularist ideology was taken up with alacrity by Syrian and Iraqi Muslims in large numbers. Nor is it true that a separation of religion and state never occurred in Islam, in contrast to Christianity. Ira Lapidus dates such a separation from the classical period of Islamic civilisation."

"A final question," Cole adds, "has to do with Europe, the explicit contrast for the Muslim Middle East in this book. Why does Lewis think things 'went right' in the West? I should have thought that the slaughter of the First World War, the rise of fascism and communism, the sixty-one million butchered in the Second World War, the savage European repression of anti-colonial movements in places like Vietnam and Algeria, and the hundreds of millions held hostage by the Cold War nuclear doctrine of 'mutually assured destruction'—that all this might have raised a few eyebrows among emeriti historians looking for things that went wrong."[26]

On the subject of democracy and on the general political scene, Lewis wrote some years ago in an article titled "The Revolt of Islam." Modernization in politics, he noted, had fared no better—perhaps even worse—than in warfare and economics. "Many Islamic countries have experimented with democratic institutions of one kind or another. In some, as in Turkey, Iran, and Tunisia, they were introduced by innovative native reformers, in others, they were installed and then bequeathed by departing imperialists. The record, with the possible exception of Turkey, is one of almost unrelieved failure. Western-style parties and parliaments almost invariably ended in corrupt tyrannies, maintained by repression and indoctrination. The only European model that worked, in the sense of accomplishing its purposes, was the one-party dictatorship. The Baath Party, different branches of which have ruled Iraq and Syria for decades, incorporated the worst features of its Nazi and Soviet models. Since the death of Nasser in 1970, no Arab leader has been able to gain extensive support outside his own country. Indeed, no Arab leader has been willing to submit his claim to power to a free vote. The leaders who have come closest to winning pan-Arab approval are Qaddafi in the seventies and, more recently, Saddam Hussein. That these two, of all Arab rulers, should enjoy such wide popularity is in itself both appalling and revealing."[27]

A rather different perspective on the subject of democracy in the Muslim world is offered by Fathullah Gülen, a religious teacher in Turkey. "If we want to analyze religion, democracy, or any other system or philosophy accurately," he writes, "we should focus on humanity and human life. From this perspective, religion in general and Islam in particular cannot be compared on the same basis with democracy or any other political, social, or economic system. Religion focuses primarily on the immutable aspects of life and existence, whereas political, social, and economic systems or ideologies concern only certain variable, social aspects of our worldly life. The aspects of life with which religion is primarily concerned are as valid today as they were at the dawn of humanity and will continue to be so in the future. Worldly systems change according to circumstances and so can be evaluated only according to their times. Belief in God, the hereafter, the prophets, the holy books, angels, and divine destiny have nothing to do with changing times. Likewise, worship and morality's universal and unchanging standards have little to do with time and worldly life."

"Democratic ideas," Gülen continues, "stem from ancient times. Modern liberal democracy was born in the American (1776) and French Revolutions (1789–1799). In democratic societies, people govern themselves as opposed to being ruled by someone above. The individual has priority over the community in this type of political system, being free to determine how to live his or her own life. Individualism is not absolute, though. People achieve a better existence by living within society and this requires that they adjust and limit their freedom according to the criteria of social life.

"The Prophet says that all people are as equal as the teeth of a comb. Islam does not discriminate based on race, color, age, nationality, or physical traits. The Prophet declared: 'You are all from Adam, and Adam is from earth. O servants of God, be brothers [and sisters].' Those who are born earlier, have more wealth and power than others, or belong to certain families or ethnic groups have no inherent right to rule others."

Islam also upholds the following fundamental principles:

1. Power lies in truth, a repudiation of the common idea that truth relies upon power.
2. Justice and the rule of law are essential.
3. Freedom of belief and rights to life, personal property, reproduction, and health (both mental and physical) cannot be violated.
4. The privacy and immunity of individual life must be maintained.
5. No one can be convicted of a crime without evidence, or accused and punished for someone else's crime.
6. An advisory system of administration is essential.

All rights are equally important, Gülen adds, and an individual's right cannot be sacrificed for society's sake. "Islam considers a society to be composed of conscious individuals equipped with free will and having responsibility toward both themselves and others. Islam goes a step further by adding a cosmic dimension. I see humanity as the 'motor' of history, contrary to fatalistic approaches of some of the nineteenth-century western philosophies of history such as dialectical materialism and historicism. Just as every individual's will and behavior determine the outcome of his or her life in this world and in the hereafter, a society's progress or decline is determined by the will, worldview, and lifestyle of its inhabitants. The Quran (13:11) says: 'God will not change the state of a people unless they change themselves [with respect to their beliefs, worldview and lifestyle].' In other words, each society holds the reins of its fate in its own hands. The prophetic tradition emphasizes this idea: 'You will be ruled according to how you are.' This is the basic character and spirit of democracy, which does not conflict with any Islamic principle."

As Islam holds individuals and societies responsible for their own fate, people must be responsible for governing themselves. The Quran addresses society with such phrases as: "O People!" and "O believers!" The duties entrusted to modern democratic systems are those that Islam refers to society and classifies, in order of importance, as "absolutely necessary, relatively necessary, and commendable to carry out." The sacred text includes the following passages: "Establish, all of you, peace" (2:208); "spend in the way of God and of the needy of the pure and good of what you have earned and of what We bring forth for you from earth" (2:267); "if some among your women are accused of indecency, you must have four witnesses [to prove it]" (4:15); "God commands you to give over the public trusts to the charge of those having the required qualities and to judge with justice when you judge between people" (4:58); "observe justice as witnesses respectful for God even if it is against yourselves, your parents and relatives" (4:135); "if they [your enemies] incline to peace [when you are at war], you also incline to it" (8:61); "if a corrupt, sinful one brings you news[about others], investigate it so that you should not strike a people without knowing" (49:6); "If two parties among the believers fight between themselves, reconcile them" (49:9). To sum up, the Quran addresses the whole community and assigns it almost all the duties entrusted to modern democratic systems.[28]

A fairly concise summary of the subject of democracy and Islam today is provided by Larbi Sadiki. The Arabs, he writes, "will be divided well into the third millennium over how to be democratic while remaining sensitive to the Arabo-Islamic *turath* (cultural heritage)—how to be simultaneously genuinely democratic, genuinely Arab and genuinely Muslim. *What* and *how much* modernity and tradition will foster that hybrid democratic, Arab, and Muslim identity."

The current debate will also set Arab against non-Arab, he adds, "Islamists represent one formidable political configuration for which the quest of *what* and *how much* modernity and tradition are real issues for both the Islamization and democratization of Arab societies and polities. The notions of cultural specificity and exceptionalism encountered in certain western discourses find resonance in the Islamist perspective. In both, the difference between the 'self' and the 'other' becomes the essence of identity and therefore a non-negotiable given. In both, specificity spells exclusion. Certain western discourses claim democracy to be a western cultural-civilizational byproduct unsuited to the 'other' while others claim it to be a universal *telos*. Advancing discourses of cultural particularity and universalism of their own, Islamists reject exclusivist western discourse by reading democracy into Islamic sources and retort to universalists in the West by upholding their right to borrow that kind and that amount of democracy that befits culture, history, and local values. . . . "

As hinted at by certain Islamist leaders, Sadiki explains, democracy needs cultural reconstructing if it is to coexist with Islamic values. "Its individualism has to be balanced with Islam's emphasis on the community, and its secularism has to yield to the radically different precepts of temporal and spiritual oneness, and an imagining of political legitimacy in which the will of man is subordinate to the will of God."[29]

Professor Gurdun Kramer, a well-known specialist on the subject, writes in an essay titled "Islamist Notions of Democracy," that a growing number of Muslims, including a good many Islamist activists, have called for pluralist democracy, or at least for some of its basic elements: the rule of law and the protection of human rights, political participation, government control, and accountability. "The terms and concepts used," she adds "are often vague or deliberately chosen so as to avoid non-Islamic notions. Many speak of *shura*, the idealized Islamic concept of participation-qua-consultation; others refer to 'Islamic democracy,' just as in the 1950s and 1960s they would have talked about 'Arab' or 'Islamic socialism'; still others do not hesitate to call for democracy."[30]

But, she asks, is there an Islamic path to a pluralist democratic society? And how can it be analyzed? There is, she writes, general agreement among Muslim authors that Islam is comprehensive or, as the commonly used modern formula has it, that it is religion and state or religion and world. This formulation, she asserts, signals the rejection of secularism as it was advocated by the Egyptian scholar 'Ali 'Abd al-Raziq in his book *Islam and the Roots of Government*, published in 1925, shortly after the abolition of the caliphate. "Almost three generations later" she adds, "his claims—that Muhammad was a prophet and not a statesman, that Islam is a religion and not a state, and that the caliphate was from the beginning based on force—still provoke outrage. For these authors there can be no doubt that Islam comprises faith, ethics, and law as it was set forth in the Qur'an, exemplified by the life of the Prophet Muhammad and his Companions (the *sunna*), and later developed by Muslim theologians and jurists (the '*ulama*' and '*fuqaha*') into the *shari'a*."

The fact is, however, that "at the core of much of contemporary writing are a number of shared assumptions: that all people are born equal, having been installed as God's viceregents on earth (*isikhlaf*); that the government exists to ensure an Islamic life and enforce Islamic laws; that sovereignty (*siyada, hakimiyya*) ultimately rests with God alone, who has made the law and defined good and evil (*al-ma'ruf wa'l-munkar*); that the authority (*sulta*) to apply God's law has been transferred to the community as a whole, which is therefore the source of all powers (*asl al-sultat*); and that the head of the community or state, no matter whether he (and they specifically exclude women from that function) be called imam, caliph, or president, is the mere representative, agent, or employee of the community that elects, supervises, and, if necessary, deposes him, either directly or via its representatives."[31]

Can Muslim Arabs adopt democracy, asks the Palestinian Arab scholar Shukri B. Abed. His answer: "Democratizing the political system without changing the reality it reflects will sooner or later backfire. We ought, therefore, to ask: Can a democracy, be it the most primitive or the most advanced type, succeed when conditions of enormous disparity prevail, as is the case within and among the various Arab countries? Can the Arabs really have western–style democracy as their model when threatened with territorial divisions and when facing growing Islamic resurgence, partly in reaction to this very same western orientation?"

"The West," Abed concludes, "can only do the citizens of the Arab world irreparable harm by hurrying the process and cutting short the debates of the Arabs before they have fully explored all the nuances of this immensely complex issue and settled on a type of government that is right for them."[32]

An anecdote cited by Elie Kedourie in a way illustrates the difficulty. In a brief study of the genesis of the Egyptian constitution of 1923, Kedourie cites a passage from the memoirs of Sir David Kelly, acting British High Commissioner in Egypt. In his memoirs Kelly recounts how King Fu'ad, in conversations with him in his last years, used to condemn the British for having "imposed a constitution of the Belgian model" on the Egyptians, who the king said were completely unsuited for parliamentary government on these lines. Great Britain's interest in Egypt, Fu'ad told the British official, was purely strategic; why had the British not been "content to leave him to run the country, as he well knew how to do. . . ."[33]

What Fu'ad was complaining about, we gather, is the complex nature of party politics and an electoral system with which he found it difficult to cope. Whether or not this reflects on the subject of the relevance or suitability for the Muslim Middle East of democracy as the West perceives it is a question that obviously constitutes an important aspect of the subject of the present survey. Put simply, the question is whether Islam and democracy can coexist. Two well-known students of Islam, John L. Esposito and John O. Voll, believe the two can indeed coexist, though they contend that "democracy" is capable of multiple interpretations and applications, and that "there may be alternative and rival uses of the term." According to them:

> However different their understanding and usages, calls for democratization, political participation, and Islamic democracy demonstrate the contemporary currency of democracy in many Muslim societies. While some remain convinced that democracy is un-Islamic, or that it is simply another attempt by the West in the post–Cold War era to achieve ideological and political hegemony in the name of a New World Order, many Muslims have made advocacy of democracy the political litmus test for the creditability and legitimacy of regimes.[34]

Esposito and Voll, then, tend to give a straightforwardly positive answer to the question whether Islam and democracy are compatible. In a 1994 brief but concise joint paper titled "Islam's Democratic Essence," the two professors maintain that the Islamic heritage "contains concepts that provide a foundation for contemporary Muslims to develop authentically Islamic programs of democracy." They cite a number of Islamic concepts that have a key role in the development of Islamic democracy: consultation (*shura*), consensus (*ijma'*), and independent interpretive judgment (*ijtihad*). These terms, they add, have not always been identified with democratic institutions, and even today have a variety of usages. "Nonetheless, like reinterpreted concepts such as citizen and parliament in the western tradition, they have become crucial concepts for the articulation of Islamic democracy."[35]

Following is a brief summary of the concepts they list and their meanings and relevance:

> *Consultation.* Advocates of Islamic democracy have sought to broaden the traditional understanding of consultation, understood to be by the ruler with his populace. . . . The popular caliphate in an Islamic state is reflected especially in the doctrine of mutual consultation (*shura*). All Muslims as vice regents (agents of God) delegate their authority to the ruler and it is their opinion that must be sought in the conduct of state.
>
> *Consensus.* The Prophet Muhammad is believed to have said, "My Community will not agree upon an error." Accordingly, consensus has for centuries provided the ultimate validation of decisions in Islam, especially among Sunni Muslims. "Sunni Islam came to place final religious authority for interpreting Islam in the consensus (*ijma'*) or collective judgment of the community." Subsequently, "consensus played a pivotal role in the development of Islamic law and contributed significantly to the corpus of law or legal interpretation." However, only learned scholars (the *ulama*) had a role in reaching consensus; the general public had little significance. When the scholars reached consensus on a subject, it usually ended the debate.
>
> *Independent judgment.* Many Muslim thinkers believe the exercise of informed, independent judgment to be the key to implementing God's will. Virtually all Muslim reformers of the twentieth century show enthusiasm for the concept of independent judgment.

"Consultation, consensus, and independent judgment," Esposito and Voll concludes, "provide the basic concepts for understanding the relationship between Islam and democracy in the contemporary world, and an effective foundation to build an Islamic basis for democracy."

"Many Muslims are reluctant simply to adopt western democratic models, preferring to establish authentically Islamic democratic systems," the authors write. "While not inherently anti-western, their effort does imply that western-style democracy has significant limitations. In particular, Muslims often bring up a contrast between the materialist West and the morally concerned Muslim world. Muhammad Iqbal believed that democracy was the most important political ideal in Islam. It is the basis for Islamic state and society, rooted in the absolute equality of its members and the doctrine of the unity of God. . . . Although Iqbal recognized democracy as an ideal, he denounced its implementation in the West, for western capitalism, secularism, and materialism lacked spiritual and ethical values. Despite such criticisms, the western experience has great influence on the Islamic debate. Muslim thinkers of earlier in the [twentieth] century argued that major concepts in western democracy have their analogs in the Islamic tradition. Simple correlations, like identifying *ijma'* with public opinion, lie at the core of the analysis of some of the first discussions of democracy and Islam by the Egyptian authors 'Abbas Mahmud al-'Aqqad and Ahmad Shawqi al-Fanjari."

> Many Muslims are actively engaged in defining Islamic democracy. They believe religious resurgence and democratization are complementary; they are contradictory only if democracy is defined according to specific western standards. Muslims need to develop Islamic programs of democracy, for this allows them to escape simply borrowing western-based definitions of democracy. Doing so shifts the debate from the legitimacy of importing foreign political institutions to the best way of increasing popular participation.[36]

Two ripostes to the two Islam scholars and given in the same issue of the *Middle East Quarterly*, are worth mentioning. Patrick Clawson argues in his rejoinder that "liberty is the thing, not democracy." The two authors, Clawson writes, "have misunderstood the thrust of American concern about democracy. When they look around the world, Americans want so see more than democracy—multiple parties, free elections, and a legislature with real power; they also want to see the other desirable features they assume come with democracy, such as freedom of speech, an impartial judiciary, and a more-or-less free-enterprise economy. Indeed, the U.S. government officials cited by Voll and Esposito make just this connection."

> Democracy describes, in fact, only the system of politics Americans wish to encourage, the means to an end. The end is liberty. . . . *Liberty* brings to mind a host of associations for Americans, from "Life, Liberty and the pursuit of Happiness" in the Declaration of Independence and the Liberty Bell to the American Civil Liberties Union to the Libertarian movement. The defense

of liberty stirs Americans in a way that democracy does not: they nearly all proudly proclaim "this is a free country," while well over half stay away from the polls.

Emphasis on liberty addresses the fundamental political problem of the modern world: excessive power in the hands of the state. The Founding Fathers worried about the tyranny of the majority; James Madison argued that the best government would be that which places "the greater obstacles opposed to the consent and accomplishment of the secret wishes of an unjust and interested majority." Madison's concern—there being no inevitable connection between a democratic government and freedom—speaks to contemporary problems. Current events on the fringes of the ex-Soviet bloc—from Bosnia to Nagorno-Karobach—demonstrate all too well how, in societies lacking in liberty, despotism can come from elected governments: the democratic will of the people may be to expel or slaughter unpopular minorities. It is entirely possible that the majority decides to reject freedom as it exists in the United States. It can choose not to separate mosque and state, not to assure men and women equality before the law, and not to respect the rights of minorities to live in peace (indeed, not to live at all).[37]

The other rejoinder to Esposito and Voll, a little more convincing, comes from the executive director of the Washington Institute for Near East Policy, Robert B. Satloff, and titled "One Democracy." There is, Satloff asserts, "no Islamic democracy, just as there is no Christian or Jewish democracy. There is, on the one hand, democracy—the notion that sovereignty belongs to the citizenry. And there are, on the other hand, religions such as the Abrahamic monotheisms, which (to varying degrees) cite the Divine as the source for a wide array of precepts that dictate man's earthly actions. By definition, the twain don't meet. Western civilization has, over the past four hundred years, recognized this fact and developed a number of mechanisms to balance the conflicting desires of devotion to the sovereignty of God and reverence for the sovereignty of man. These mechanisms take different forms. . . . Democracy has taken root among many millions of Muslims throughout the world. For Muslim democrats, the suggestion that they search their past for some authentic form of Islamic democracy is an act of towering condescension. That they are not in political ascendance is tragically clear. But they do exist and they even govern in some places, like Ankara and (with difficulty) Irbil, and they deserve the West's active support. Muslim democrats do not want American policy makers 'to transcend a narrow, ethnocentric conceptualization of democracy,' as Professors Voll and Esposito urge."

To the contrary, argues Satloff. "They want us to celebrate our understanding of democracy as they would if they could, and they want us to proselytize it so that maybe they eventually can. The essence of that narrow, ethnocentric conceptualization of democracy is not the Westminster or the presidential system; it is a series of basic principles—the rule of law; an independent judiciary; freedom of speech, religion, press and assembly; minority and property rights; the right of the ruled to participate in the selection of their rulers. To dilute these principles in search for Islamic activist democratic principles in some sort of pluralistic global vision does a disservice not only to our own blood-drenched history, but also to the ongoing battles waged by democrats in the Muslim world every day."[38]

THE WAY OUT

Toward the end of *What Went Wrong?* Lewis devotes a few pages to the subject of responsibility and "blame." "Who did this to us?" he writes, "is of course a common human response when things are going badly, and there have been indeed many in the Middle East, past and present, who have asked this question. They found several different answers. . . ."

"It is usually easier and always more satisfying to blame others for one's misfortunes," Lewis adds. For a long time, the Mongols were the favorite villains; then the Turks, followed by the French, the British, the United States, "the Jews"—a borrowing from European anti-Semitism. The point has often been made that if Islam is an obstacle to freedom, to science, to economic development, how is it that Muslim society in the past was a pioneer in all three, and this when Muslims were much closer in time to the sources and inspiration of their faith than they are now?

> For those nowadays known as Islamists or fundamentalists, the failures and shortcomings of the modern Islamic lands afflicted them because they adopted alien notions and practices. They fell away from authentic Islam, and thus lost their former greatness. Those known as modernists or reformers take the opposite view, and see the cause of this loss not in the abandonment but in the retention of old ways, and especially in the inflexibility and ubiquity of the Islamic clergy. These, they say, are responsible for the persistence of beliefs and practices that might have been creative and progressive a thousand years ago, but are neither today.

A more usual approach to this theme, Lewis adds, is to discuss not religion in general, but a specific problem: the place of religion and of its professional exponents in the political order. "For these, a principal cause of western progress is the separation of church and state and the creation of a civil society governed by secular laws. For others, the main culprit is Muslim sexism, and the relegation of women to an inferior position in society, thus depriving the Islamic world of the talents and energies of half its people, and entrusting the crucial years of the upbringing of the other half to illiterate and downtrodden mothers."

At the present day two answers to this question command widespread support in the region, each with its own diagnosis of what is wrong, and the corresponding prescription for its cure. "The one, attributing all evil to the abandonment of the divine heritage of Islam, advocates a return to a real or imagined past. That is the way of the Iranian Revolution and of the so-called fundamentalist movements and regimes in other Muslim countries. The other way is that of secular democracy, best embodies in the Turkish Republic founded by Kemal Atatürk."

Meanwhile the blame game—the Turks, the Mongols, the imperialists, the Jews, the Americans—continues, and shows little of sign of abating. For the governments, at once oppressive and ineffectual, that rule much of the Middle East, this game serves a useful, indeed an essential purpose—to explain the poverty that they have failed to alleviate and to justify the tyranny that they have intensified. In this way they seek to deflect the mounting anger of their unhappy subjects against other, outer targets. "But for growing numbers of Middle Easterners it is giving way to a more self-critical approach. The question "Who did this to us?" has led only to neurotic fantasies and conspiracy theories. The other question—"What did we do wrong?"—has led naturally to a second question: "How do we put it right?" In that question, and in the various answers that are being found, lie the best hopes for the future."[39]

One interpretation, and vision, of Islam and the modern Muslim state is that presented by the former crown prince of Jordan, Prince Hasan bin Talal. In an article he contributed to the London-based Arabic daily *Al-Hayat*, Prince Hasan touches upon a number of aspects of this subject. His thoughts and suggestions, coming as they do from the heartland of the Muslim-Arab Middle East, offer some timely answers to the questions posed by Lewis in his concluding remarks, and they seem to me to provide a fairly fitting reply to the advocates of the modernization-equals-westernization school of thought.

"In constructing the modern Islamic state," Prince Hasan writes, "it is imperative on Muslims not only to use the early model of the Islamic state but to ask whether we have lived up to that which we have inherited from our forefathers in terms of wisdom, civilization, and experience. It is also imperative to understand modern dynamics that govern us—in addition to the need to face up to the challenges brought about by globalization, mass communications, technological achievements, mass culture and human rights."

> *On women's rights.* "The Islamic state is not isolated from the world and is
> not secure from pressing world problems—hunger, poverty, and disease.

Half the world population is women and another 10 percent are disabled. If we fail to integrate these two elements into society we would lose more than 50 percent of potential human thought product. The Prophet Muhammad and his companions believed that heaven was under the feet of women."

On the separation of state and religion. "Our unique historical experience that relates to religious states shows the benefit of separating church and state for the benefit of all people. We need to distinguish between a religious government that seeks the well-being for all irrespective of their religions and the one which aspires to implement a single religion or secular point of view. Whenever theocracy is mentioned, people the world over, think of Iran. I like to remind them of the European theocracy, known as 'The Vatican.'"

On waging wars. "In the construction of the modern Islamic state it is important to bear in mind that the Quran is devoid of any reference to a war of aggression or the promotion of violence. Even in circumstances in which Islam condones war it is in the defense of the oppressed and the victims of exploitation not for the purpose of attaining power. The right to wage war is only 'for the sake of Allah.' [In other words] it is for justice and protection of the rights of the poor and the exploited. It is essential that conflicts, including those within the contemporary Islamic world, are resolved peacefully. The alternative will require an unwelcome arms race accompanied by a deterioration in the social and economic standards and a slowdown toward achieving human security."

On economics. "In reviewing the various aspects of the modern Islamic state, it is important to discuss the interdependence between capacity, armament, and debt, and how this crazy knot prevents a future of sustainable peace. There is a need to go back to the basic meanings on issues such as poverty. The modern Islamic state can take the initiative in the field of economics and politics by placing the well-being of people at the center of policy making, both national and international. Do we need wars to remind us of our common humanity? Why can't we build the means for defending peace during peaceful times? Why have international efforts in recent decades focused on peace keeping rather than peace making? Can we not speak of crisis prevention that crisis management? The modern Islamic state is a good example for putting an end to dehumanization, which we have witnessed, in the last century."[40]

NOTES

1. Quoted in Nissim Rejwan, *Arabs Face the Modern World: Religious, Cultural, and Political Responses to the West* (Gainesville: University Press of Florida, 1998), 29.

2. Quoted in Rejwan, *Arabs Face the Modern World*, 30.

3. Bernard Lewis, *What Went Wrong?: western Impact and Middle Eastern Response* (New York: Oxford University Press, 2002), 151, 152.

4. Lewis, *What Went Wrong?* 151, 152.

5. "Arabian Nightmares," *The National Interest*, Washington, D.C., Spring 2002, 136–37.

6. "Arabian Nightmares," 138–39.

7. Lewis, *What Went Wrong?* 73–74.

8. Lewis, *What Went Wrong?* 81.

9. A few of the author's friends and acquaintances, Muslims and Jews, studied in or graduated from such a conservatory—*Ma'had al-Funun al-Jamila,* founded in Baghdad in the late 1930s.

10. Lewis, *What Went Wrong?* 147–50.

11. Lewis, *What Went Wrong?* 151–52.

12. Samuel P. Huntington, "The West: Unique, Not Universal," *Foreign Affairs*, Washington, D.C., November–December 1996, 29.

13. Dana Buntrock, "Without Modernity: Japan's Challenging Modernization," *Architronic* 5, no. 3, 1.

14. Buntrock, "Without Modernity," 23.

15. Buntrock, "Without Modernity," 24.

16. Buntrock, "Without Modernity," 24.

17. Deepak Lal, "Does Modernization Require westernization?" *The Independent Review* (summer 2000): 22.

18. Huntington, "The West: Unique, Not Universal," 35–36.

19. Jamal Ali Ahmad, *Occidentosis: A Plague from the West* (Berkeley, Calif.: Mizan Press, 1983), 94–98.

20. Ahmad, *Occidentosis,* 117–18.

21. Peter J. Leithart, "Testing the Modernity Thesis," *Premise* (1995): 4–5.

22. Leithart, "Testing the Modernity Thesis," 5.

23. George Kneller, *Educational Anthropology* (New York: Wiley, 1965), 9, 10.

24. Huntington, "The West: Unique, Not Universal," 29–30.

25. Lewis, *What Went Wrong?* 103.

26. Juan R. I. Cole, "A Distorted Picture of the Islamic World," *Global Dialogue*.

27. Bernard Lewis, "The Revolt of Islam," *The New Yorker*, November 19, 2001.

28. Fathullah Gülen, "A Comparative Approach to Islam and Democracy," *SAIS Review* (summer–fall 2001): 133–36.

29. Larbi Sadiki, "To Export or Not to Export Democracy to the Arab World: The Islamic Perspective," *Arab Studies Journal* (spring 1998): 71–72.

30. Sadiki, "To Export or Not to Export Democracy to the Arab World," 73.

31. Gurdun Kramer, "Islamic Notions of Democracy," in *Political Islam: Essays from Middle East Report*, Joel Beinin and Joe Stork, eds. (Berkeley: University of California Press, 1997), 71–72.

32. Shukri B. Abed, "Democracy and the Arab World," in *Democracy, Peace, and the Israeli-Palestinian Conflict*, Edy Kaufman, Shukri B. Abed, and Robert L. Rothstein, eds. (Boulder, Colo.: Lynne Rienner, 1993), 206–7.

33. Elie Kedourie, "The Genesis of the Egyptian Constitution of 1923," in *The Chatham House Version, and Other Middle Eastern Studies* (New York: Praeger, 1970), 160.

34. John O. Voll and John L. Esposito, "Islam's Democratic Essence," *Middle East Quarterly* (September 1994): 7.

35. John L. Esposito and John O. Voll, *Islam and Democracy* (New York: Oxford University Press, 1996), 193. Quoted by Gabriel Warburg in *Middle Eastern Studies* 35, no. 3 (July 1999): 184.

36. Esposito and Voll, *Islam and Democracy*, 7–10.

37. Patrick Clawson, "Liberty Is the Thing, Not Democracy," *Middle East Quarterly* (September 1994): 12–13.

38. Robert B. Satloff, "One Democracy," *Middle East Quarterly* (September 1994): 18–19.

39. Lewis, *What Went Wrong?* 156–59.

40. Hasan bin Talal, "The Modern Islamic State," *Al-Hayat*, London, August 27, 2002.

Index

About the Contributors

Ömer Çaha is professor of public policy and politics at Fitah University in Istanbul, Turkey. He is the author of numerous books on Islamic politics and society.

Sandra Halperin is a senior lecturer in international relations at the University of Sussex in the United Kingdom. Her principal research interests focus on the causes and conditions of war and peace: macro-political economy; comparative political development; and Middle East politics. Her publications include *In the Mirror of the Third World: Capitalist Development in Modern Europe* (Cornell University Press, 1997); *Global Civil Society and Its Limits*, co-edited with Gordon Laxer (Palgrave/Macmillan, 2003); *War and Social Change in Modern Europe: The Great Transformation Revisited* (Cambridge University Press, forthcoming); and articles on nationalism, ethnic conflict, state-building, and Islam.

Wadood Hamad is an activist and writer living in Vancouver, Canada.

Lauren Langman is professor of sociology at Loyola University of Chicago. He is current chair of the Alienation Research section of the International Sociological Association and was former chair of the Marxist section of the American Sociological Association. He works in the Frankfurt School tradition and has written on identity, globalization, nationalism, and, more recently, on carnival-spectacles.

Douglas Morris is completing a Ph.D. in sociology at Loyola University of Chicago. He has an M.A. in social research from West Virginia University. He and Lauren Langman have co-written a number of papers on Islam and modernity, and on social movements and the Internet.

187

Haroun Er-Rashid is professor in the School of Environmental Science and Management at Independent University, Bangladesh. He has worked for the Civil Service of Pakistan and after 1971, for the Government of Bangladesh. He has also been with the World Bank and the Food and Agriculture Organization of the United Nations for more than a decade. His publications include many articles on environmental, geographical, and political issues and three books, the latest of which is *Clash of Cultures: Lessons from Bosnia.*

Nissim Rejwan is a research fellow at the Harry S. Truman Institute for the Advancement of Peace at Hebrew University, Jerusalem. His books include *Arabs Face the Modern World* (University Press of Florida, 1998), *Israel's Place in the Middle East* (University Press of Florida, 1998), *The Many Faces of Islam* (University Press of Florida, 2000), and *Baghdad Exit: A Memoir* (University of Texas Press, forthcoming).

Michael J. Thompson teaches political science at Hunter College, City University of New York and is also the editor of *Logos: A Journal of Modern Society & Culture.*

Farzin Vahdat teaches social theory and social studies at Harvard University. He received his Ph.D. in sociology from Brandeis University in 1998. His intellectual interests include the theoretical approaches to the development of modernity in the West and the Middle East, critical theory and Islam, and modernity. His articles have appeared in journals such as the *International Journal of Middle East Studies, Critique,* and the *Scandinavian Journal of Middle Eastern Studies.* His book, *God and Juggernaut: Iran's Intellectual Encounter with Modernity* (Syracuse University Press, 2002), explores the development of modern ideas and institutions in Iran by drawing on critical theorists' assessments of modernity, particularly those articulated by Kant, Hegel, Frankfurt School theorists, and Habermas.